WILD AND FAIR
TALES OF HUNTING BIG GAME IN NORTH AMERICA

WILD AND FAIR
TALES OF HUNTING BIG GAME
IN NORTH AMERICA

SELECTED AND EDITED
BY
THOMAS MCINTYRE

Safari Press

McIntyre, Thomas

First edition

Safari Press Inc.

2008 Long Beach, California

ISBN 1-57157-248-1

Library of Congress Catalog Card Number: 2006927700

10 9 8 7 6 5 4 3 2 1

Printed in China

Readers wishing to receive the Safari Press catalog, featuring many fine books on big-game hunting, wingshooting, and sporting firearms, should write to Safari Press Inc., P.O. Box 3095, Long Beach, CA 90803, USA. Tel: (714) 894-9080, or visit our Web site at www.safaripress.com.

*This book is dedicated to
the memories of
Bob Jones and Bill Wise,
wild, fair, and now free.*

TABLE OF CONTENTS

INTRODUCTION

North America was never discovered. It was hunted. North America's earliest inhabitants found their way across Asia, into Alaska, and then throughout the continent in a sequence of hunts, advancing by the lengths of their spear casts and the flights of their arrows. The first settlements on this land were the camps of hunters, the first lights hunters' fires.

The North America in which Europeans eventually arrived, though, was far more cultivated than the history books imply, the Native Americans having turned their hands to shaping the earth intensively to meet their needs, with fire one of their foremost implements. The culture that the Europeans brought (aided by spirituous liquor, black powder, and microbes) halted those manipulations of the environment by the blunt force of ending untold numbers of Native American lives. During the succeeding two centuries, the vast and depopulated interior of the continent reverted to the state it had enjoyed prior to the advent of humans: Teeming herds of animals that would render the early European pioneers dumbfounded, and not a little apprehensive, reappeared on the land.

Before long, however, the mule and the plow, speckled cattle and the festive cowboy, the railroad, and the market gunner had almost utterly banished big game from North America. Then a rather strange trend began, as amateur hunters (in the pejorative term of the day, men who hunted for "sport") convened to save and restore the large mammals of the continent—not for themselves alone but also for the public as a whole.

Up until that time, the latter portion of the nineteenth century, the big game that had been preserved in other parts of the world had invariably been protected for the exclusive benefit and amusement of a ruling aristocracy. These North American sportsmen, however, possessed the native wit to see that the sole hope for both the animals and the honorable pursuit of them resided in ensuring that everyone, not merely a privileged elite, held a stake in the continued existence of wildlife.

And so ethics were enunciated, laws enacted and enforced, reintroduction efforts undertaken, and against monumental odds the return of big game was accomplished. You only need look around you today, in almost every region of this continent, to see how great has been the success of that enterprise.

In fact, it is still quite possible to measure one's progress across North America in figurative (and sometimes literal) bow shots. There are so few other places on earth where that is still true that it creates an almost palpable sorrow for what we humans have lost. But it has not been entirely lost here—which makes the telling of the tale all the more worthwhile.

Thomas McIntyre
Sheridan, Wyoming

THIRTY YEARS WITH *CERVUS* CANADENSIS

BY
DAVID E. PETZAL

At the time of the European arrival upon this continent, the American elk, or wapiti, was the most widespread species of ungulate, native to the East as far as what is now Massachusetts, the West as far as California, the North nearly as far as the edge of the Northwest Territories, and the South to Hidalgo, Mexico. Perhaps that is what inspired Dave Petzal—currently deputy editor and for as long as anyone can remember a virtual promontory in the offices of Field & Stream *magazine—to write about it. The keener suspicion, though, is that he chose to write about the elk for the same reason he chooses to hunt it: Despite his laments about the rigors of the pursuit, for him wapiti has always been the best game in town.*

Elk are deer, except more so. Deer in rut smell musty and unpleasant, like lathered hansom cab horses. Elk, on the other hand, will make your eyes water. There is a sickly, sweetish taint to them, as overpowering as mules that have spent a hot day plowing under rotten cabbages. The very biggest deer weigh in at three hundred pounds; the very biggest elk can quadruple that. Deer, if shot fatally, can run perhaps two hundred yards but usually give up after a hundred or so. Elk have a vitality that defies belief; they can run incredible distances after absorbing a mortal wound. Big deer antlers are impressive, but big elk antlers inspire nothing short of awesome.

Whitetails are perfectly comfortable in civilized surroundings; indeed, the closer to man and his crops, the better they like it. Mule deer are not quite so congenial, and you will find only a comparative few in the really rugged mountain country that elk prefer. Deer almost never give you a chance to see what you are made of; elk provide every opportunity for self-examination. And, oddly enough, elk hunts seem to provide better and more vivid memories than deer hunts.

I can remember hunting elk in southwestern Montana, where snowstorms are frequent and in earnest. Wet weather would sweep in from the Pacific, cold air would come down from Canada, and the world would turn white. This one was a major blizzard, and I stood on a mountainside watching it: a black wall that extended from the ground up into the sky. It looked like doom itself, and the only other time I've seen anything like it was when the whole lower end of Manhattan Island was blanketed by a similar wall, gray-green and made of dust and smoke.

That kind of snow is what elk hunters pray for: two or three feet of it on the ground, followed by below-zero temperatures. Then, after a day, the elk come down from the high elevations to where you can get at them. And I did get at them.

I remember killing a six-point bull close to dark on a bitter cold day and having to leave the field-dressed carcass for the night and part of the next day while a friend and I organized a packhorse to come and carry out the critter. We managed to butcher the rock-hard meat and get it on the packsaddle, but there was no way to get the caped head on the horse as well.

Being a macho guy at the time, I tied the head to a pack frame and began the two-mile trek down the mountain, the solidly frozen head riding awkwardly on my back. I was unaware at the time that the heat from my body was thawing the rock-hard meat in the head and neck, and by the time I got to the bottom I was soaked in blood from the waist down. A friend of mine took my bloodstained pants to the laundromat. She threw them on the floor with the other clothes to be washed, and the woman next to her took a look at the mess and reeled, clutching at a dryer for support.

"Elk," said my friend sweetly.

There is a memory I will always associate with elk hunting that is not about elk. In Montana, I hunted with a friend whose wife was a seriously good cook and who made spaghetti with a wallop, thanks to a generous helping of jalapeno peppers. Late one afternoon my friend and I returned to their cabin to find markings in the snow that defied description. It looked as if some kind of death struggle between two large animals had taken place—say, a grizzly trying to kill an elk in hand-to-hand (as it were) combat. But there was no blood or fur.

We asked his wife what the hell had gone on outside the cabin. She was evasive at first, and it was obvious that she was hiding something. Finally the truth came out. While chopping up chilies for her killer spaghetti sauce she had had to go to the outhouse, and while thus engaged she had gotten chili oil on what the Monty Python crew would call her "nasty bits." The pain was excruciating, and the only thing that helped was to drag her hindquarters through the snow, round and round, till the fire went out. The story was not as dramatic as a grizzly-elk fight to the death, but it was just as entertaining.

There was one fight almost to the death that I did get to see. It was between two huge bulls at twilight on a New Mexican mountain meadow. They were five hundred yards away and were having at it with maniacal intent. This was no sparring match; these two monsters were cracking head with full force, much as bighorn rams do, and tearing up the ground with their hoofs. Nearby, a cow looked on, waiting to see who would win her favors.

In the reddish glow of twilight, the scene had an uncanny quality, as though I were witnessing a scene from prehistory—as indeed I might have been. So violent was the struggle they fought in a cloud of dust, clods of earth flying, that the *crack* as their antlers locked carried clear across the meadow.

Then one of them simply broke off and ran, beating a retreat out of the meadow into the bordering pines. The winner stood there, flanks heaving, stunned, probably, at the suddenness of its victory. And in that moment I fired. And missed. The elk was a quarter-mile away (498 long cowboy paces, as it later turned out). It heard the shot but, because of the great distance, couldn't tell where the sound was coming from; it stood rooted to the spot, unsure of what was happening and unwilling to abandon the cow.

And then my next bullet did what the other bullet couldn't—it broke the elk's back. Its hindquarters dropped. I ran up and killed it with a shot to the heart. This was the

biggest-bodied elk I've ever seen, a 6x7 that scored 338 B&C points, even with two tines broken off in the fight. The animal weighed well over 1,000 pounds, and it was so heavy that it broke the winch on the pickup truck.

The head hangs on my wall today, staring at me sternly with glassy amber eyes. And I will always wonder if I should have fired. This was a once-in-a-lifetime trophy, and at the time I wanted it so badly I would have tried to take it with a knife. But, on the other hand, this elk had just won what was probably the fight of its life and was entitled to the spoils of battle; maybe I should have let it live. Then I reflect that nature, of which I am a part, is just as unfair to elk as to every other species.

But there was another elk that I did not shoot, and that was in Colorado last fall. It was a 4x5 bull that had run up a canyon to escape a group of hunters; he was standing with its little group of cows, flanks heaving and steam blowing from its nostrils in the morning cold. I was sitting across the canyon with my cross hairs on its chest, and I could see what it was thinking as it labored to catch its breath:

Wow, that was a little too close for my liking. As soon as I get my wind, we'll go up onto the flats and put some distance between them and us.

I simply couldn't put a bullet into that elk just at the moment of its escape. As it happened, I did not get another chance at an elk on that hunt, even though I worked hard and did everything right. And I have no regrets.

Hunting elk is rather like playing for the Green Bay Packers in Vince Lombardi's time. It involves a mixture of bitter cold, superhuman effort, and playing hurt. On one horseback hunt in Montana's Bangtail Mountains, it got so cold that the outfitter and I had to stop hunting to build a fire. Usually, if you're working hard enough, you don't feel the dry cold of the Rocky Mountains, but this day was just awful. We were so frozen that we couldn't go on.

And as we stood shivering, trying to catch some warmth, the outfitter, who was as capable an outdoorsman as I've known, looked out on the dark pines, the rocks, and the snow, and said, "I love this country, but it scares the hell out of me."

In Wyoming, years ago, I got kicked in the face by a horse named Trooper. It did not kick me out of meanness, but rather it lost its footing on loose volcanic rock and hit the ground. I dived out of the saddle, and the horse and I flailed around on the ground trying to get back onto our feet. In the process, Trooper's hoof and my nose tried to occupy the same space at the same time.

I got the best bloody nose I've ever had, and my lower teeth were driven through the skin below my lip. However, the code of the West dictated that I mop up the blood and carry on, so I got back onto Trooper and we made it to the top of the mountain. There were no elk whatsoever; instead, we found chest-deep snow that was heavily crusted.

Then Trooper and the outfitter's horse did something I had never seen before and have never seen since: They quit. They simply groaned, sagged onto their sides, and quit. So we got off and walked ahead, breaking trail until we got clear of the drifts and could ride back down the mountain.

Now a good outfitter will never give up if he and his client are still breathing, so the fellow suggested that we stable the horses, get in a pickup, and drive to a sagebrush meadow where elk had been known to cross at twilight. And in the below-zero cold, with perhaps five minutes of shooting light left, that was what we did.

The outfitter was half my age, long-legged, used to thin air, and tough as saddle leather. I was middle-aged, unable to breathe through my nose, still swallowing blood, and pretty played out from breaking trail for our nags. We parked the truck next to a steep bank that ran perhaps seventy-five yards from the roadside to the edge of the meadow. It was covered by a snowdrift five feet deep whose surface had frozen hard. The outfitter volunteered to climb the snowbank and take a look while I waited at the bottom, and so I stood there, praying there would be no elk. Just then his head appeared over the crest of the snow, a smile of pure delight on his face. He crooked a beckoning finger.

I can remember thinking, *I'm going to die here.* But I was an elk hunter, wasn't I? So I started to climb. It was the kind of snow in which the crust cracks under you and you sink to your neck in powder. Then you dig yourself out, get back onto the crust, take another step, and go in again. I did that for seventy-five yards before arriving at the top alive. There, some five hundred yards away, was a five-point bull, and I killed it. I didn't have to hunt elk the next day; that was the best part.

Like childbearing pains, the memories of elk-induced suffering eventually fade, and you tend to remember only the triumphs, even though they are far outnumbered by the failures. I think back to a Montana elk hunter I knew by the name of Tommy Sicard. He was a jack-of-all-trades, an alcoholic, and a ferocious elk hunter. Even when he was in his fifties, there were hard-case twenty-year-olds who could not keep up with him.

But Tommy heaped more abuse on his body than it could take, and he ended up feeble and dying. I met him when he was near the end, at the home of a friend. It was snowing that day, and Tommy was sitting in a corner watching the flakes drift down. He was probably thinking that if the snow kept up it would drive the elk to where they might be hunted—and that he would never again be the one hunting them.

In a fervent whisper, he said, "God, how I miss them mountains."

He is in a place now, I hope, where he is young and strong and has steel springs for legs, and there are big elk to chase and good tracking snow. I think of Tommy when there are no elk, or when I have to force myself out of a sleeping bag at 3:00 A.M., or when riding a horse sets my arthritis on fire, or when I wonder why I need to kill another elk.

Tommy could tell you the answer: because elk are the greatest of all our big-game animals, and because there is no better way to spend your time on earth than hunting them, and because one day, there will be no more hunts for you, for elk or for anything else.

And that is a pretty damn good answer.

THE GREAT BUBBA BROTHERHOOD HUNT

BY

DAVID PETERSEN

David Petersen views the wapiti as an object of veneration in about as many meanings of the word as can be conjured. To list but a few, it represents the "meat from God" that Aldo Leopold talked about, and it is a talisman of the wider wild in which it originates. And in case you worry that there is any, in Ortega y Gasset's words, "affected piety" lurking around Petersen's regard for the great deer, the following piece will dispel such notions. Clearly, the elk also represents for his friends and him a high old time when they set out to hunt it.

When I sneaked a glance his way, I saw that the Yankee was staring blissfully into the treetops, oblivious to the 5x5 bull elk posing broadside in a lemony patch of sunlight a rock's toss away. Nothing for it but to try whispering across the twenty yards separating the Yank and me.

"Steve!"

My friend's only reaction was a bemused yawn. Captivated by the comic antics of two immature magpies in the fir boughs above him, he clearly hadn't heard me—no more than he'd spotted the bull.

"*Steeeve!*" I hissed, upping the volume to the reckless edge of disaster. "There's a big *bull*, right over *there!*"

Still no response from my friend from Connecticut, his face tilted peacefully skyward as if in prayer—a tactic I was seriously considering.

The bull, meanwhile, had gotten the message that something weird was going on. Its reaction was to go from watching the birdwatcher to glaring at me. But amazingly, it held its ground.

At this juncture, cross-eyed with frustration, I stood and pumped a thumb frantically elkward, like a hitchhiker in a blizzard, commanding in too loud a voice: *"Steve! Will you please shoot this beautiful bull?"*

Unhearing, unseeing, unsmelling sat the hunter, aloft in his mental birdland, though the barnyard stench of the rutting bull could have set off a smoke alarm.

The wapiti reacted by promptly showing me the north end of a southbound bull. And even as it thundered away, the Yankee hadn't a clue.

This was the second morning of our second hunt together. I'd guided Steve for a week the year before, but the wapiti had gone to ground then, and we hadn't seen a one. And now, like a thousand-dollar bill skittering along a breezy street, this gift bull had come our way—only to escape our clumsy grasp and blow right on by, indeed, like paper on the wind.

After indulging in a brief tantrum of muted cursing, I sagged over to where Steve was sitting—looking rather forlorn now, since his precious birds, amid all the excitement, had finally flown the coop. "Well," I said with feigned equanimity, "you won't likely be getting another chance like *that.*"

"What?" said Steve with a start, like a man jolted awake from a dream. "Did I *miss* something?"

By now you may be thinking that my pal Steve is not the sharpest arrow in the quiver. Think again. His handicaps that morning were inexperience in hunting big game and an incompetent guide. Steve had yet even to glimpse one of the semimythical creatures that litter the woods each night with piles of acorn poops and big cloven tracks yet can magically go unseen when hunted, hour after day after week. In my friend's brief experience with elk, he'd seen precious little reason to remain alert.

Besides, Steve had a twenty-year elk-hunting expert at his side—or should have. I'd forgotten that my hunter was a bit hard of hearing. We should have been sitting closer together, within easy whisper and hand-signal range—my fault, and our ultimate undoing. So while the Yankee loves his birds, he is no birdbrain. In fact, Steve is Dr. Stephen R. Kellert, a world-renowned Yale sociobiologist and writer who, just weeks before, had delivered the keynote address to a global conference of scholars in Hong Kong. Nor is he any babe in the woods. On a recent vacation in the Northwest Territories, for a typical example, he had camped, fished, and floated one of the lonesomest rivers on the continent.

And so it was, that at 9:30 A.M. on this Sunday, 4 November, Steve Kellert greeted my gentle scolding with an earnest, "What? Did I *miss* something?"

After explaining precisely what he had in fact missed, and why, I suggested that we give this wooded point overlooking a dry gully a couple more hours of silent scrutiny. Besides being laced with fresh sign, this sweet spot was two steep miles up a convoluted mountainside accessible only by internal combustion engines of the heart-and-lung variety. Consequently, we three Bubbas had it all to ourselves—just me, Steve, and Thomas D. I. Beck, who was off hunting this morning alone, as is his preferred way.

Returning to the hunt with fresh resolve, Steve chose a huge, roan-barked ponderosa to sit beneath, in deep shadow with a sweeping view across the gully, up the far hill, and into the aspens beyond. I found my own pool of shade just a few yards away, within solid whispering range.

Time passed, but not all that much of it, and it was I who was lost in the ozone when the Yankee shouldered his 7mm Weatherby Magnum, braced elbows on knees, leaned into a 3X Leupold scope and . . . *Ka-WHUMP!*

What? Did I *miss* something?

Happily, Tom Beck was hunting near enough to hear the shot and deduce our location. Not so happily, and in accordance with Murphy's Law, Steve's first elk chose to expire in the narrow, brushy bottom of the gully, belly-up and intractable. Even so, by the time Tom arrived—having optimistically hiked a mile down to camp, then back up while bearing meat bags and three pack-frames—Steve and I were all but done converting a quarter-ton animal to what later would scale at 173 pounds of boneless meat.

As we tended to man's oldest profession, Steve recounted for Tom how he'd spotted the lone cow ghosting toward us through the aspens. Wisely, he'd waited for the animal to enter the gully and drop momentarily out of sight before slightly readjusting his position for the shot. "The instant she topped out on this side, she smelled a rat and put on the brakes. When she looked at me and started to turn away, I knew it was then or never."

Steve had the cow dead to rights in his scope, and her instincts, good as they were, proved just a moment too slow. Thus was our birdman redeemed.

What Steve neglected to recall for Tom were the profoundly mixed emotions he'd struggled to express to me when we first laid eyes on the hugely gorgeous animal he had just killed, its eyes still bright and seemingly alert, mirroring the midmorning sun, although it was utterly dead. Because such heavy feelings rising in the emotional wake of a kill are scorned by some as touchy-feely nonsense, they often go unspoken. But as one who has killed many big-game animals across many years, and guided others to do the same, I feel qualified to testify that feelings of the sort professed by Professor Kellert beat at the very heart of the hunt for all of the truest and best hunters I have known. Where is the nonsense in acknowledging honest respect and gratitude to the animals we kill? What's so damn touchy-feely about honoring our visceral connection to the animals and the places we hunt? Tom Beck, his crusty tough-guy exterior hiding a huge heart within, didn't need a retelling to know how Steve Kellert felt. He could see it in the trembling, in the moist gleam of his eyes, in the beaming smile informing the Yankee's face.

By deboning the meat and shouldering heavy loads, we determined to complete the pack-out in one mulish haul. As we tottered down the rocky, ankle-twisting slope, Tom and I helped distance ourselves from the discomfort by poking fun at the increasing number of sissy hunters, many of them half our age, who argue that without horses you must have an ATV to retrieve an animal as big as an elk. "*Har-har-har. Ho-ho-ho.* What a bunch of *wimps!*" crooned the enigmatic Beck.

An odd bird, my pal Tom. Like Steve, Tom is highly educated, an intellectual in fact whose I.Q. is higher than Satan's body temperature. But Beck has Florida swamp-rat roots and delights in turning his inner Cracker on and off to fit the occasion. Relaxed

© JUDD COONEY   ANDREW WARRINGTON 93

among friends, he's pure Bubba. But in front of an auditorium full of people, at a wildlife commission meeting or scientific conference, the preeminent wildlife research biologist's vocabulary is stunning, his diction flawless, and his arguments unimpeachable. As a fellow wildlife professional once succinctly summed him up: "Tom Beck is an intellectual in overalls."

Soon enough, with only one brief sit-down break and a few standing pauses, we were back at camp, snapping hero pictures in front of Tom's white canvas wall tent.

In unanimous agreement that handling one elk a day is plenty enough, us Bubbas lounged around camp the rest of the afternoon, dining that evening on Chef Tom's chicken-fried pronghorn with stir-fried veggies and spuds. Dessert, as usual, was Tennessee sour mash. And through it all we jawed about .. . well, what might such an odd-lot bunch as we three—an Ivy League university professor, a world-class field biologist who wrestles bears and bureaucrats for a living, and an unemployable hunting bum whose only apparent credentials are BS and SOB— what had we three in common to jaw about?

Women! Food! Drink! Music!

But mostly, we talked about hunting.

It was while treading this latter trail of gab that the modestly oiled Yank asked the well-greased Anti, "What do you plan to do when you retire next summer?"

"Hunt more!" came the explosive response, feigning outrage.

"Hell, Tom," I interjected, "you already hunt more than anyone I know who doesn't get paid to."

Which accidental invitation prompted the Antihunter, not widely famous for modesty, to launch into an accounting: "Well, let's see—this year I opened with archery elk season but didn't kill anything because nothing worth an arrow showed up."

Beck's "nothing worth an arrow," I interrupted to tell Steve, included two record 6x6 bulls standing broadside at ten yards. For his steadfast and superhuman refusal to kill prime breeding bulls, bucks, or even tom turkeys, some folks say Beck is crazy. I think he's crazy, too, but for entirely different reasons.

"Anyhow," the Anti rolled on, "so far this year I've killed a muley doe with my bow, a rifle doe antelope—the one we just bet on— a fall turkey, and a dozen blue grouse, including three I popped with a .22 while helping my wife pack out her cow elk. After this hunt I'll have just enough vacation time left to duck down to Arizona for a Coues whitetail hunt over Christmas. Then . . . well, you know, a man has to work *sometime*. But when I retire . . . "

"Well, then," interrupted the Yankee (it had been Tom who'd hung that teasing moniker on Steve and now, I sensed, payback was at hand), "if you hunt so much and so successfully, why does Dave call you the Antihunter?"

To spare the bashful Beck another bout of boasting, I explained to Steve that, in his overlapping roles as a senior Colorado Division of Wildlife biologist, gonzo hunter, and poker of sacred cows, Tom frequently voices personal, professional, and political opinions that seem almost calculated to ruffle feathers. For an instance, to a national convention of professional wildlife managers in Wyoming, Tom recently delivered a speech under the subtle title "The Amorality of Wildlife Management," to wit:

> The notion of fair chase is key to the nonhunting public's tolerance of hunting. Most of our critics are not antihunters but just concerned people predisposed to object to what they perceive to be unfair. It's difficult, for instance, to condone the orphaning of bear cubs in the spring. And anyone who's witnessed a pack of hounds tearing apart a bear or lion cub is going to find it difficult to condone hounding. And where is the sport in shooting a bear with its head stuck in a bait bucket of Twinkies? Most hunting can be ethically defended. Some cannot. Change, where necessary, is our only hope for survival. Antihunters may hold a spotlight on our behavior, but through our behavior *we* control what they see.

Enraged by such blasphemy, Beck-bashers from the bait-head ranks have repeatedly and publicly accused him of being an antihunter in camouflage. "And that," I concluded for Steve, "is how our buddy Beck earned his Anti moniker."

Later, as we wobbled off to bed, Dr. Kellert commented poetically on the "preternatural pinkness of the moon," forecasting eloquently that it "presages snow or rain." Then he shocked us with the announcement that with his elk hunt now finished, he really had no choice but to return to Yale in order to address "nagging obligations" there.

"Now why would you go and do *that*," Tom teased, "when you could stay here and enjoy our fine company, cook our meals, wash our dishes, and help us pack down the elk I aim to kill tomorrow morning?"

"It's a tough choice," quipped the wily Yank, ducking into the shelter of his tent.

Come morning, we packed Steve's gear and meat down to the vehicles. While I drove Steve to the county airport, Beck hauled the elk meat home to his house, seventy miles away, there to age in a refrigerator reserved specifically for the purpose. A week later Tom and I would cut, wrap, freeze, pack with dry ice, and FedEx a huge insulated box of wapiti meat to New Haven, C.O.D.

Back on the mountain that evening, my old friend and I enjoyed leisurely solo hunts, but to no avail.

Tuesday morning, 6 November, and all was changed. Steve's "preternaturally pink moon" had in fact "presaged snow and rain"—a little of both, continuing through the night. Gone at last was the noisy carpet of fallen leaves that had forced us to walk short and sit long. Taking full advantage, Tom loaded his pack with a day's provisions and melted silently into the soggy woods, beneath the breaking clouds.

As for me—with a freezer already fat with a bow-killed wapiti, a rifle pronghorn, grouse, and rabbit—my motivation to kill another elk was nil. The hunt itself, the friends, the camp, the conversation and laughter, even the gutting and the packing—these were my prey this time out. Unless, of course, I stumbled onto a yummy calf—"spoon meat" Beck (a fellow trophy meat hunter) calls it, and sweeter than any veal. But no calf was forthcoming, and in obedience to my apathy I returned early from my walkabout and was relaxing outside the cook tent in the warming sun, devouring poet and wild-game gastronome

Jim Harrison's deliciously ornery *The Raw and the Cooked*, when I was assailed by a croaking Cracker voice crooning from the nearby woods: "I reckon you'll need your packframe, a sharp knife, and a coup'la meat bags."

Back up the mountain, above where Steve had taken his cow, the Anti described his hunt as Tom and I strapped our initial loads of meat to our packs:

"I was sneaking along a ways below here when I heard a bugle. At first I thought it was some poor Joe hunter who'd watched too many elk-calling videos. But then came an excited bull-squeal that was clearly the real thing. A bull bugling after the rut means he's found at least one cow still in heat. Since one cow was all I needed to ensure my family's winter meat supply, I started toward the call and ran smack into a whole herd, maybe two dozen animals, contouring east and moving fast. I could see flashes of head and hide through the trees but no clean shot. So I hunkered down and cow-called: *Meeew, chirp, meeeww*. The main herd with the bull kept going, but half-a-dozen animals broke off and started toward me, chirping as they came. Then, inexplicably, they stopped and began feeding. But still no shot. Finally, this two-year-old grazed into the open at seventy yards, and when she raised her head with a mouthful of *Carex*, I took her front-on through the brisket. She died on her way to the ground." Indeed, her last bite of sedge was still in her mouth.

And so ended the Great Bubba Brotherhood Hunt, a meaty conclusion to a good sporting year for the infamous Antihunter, the suavely debonair Connecticut Yankee, and, by default, for the third member of this rude and motley crew—the one they called Elkfart.

TROPHIES

BY

TED KERASOTE

It's difficult to name someone who writes more lucidly and seriously (which is not to say somberly) about hunting in these latter days than does Ted Kerasote. In this tale of pronghorn hunting, and remembering an elk hunt past, Ted offers an understanding of why a true hunter's emotional reach should always exceed his grasp, while at the same time eloquently expanding the definition of what it means to bring an animal "to possession."

This is the hunter's sweetest story: to bring back the unusual and have it remind us of our connection to country. It's what goes beyond the meat—these trophies. They last when the freezer has been emptied, and perhaps they don't have to be horns or antlers. Sometimes they can be nothing more than a single, clear thought, seen like a cairn that changes our direction.

Playing with these ideas, I drove toward the Oregon Buttes with my longtime hunting partner, Bob, as the big, wide, salmon-colored sprawl of the Wyoming desert opened before us. Pronghorn began to sprint alongside the sandy road. Tan and white—and sleek—they burst from arroyos and galloped toward higher ground. Panting in the heat, they left clouds of dust in the September air. Bucks with fourteen-inch horns ran by like starlings. Here and there we could spot a fifteen-incher standing sentry on a butte. Taking such an animal could put one's name in the record book.

That, of course, hadn't been my intent when we drove out for the last day of antelope season. I had intended to get a pronghorn for salami and sausage and save the elk for steaks, but the idea of shooting an antelope two minutes after starting and going home to dump it in the grinder seemed like no hunt at all. It seemed like farming, and I'm not much of a farmer. So to stay longer we played the game of those who aren't hungry—we looked harder for the bigger.

We forded a muddy wash and climbed the back of a low ridge; it might have been an enormous wave, curling over the sage. Just where it broke, we stopped. We had to. Had we gone farther, we would have plunged half a thousand feet into the canyons below. There, among the maze of rocky fins and blobby gray towers, on a knob higher than the rest, stood a wild horse, sleek and black as midnight, head erect, looking over the country. It could see a long way, as could we—a hundred miles to the horizon, etched here and there by an old surveyor's trail, a faint red line through the pale green sage, beginning nowhere and leading to openness devoid of any destination—and overhead the sky so enormous and crazy blue it made me catch my breath.

We walked a long circle away from the Isuzu, Bob spotting about three antelope to my one. Once a professional guide, now a builder, he has the sharpest eyes of anyone I know and is inspired to look. In fact, he's one of those rare people who, on foot and without the use of dogs, has actually spied a mountain lion. Thin and tan, with a gentle smile and a rim of organ-grinder's curly hair, he also loves to hunt, which doesn't necessarily mean to shoot. I have seen him carry his rifle in the field for days without ever loading it.

By chance he looked one way and I the other, and below us, at the edge of a dry streambed, I saw a buck courting two does. Instantly, I knew this buck was larger than any we had seen—larger, in fact, than any buck antelope I had ever seen in my life. I dropped behind a pile of rocks, and Bob slipped beside me. From three hundred yards off we watched the buck circle the does, nudge their rears, and chase them. "He'll go sixteen" said Bob.

I knew exactly what he meant. Inches. But more. Ever since Rowland Ward, Boone and Crockett, and Safari Club International began to publish their record books, individuals who have applied their competitive streak to hunting have taken to describing animals by the measurement of their horns and antlers, or the inches those measurements produce after being transcribed by a formula. Thus, a "185" sheep or a "390" elk puts you well up in the B&C record book, as does a "16-inch" pronghorn. All of which is understandable: People love numbers. Numbers seem to give us a precise way to measure our accomplishments and help us to forget that there aren't exact ways to measure the ambiguous parts of ourselves, such as conscience, sympathy, or love.

I looked at my watch. We had been out two hours, which didn't seem long enough. Nevertheless, sixteen-inch antelope don't come along every day. Just as I put the cross hairs on the buck, the does broke from it, galloping off another three hundred yards into some willows, and the buck followed. I was relieved. Now we'd have a stalk.

We hurried to where a ramp of steep clay led off the ridge. Dropping out of sight, we circled behind some tall, eroded fins, crawled across a salt pan, and found ourselves in the wash that led directly to the antelope. I plucked some grass, tossed it, and watched it drift sideways from us. Slowly, we began. I knew that within fifteen minutes we would be in range, and I slowed down. It seemed that we had just started. Placing my feet carefully, I noticed some elk spoor, and I was surprised to see that the big deer were out here in the desert. Stooping to pick up a pellet, I thought of the forested valleys and yellowing parks I hunted in the Gros Ventre country to the north, which is my home.

The Gros Ventre country. How many days and weeks and months and years had I spent there, until the game trails between the game trails had become familiar, and I could walk to places by starlight? I had a great sense of patience there, not because I am a patient man, but because I have loved that place more than most. In fact, once for no other reason than an overwhelming desire to do so, I lay on the sun-warmed grass and put my nose in the earth, breathing in a deep draft as if the land were a woman. It smelled of chlorophyll, tubers, and roots—my roots. I think I have been patient in that country because I like being out in it, a strange turn of phrase that neatly explains being outside one's normal shelter while being immersed in a home. There, out in the country, shooting in a hurry is a foolish business, for then the being-out-in-it is over. Last season I had passed on four-point elk there, then a five-pointer, and even a six-pointer, the last with Bob by my side. He, too, had raised his rifle at the bachelor club of bulls and had not fired.

The following week, after sleeping at the trailhead, I had walked back to the valley in which we had seen the bulls and which had become familiar over many summers and falls. Bob had had to work. As I set off, I saw the print of a grizzly in the frozen mud, an eleven-year-old male that frequented the area. Then I shut off my headlamp and walked by starlight, listening to the increasing hush of the creek below me.

I was too early, an hour early, which is exactly what I had intended. I sat drinking tea from a vacuum bottle until the black sky turned charcoal gray. Then I slipped into the meadow and saw them—fifty cows and a half-dozen bulls. Leaving my pack and taking only the rifle, I crawled the last two hundred yards on my belly, then ever so slowly turned into a sitting position in the midst of the elk.

A four-pointer walked within twenty yards of me, stared at me, walked on. The six-point bulls were mixed among the cows and occasionally bugled to one another, their voices turning to steam in the cold. But it was the end of the rut, and their challenges weren't bellicose.

From one to the other of the bulls, I trained my glasses. How could I choose? I lingered on the largest. Why is larger always better? From the largest I turned away, finding a bull whose antlers were more symmetrical. Perhaps symmetry said more clearly what I felt about this country—its shape of wholeness and peace, and how elk seem a distillate of the country's water, grass, and air: whole, clean, solid. The bull also stood close, within fifty paces, so I knew that I could hit it in the neck. It cropped some grass, and when it looked directly at me, I fired. When the scope returned to where the bull had been, I could see only the tip of one antler sticking toward the dawning sky.

The cows and other bulls looked up, startled, then continued to graze while slowly moving off. I didn't rise until they were out of sight, then walked to the bull and saw that it had been killed so suddenly it still had grass sticking from its mouth. The right hoofs lay in the prints where it

had been standing. I touched the smooth, ivory tips of the antlers. A 6x6.

As I cleaned it, a flock of trumpeter swans flew overhead, honking, and another herd of elk, led by another 6x6, forded the river. It stopped and bugled.

Six-by-six. I felt the antlers again—their rough cornices around the pedicles, the polished tines, this benchmark and symbol of arrival, like an under-three-hour marathon for the runner, a twenty-thousand-foot peak for the mountaineer, or a Class V rapid for the kayaker: what Aldo Leopold called a *certificate* (his italics), what you bring home, a testing that you've been somewhere and done something, that you've exercised, as he said, "skill, persistence, or discrimination in the age-old feat of overcoming, outwitting, or reducing-to-possession." Except that in hunting, the certificate you bring home is dead. No one else can run or climb or boat it. It's not a time on a clock, an eternal mounting, or an endlessly flowing rapid. It is finite, removed from everyone else's enjoyment, particularly its own.

That's why it has always seemed important to me that we examine what we're doing out in the country, to be aware before we send the shot on its way. It is important to believe that we have spent enough time there, watching, listening, intermingling, and to know that what we are doing—killing— is not only imperfect and unclear but can also be done respectfully only when we remain unsure and somewhat doubtful—not so doubtful that we won't do it, but doubtful enough to know that converting animals into food will never be a joyful business, that it will always be undercut by sorrow. It is the basic constituent of the web in which we live, and why some of us go back and back. Being out-in-it isn't the model of what is. It is what is.

From the steep bank of the streambed I could see nothing more than the antelope's horns above the sage, fifteen yards off— about as close as you ever get to a pronghorn. Dropping back, I circled in order to come at it from the side. As I crawled along, a short-eared owl flapped from the willows and flew over my head, turning its wise monk's face to look down at me—a portent, I thought, and a reminder to be cautious.

I eased over the bank, and the three antelope jerked up their heads, black eyes bugging—for only a half-second. They leapt a small hill and ran against the sky full tilt. I put the rifle on the buck, slipped off the safety—ninety yards, offhand, running—and let it go.

"You'll never get a chance like that again," said Bob, walking up to me.

And I didn't. But I got another, almost as good and, in some ways, better.

We hiked back to the car and made a wide circle across the plains. A herd of wild horses—twenty-five of them, with three colts—crossed before us: cinnamon and sorrel creatures with long manes and sweeping tails that gazed over their shoulders at us with regal curiosity.

The sky became a soft and ruffly blue, the hills a wounded red. On a bluff we spotted a herd of does and one large buck—fifteen inches if an inch—overseeing them.

My luck seemed enormous, but somehow it didn't please me. I wanted to camp in this place, spend a few days here—but I didn't have the time. Knowing that, and feeling uneasy, I could have gone home without even trying for the buck. But Bob wanted me to take it. Not that he said it in so many words. It was just the feeling I got from him: This was his spot, and I was his friend. He had been here the weekend before, had camped out, and had taken a good antelope—over fourteen inches. Now he wanted me to do the same.

So we stalked up a dry stream, peeked over its top, and saw the herd four hundred yards off.

"Might as well take him," he said.

The antelope seemed too far away. Not really. But I was being obstinate—and careful. So I crawled—through the sage, across a cactus field, over some shale—using every little depression to shield my passage until I was about 120 yards from the pronghorn and had spent about forty-five minutes.

Lying on my belly, I watched it through the scope—white and tan, moving among its harem with head high, horns polished, strutting, chasing off young bucks, rounding up straying females. A baron.

23

The setting sun began to flare in the scope, and I waited for the does who shielded the buck to step aside. Finally they did—and still I watched, wondering why I couldn't shoot when I had had no problem with the elk whose antlers now hung in my cabin. I knew, as well, that within the next month I would shoot again—when the right elk crossed my path.

Suddenly the antelope stared at me—stared for three long seconds—then wheeled and trotted off, the does and young bucks following. I stood and watched them go.

Turning around, I saw Bob walk toward me. He looked dejected, binocular hanging from his hand and a sour expression on his face. It was the last day of antelope season, and now I'd have no chance until the following year.

As he came up to me, I asked, "Are you mad?"

"No," he said. "Why didn't you shoot?"

"Does were in the way."

He looked at me, then quickly began to walk to the car. I emptied the rifle and followed him. Walking through the sage, I was sorry that I hadn't pleased him. He was my friend, and who doesn't like to please a friend? And then I thought of my friends far and wide, and what they would have said had I put one in the book. Who doesn't like applause?

Bob reached the car and took a pop from the cooler. I stopped and looked up the long valley where the pronghorn had gone. Still running, they were now well into a canyon, its walls deep in shadow. The rumps of the last three animals were lit like fireflies.

Then they disappeared, and I thought about how next year I'd come back and camp. After you've gone to bed in a piece of country and woken up in it, and spent another day walking through it, you may know it well enough to take home a trophy—at least the kind that makes you reflect on what you really want to hang on the wall.

GORILLAS

BY

CHRIS MADSON

Why such a title? Because for many, the trophy mule deer is the undisputed eight-hundred-pound gorilla of Western big-game hunting. Chris Madson never comes right out and says that, but he does offer a concise yet detailed portrait of our grandest deer, one that shows why the mule deer ably holds its own against, and for more than a few surpasses, such behemoths as the elk and moose in the estimation of hunters.

It was my parents' fault. If they had followed their hearts, I might have been born in Wyoming. As it was, I first saw the light of day far from here and will never be able to claim the coveted title of native.

I've done what I could to compensate for this defect in my background—I started visiting the West not too long after I could walk, and as soon as I could figure out a way to make a living here, I resettled. Still, in more than twenty years of full-time residency, I've come to see subtle but crucial differences in point of view between natives of the West and immigrants. The distinction is nowhere more obvious than in the concept of a "trophy."

There are many spectacular representatives of the ungulate clan in the Rocky Mountain West, all of which have their devotees. I've stood in front of the Chadwick ram at the Buffalo Bill Historical Center with good friends and marveled at the mass, sweep, and symmetry of those magnificent horns. We've shared the binocular at the oxbow of the Snake to get a better look at the span of the palms on an exceptional bull moose and studied the racks of the dominant harem bulls when the elk gather along the Yellowstone and Madison.

The admiration is genuine and unreserved, but when it comes down to picking favorites, the natives of my acquaintance always seem to settle on mule deer. Show one of them a picture of a muley with a thirty-five-inch spread and he lapses into several minutes of trance, staring through the page into another time and place. Just about the time you're thinking of calling for an ambulance, he fixes you with a glittering eye, like the Ancient Mariner, and says, "He reminds me of a buck I saw up the Gros Ventre"—or words to that effect. That is your cue to get comfortable; you are about to hear an extended parable on the wages of sin and the abiding disappointments of life.

Trophy mule deer are valuable for much the same reason that other commodities are valuable—there is high demand for a tiny supply. Big bucks are scarce for several reasons. First, they are unusual genetically. An imposing rack has obvious advantages during rut, since it impresses the ladies and tends to intimidate other bucks.

Some of this reaction is a hard-wired rule of mule deer behavior, but it rests ultimately on the basic reality that a buck with a big rack is mature and extremely healthy. His antlers suggest that he is likely to be tough in a fight and that his offspring will be equipped to survive to a ripe old age. That information is important to potential rivals and mates.

If there were no disadvantages to a large rack, mature mule deer bucks would have headgear as big as an elk's, but growing a large rack imposes an obvious hardship on the animal. It takes a lot of nutrition and energy to grow antlers. Most bucks mobilize calcium and other minerals from other parts of their skeletons to build the bone in their antlers—up to ten pounds of bone in a really big rack. Combined with the exertions of the rut, a trophy buck's outstanding headgear puts it in a precarious balance between reproductive success and failure to survive.

A big rack is generally a reflection of good year-round habitat and a deer population that isn't eating everything that's available. It's also a sign that winters haven't been too severe, since a buck won't grow its biggest racks until it's more than five years old.

So genetics, good forage, and a little luck with the weather all play a part in producing an exceptional mule deer. The big bucks share one other trait that is best appreciated by the people who pursue them—they are invisible. The late Erwin Bauer, one of America's most experienced wildlife photographers, told of seeing the biggest mule deer buck of his life high in the Teton Range on a cold November afternoon. A year later, he saw a second giant buck on the same trail. He said that the sightings confirmed "an old supposition—that the biggest mule deer, at least those with the finest antlers, are not scattered equally wherever the species exist. Instead they are found in just a few, sometimes small, areas where all conditions for health and growth are right. Almost without exception these are not areas where other mule deer are very plentiful."

The big bucks spend most of their time in places people seldom visit. Often those refuges are at timberline or above; sometimes they're in sagebrush breaks or badlands. Always, there is a back door, a way for a buck to slip away from an approaching threat without being seen.

A number of years ago I was hunting the north side of the Ferris Mountains, a small, mostly perpendicular range that rises out of the sagebrush in central Wyoming. There were other hunters on the lower slopes. I wanted to get away from them, but about two-thirds of the way up the steep slope, a sixty-foot rim wound through the trees, barring the way to the top.

The second morning of the hunt I was walking the contour a hundred feet below the rim when I came on two sets of fresh elk tracks in the snow, heading straight up. The elk seemed to know where they were going, and I figured I could probably climb anything an elk could, so I followed.

The trail led to a crack in the rim not much wider than my shoulders. I scrambled up through the rock and emerged on the ridge that led to Ferris Peak, the highest point in the range. I picked my way up, turning every now and then to enjoy the view of the Sweetwater Valley and the jumbled ridge of the Granite Mountains to the north.

A pink granite boulder the size of a van sat in the talus at the summit, and as I eased around it I found myself face to face with one of the largest bighorn rams I had ever seen. We stared at each other for almost a minute while it tried to figure out how I had managed to get so close, then it turned slowly and eased down the south side of the ridge and out of sight.

I followed for a while, convinced that this was an exceptionally good place for a big buck, but the ridge sharpened until I was spending more time watching my feet than hunting. I decided to go back the way I had come.

Hunting has a way of teaching hard lessons, and I have a way of forgetting them. It had been half an hour since I had left the summit, and I should have known there was a chance that something had moved in behind me. Nevertheless, I walked back to the peak with my eyes down, secure in the conviction that I had already worked this ground.

It jumped out of the shade of a limber pine no more than forty yards from me. Its rump looked about an ax handle across, and as it bounced away its antlers stuck out at least a foot farther on either side, then turned up. And up. And up. I managed to unsling my rifle before it disappeared in the low pines below, but I knew I wasn't good enough to shoot it in the head and didn't want to hit it in the rear. So I sat down to watch the far slope.

The buck appeared on the far wall of the mountain a couple of minutes later, about six hundred yards away, on a faint trace that crossed a scree slope under the cliff. It went as far as the next buttress of stone, well out of rifle range, then stopped in the shade to examine its back trail.

The two of us were motionless for about five minutes. I watched through my binocular, and after a while the buck seemed to relax. A stalk was in order. All I had to do was ease off my rock and crawl down to the first of the pines, not more than fifty feet. With the trees for a screen, I could get on the other side of the canyon below and get to within 250 or 300 yards. With a good rest on my daypack, I could take the shot. I started to ooze down off my seat.

I made it about eight inches. The dot on the other side turned its head and disappeared around the buttress. After another three or four minutes, I picked up a speck about a mile away on the

mountain face, still moving steadily. It traversed a couple of avalanche chutes, scrambled over more scree, and finally vanished over the far ridge, maybe three miles to the east. I assumed that that it stopped running eventually, but it showed no sign of slowing down while I watched.

I ate a candy bar to console myself, slung my rifle, and started down to find the crack in the rim and supper, pondering my mistakes. It occurred to me that there wasn't much shame in the outcome. I was an amateur; my opponent was clearly a professional. My thoughts settled at last on the mantra of generations of mule deer hunters as they have walked back to camp without meat: "He didn't get that big by being stupid."

It made a lot of sense but wasn't much comfort.

THE HOME PLACE

BY

MARY ZEISS STANGE

"Hunting in your own backyard," writes the novelist Thomas McGuane, "becomes with time, if you love hunting, less and less expeditionary." What might it become, then, when it is the deer's backyard? Some would argue that anywhere a deer stands (like wherever the gambler hangs his hat) is his home. But any decent hunter knows better—that there is one place a deer is always circling its way back to, even if that circle takes all of a season or a year to close. Mary Zeiss Stange's story is about tracing such a circle, and how it is one that can come to surround our lives as well.

When Porkypine Johnson surveyed his 160-acre stake, the deed in his pocket signed by President Woodrow Wilson himself, he couldn't believe his good fortune. Running right through its center was a half-mile worth of creek drainage, a lush and secluded ravine, with ponderosa pine woods banking its deep sides, and thickets of wild rose and plum, buckbrush and buffaloberry. A few miles off was a county road that was barely a road at all. This was the perfect place, pioneering Porkypine knew, to realize his dream and make his fortune. And so he built a shack, set up his still, and, local legend has it, went on to produce some of the finest moonshine Carter County had ever seen.

By the time Prohibition hit, he was operating a speakeasy that drew its clientele from ranches for miles around. Cowboys and their lady friends drank and danced into the night, secure in the knowledge that the revenuers weren't likely to venture this far into the remoteness of southeastern Montana.

Porkypine Johnson—if he did indeed exist—is long gone now, as are the family that subsequently tried, and failed, to make a go of it, raising pigs on his little tract of land. Either they left no descendants, or their kin moved on to more profitable pastures. But remnants of their presence remain. The log cabin still bears traces of human habitation: a cracked fragment of mirror on the wall, a hole in the roof where a stovepipe used to be, scraps of linoleum flooring and tar paper insulation. There are ruins of a granary and of pigpens, along with the rusted hulk of a Ford motorcar and coils of now antique barbed wire.

These days, Porkypine's homestead is the stomping ground for less rowdy species. One almost invariably sees mule deer and turkeys there, and sometimes whitetails. It has always been one of the favorite hunting spots to which my husband, Doug, and I return, generally late in deer season, when we both have filled our deer A-tags with bucks taken in more challenging country and are looking to shoot does. We've seen some nice enough bucks there, too, on occasion. Indeed, several years ago Doug shot a hefty 4x4 muley about a quarter-mile up the creekbed from the ruined buildings, and a few years later we spied a very impressive buck contentedly grazing right next to the cabin in the waning hours of the last day of deer season—when all that either of us held was an antlerless deer tag.

But those were exceptions to the rule. The majority of bucks we've sighted there have been immature. I had always viewed Porkypine's homestead primarily as doe territory. Last year that changed.

It had not been a particularly good deer season in eastern Montana. Uneven summer rains meant that grasses and browse were less plentiful than usual, and the weather was unaccountably warm well into November, when we were hit with slushy snow and sometimes gale-force winds. Mule deer numbers were rumored to be down somewhat. Whether or not that was true, most of the bucks we were seeing were young spikes and forkhorns.

Throughout the season, Doug and I hunted our usual tried-and-true buck areas: rugged buttes and badlands where big mule deer tend to hide out; pine forests and brushy draws that the local whitetails tend to favor; a broad, rolling hayfield in which both species mingle in the predawn stillness before filtering down into the trees at daybreak. Neither of us saw a buck of either species that we were willing to shoot. By Thanksgiving week, which marks the end of Montana's long deer season, we were driven to wax philosophical. We are neither of us truly trophy hunters, but we are both drawn to bigger, mature bucks—partly because of the challenge hunting them entails, partly because they have made their contribution to the gene pool while their more vigorous male offspring need the opportunity to grow and to thrive.

"I'm about ready to fill my A-tag with a big doe," Doug ventured over lunch. It was the day before Thanksgiving. We had spent all morning hunting and had seen nothing, not even a fawn. "That is, if I'm lucky enough to see a big doe, at this point." I—who usually proclaim that I'm happy enough with any deer that's a good, clean kill, yet at the same time had to admit to feeling frankly let down if the current year's buck isn't at least as impressive as last year's—reluctantly agreed.

We regrouped in the later afternoon to take advantage of the "golden hours" before dusk. One place we had not hunted recently was that stretch of creek above Porkypine's homestead. The wind was right for us, and we traced what by now had become a standard stalk, a pincer movement in which Doug works his way down through the forest on one side of the creek and I work the other. Much earlier in the season—and not for the first time—this strategy had yielded an adult doe for me. This time, though, I didn't see anything aside from immature does and fawns. Reaching the homestead (our point of rendezvous) ahead of Doug, I sat on a log in the slushy snow, musing and trying not to notice that I had underdressed for the rapidly chilling afternoon.

Before long, I heard the crack of Doug's rifle. Within minutes, he appeared and waved to me to join him. He looked reasonably pleased with himself.

"A big doe?" I asked.

"No, a buck. He's not huge, but he's, well, he's OK. He's got a few years on him," he said, smiling. We hiked several hundred yards uphill, toward the dense thicket that marks the spot where the creek emerges from the timbered hillside. Doug's deer had fallen at the edge of the creekbed. It was an older mule deer, with antlers that made up in spread what they lacked in thickness, and good body size. By the time we had it field-dressed, the rays of the setting sun were burnishing the Chalk Buttes to our east and the air was growing decidedly colder.

I was ready to call it a day. But, since we were up here anyway, Doug urged that we take a quick walk up around the rim of the ravine. "I was just up there an hour ago and didn't see anything," I protested. "Besides, I've got snow in my boots." Instantly I realized that this was pretty lame reasoning, on both counts. "Sure. Let's go," I said, shouldering my rifle sling. I was convinced that we wouldn't see anything, but then deer season was evaporating and I didn't have much to show for it.

The wind had shifted slightly, so that now we were not likely to surprise any deer that might be daft enough still to be sitting on the hillside I had threaded my way up and down so recently. We had just achieved the crest of the hill when out of the corner of my eye I caught a quick, nearly soundless explosion of snow, sage, and mule deer.

"It's the drop-tine!" Doug cried. At the same moment, my eyes were managing to focus on the deer that was now racing downhill. It was indeed the big drop-tined mule deer that we had seen, and had fantasized about, in this vicinity for two or three years now, always outside of hunting season. Every year I assumed—we both did—that some other, luckier hunter had probably taken it. A large-bodied mature buck, with thick and perfectly symmetrical 5x5 antlers, the first tine of which on either side was elegantly down-turned, this deer was absolutely gorgeous. And it was quickly gone.

We worked our way back down the hill, toward the thicket. Peering through an opening in the pines, I at first saw nothing. Then I spotted a mule deer buck, skirting a clearing about 150 yards below me. It stalked deliberately, nose down, evidently having caught the scent of a doe. It paused, lifted its head, and turned away from me. It was the drop-tine. I dropped to a sitting position and took aim, using my knee as a rest. The deer took a few steps and was mostly obscured, rump toward me, behind the tangled branches of an ash tree. I waited for one of those

eternities that last a minute or two. It took a cautious step forward and to the right. I had a clear shot, fired, and the buck fell.

When we field-dressed the buck, it was with mixed emotions that I discovered I was not the first hunter to shoot this deer. Mine, without question, was a good, clean kill: The bullet broke the spine and fragmented to puncture both lungs. But this deer had earlier been shot in the haunch, causing some internal injury and a partially healed exit wound—with a bit of gut protruding—in the belly. That it had not acted at all injured was testimony, perhaps, to the indomitable strength and spirit of this particular animal. An elder statesman in this mule deer community—its teeth were completely worn away—it had survived, and outwitted, many seasons of hunters. But it would not have lived much longer.

To judge by the placement of the earlier wound—which looked to be a few days old—we figured that this deer had probably been shot from above, and from a considerable distance. We had no way of knowing how conscientiously that earlier "sharpshooter" might or might not have tried to finish a job so clearly botched. But we did know that the deer had responded in logical fashion. It had retreated to its most familiar shelter, to lie low. It had returned to the deer-rich ravine above which we jumped him. It had, in short, headed for home.

Old homesteads, like Porkypine's, dot the American West and Midwest. They are rich in human history. Even when no artifacts remain, their setting, the buildings, and their vestigial vegetable gardens and root cellars speak volumes about what it must have been like to live—and frequently to suffer—the pioneer experience. It is obvious to anyone who has seen these places, and perhaps more so to one who has felt through them the chill of a Dakota blizzard or the heat of a Montana drought—and maybe caught a faint echo of a scratchy gramophone mingling in the autumn breeze—that spirits seem to linger at homestead sites. And so do deer, because these sites are an important element of their history, as well.

Abandoned homesteads attract deer for several reasons. The first is that, when it comes to choosing the sites for their dwellings, human beings tend to seek pretty much the same things deer do: shelter from the elements, a certain degree of seclusion to ensure some privacy, nearness to water, and a ready access route. The extent that human housing developments are gobbling up prime deer habitat across the country today surely attests to the fact that we think like deer when it comes to deciding where we like to bed down. In that regard, old homesteads represent (from a deer's point of view, anyway) the first outreaches of prairie suburbia. Whatever impact human habitation subsequently may have had, the deer were there first.

However, rather than sighing, "There goes the neighborhood," and moving on, the deer tend to stay, and with good reason. The kitchen vegetable garden, newly cultivated fruit trees, berry bushes, flower beds, salt and mineral licks put out for livestock: All are enticements to hang around. And even after the two-leggeds pack up and leave, traces of those delectables remain. Poke around many an old homestead today, and you will discover Juneberry and currant bushes, rhubarb, perhaps even volunteer squash or sunflowers that come back season after season. Years of putting out salt licks leaves trace residues in the soil, and deer scrape the surface to get to the salt. Old two-track roads and overgrown garden paths still provide ease of access and escape. Robert Frost notwithstanding, wild animals—like humans—generally prefer the road more frequently taken, especially in the snow.

In short, deer became habituated to sharing their space with humans, and then continued to reap the fruits of human habitation even after the two-leggeds had left. Hence another reason why deer tend to haunt homesteads: They have become part of "deer history," as each generation of does has passed on to their fawns the behavior patterns that led them back to the homesteads. Many deer may have no more reason than many humans do for calling a particular location "home," except that it has something to do with Mom. It is a primal place of shelter and security. And it is where you return, as my beautiful old drop-tined buck did, when what you need most is a place that feels safe.

Big, older mule deer bucks are the hardest to find, which leads most hunters to assume that you have to seek them in the hardest places to get to. But reality often gives the lie to conventional wisdom, perhaps especially in leaner years. For most of last year's deer season, Doug and I had been looking for bucks in all the wrong places, those rugged terrains where we expected to find them. Then, for the first—and very likely the last—time in many years of hunting together, we improbably shot two mature mule deer bucks, within ninety minutes and about two hundred yards of each other. That was because we finally hunted the place that any experienced mule deer might have gone first, in a difficult season. Without quite realizing it, we too had gone home.

CROSSING OVER

BY

SUSAN EWING

In the English woods, the home of Robin Hood, there is a certain begrudging respect for the poacher. His taking of the lord's (human, rather than divine) game often has a retributive quality to it, and good books, such as John Buchan's John Macnab, *have been written about his roguish exploits. Not so here. In North America, big game has always been the property of the people—that is, everyone. Poaching, then, is theft from you and me, and a good deal less admirable for that. On the other hand, there is the problem of one man locking up his land to keep the public's game away from the public. All of which makes it a more complex matter to hand down a verdict on the "poacher" in Susan Ewing's short story. It's also fair, to imagine O. Henry—had he hunted— admiring the ending, but that may be giving away too much, too soon.*

"**D**amn, Benny, you can't cross that fence. It's posted."
"I don't give a s—," Benny said. He handed his rifle to Frank, pushed down the top wire, and stepped over. "You coming?"

It was the last day of deer season, a half-hour before sunrise. Snow glimmered under a sinking moon. Frank looked toward the road before handing Benny's rifle over the fence.

"It's trespassing, Benny."

"I got grandfather rights." Benny slung his rifle over his shoulder and turned to cross the flat toward the forest drifting up the mountainside.

"God dangit, Benny. I'm on parole, you know. Son of a b----. Wait."

Frank jammed down the top wire of the fence as if he wanted to strangle it and crossed over, as Benny knew he would.

Benny shrugged and smiled. "My old man brought me here for the first time when I was ten," he said. "Handed me this rifle, put three cartridges in my coat pocket, and said we were going hunting."

Wind had scoured the snow off the cow trail, and their jeans whisked against brittle sagebrush. Frank kept checking back toward the road as they threaded their way across the scrubby flat, kicking up rabbit pellets and stray rocks.

"What if somebody sees the truck?" Frank huffed, a little out of breath. He and Benny had played basketball together at State, but that was fifteen years ago.

"It's not against the law to break down on a county road," Benny said, "especially in that old Dodge. Anyway, we're not doing anything wrong."

"Some folks would be inclined to call it trespassing," Frank said, pulling up his collar against the cold.

"What would they be inclined to call it when a doctor from Florida posts a sign that shuts a guy out of a place that's always felt like his?"

"America?"

"You sound like Dr. Florida," Benny said.

"Or Mr. Judge, who's gonna hammer our nuts. They hate it when a guy makes up his own rules."

Benny and Frank crossed the flat and climbed the slope toward the tree line. At the edge of the forest, Benny stopped and looked back over the valley. He tapped a little rhythm on the Skoal can in his front pocket and shifted his rifle. He always tried to pay attention just before the sun came up. There was a certain slippery promise in the pink light, something impossible to contain, like love or time. He waited for the restless breeze he knew would come, felt it seconds later in the stubble on his cheeks. Benny took a deep breath as he walked into the woods. The clean scent of forest expanded inside him, pushing away tension he hadn't realized was there.

When the trail split, Benny took the right fork. It was funny how you could be gone from a place for a while and still know it like yesterday, like remembering all the verses of a childhood song, each surprising line tugging up the next. This place pulled

Benny on like that: creek crossing threaded to an uphill turn and strung to a lightning-split tree and a limestone outcrop. The forest thickened and thinned around them as Benny traced his way.

Soon after sunrise low clouds rolled in, spreading a flat, gray light. The wind picked up as Benny and Frank walked out from a stand of big firs into a small clearing. Snow draped over huckleberry bushes in slumping igloos. Within Benny's memory of the tart huckleberries, a blue grouse burst from cover. It had been right here, the last fall his father came around. Benny's father had praised the boy's young Brittany, and recounted stories of his own boyhood dogs. For Benny, happiness would always smell like gunpowder and feathers.

Back in the woods, a red squirrel gripped a branch and ratcheted warning above its litter of disassembled cones.

"We're not after your stash," Benny said to the squirrel.

"What?" said Frank.

"Nothing."

They meandered for a couple of hours, finding only old sign. In the third hour, they crossed a weave of fresh mule deer tracks. Frank squatted for a better look and clicked his tongue at a set of big, splay-toed prints set among the smaller ones.

"Now that," Frank said, poking his finger into the deep track, "is a deer." He looked up at Benny and winked. "We crossed over into national forest back there, didn't we?"

"Nope," Benny said, stooping to examine the huge track. "Nice one."

Frank rolled his eyes. "Oh yes, Your Honor. We knew it was private property."

Ignoring Frank, Benny waved his hand in the direction of the tracks. "There's a good spot up this way to take a break and eat lunch."

"Aren't we going after that deer?" Frank said, hitching up his jeans.

"You bet," Benny said.

Frank shook his head and dogged Benny's steps up the trail.

Benny had a clear picture of the car-size boulder set into the hill. It had a flat face on the south side perfect for leaning against, and a downhill view of an open meadow. His father had parked

him there that first hunting trip and had left him for half a day with his .243 and three shells.

When Benny and Frank came up on the boulder, Benny saw with satisfaction that the tracks made a neat semicircle around the rock and angled uphill.

"I think they're headed for bed," he said, leaning the .243 against a stump.

The gun was covered with dings and dents and hadn't been fancy when his father had given it to him new. But if Benny's house caught fire, he would grab that gun and let everything else burn. They settled against the rock, out of the mounting wind. A sound like the river curled through the tossing treetops.

"My dad died," Benny said, unwrapping his sandwich, "a month ago. Mom heard last week."

"Wow, man. Sorry."

"It's OK. I hadn't seen him in a long time."

Benny's father had taken a job in the oil fields of Alaska when Benny was fourteen. At first he flew home at the end of each four-week shift, and he and Benny would go hunting, or fishing, or rooting around for mushrooms. Then he started flying to Arizona on his breaks, or Mexico, or anyplace, it seemed, but Montana. By the time Benny was a senior, his visits were down to one a year, but always during hunting season. Then he quit coming at all.

"We were going to buy this place," Benny said. "Him and me." A tree creaked in the wind. "He said that's why he took that job. I started stocking shelves at the IGA after school. I ended up buying a motorcycle with the money I'd saved."

Benny and Frank watched the snowy meadow below them as they ate.

"Marksons had this place for fifty years, I think," Benny said. "Did you ever know Jason? I remember when he changed his major to computer science. Moved to Seattle right after he graduated. Why would a guy want to live in Seattle when he could slide right into something like this?"

"Maybe he developed an allergy to hay," Frank said. "Maybe he wanted to make enough money so he could buy a ranch in Montana someday." He snorted at his own joke.

They fell silent, listening to the wind on the trees and a pair of passing ravens.

"Where do you think that buck is hiding?" Frank asked, after the chill of inactivity had set in.

"There's a little spring on the other side of this ridge. My old man and I found it the year I turned twelve. He shot a monster muley that day, in its bed a hundred yards from the spring. So we always checked there. He would drink a handful of water and say that was as close to communion as he was going to get. Told me he wouldn't mind being buried right there."

Benny wiped the lenses of his binocular with his handkerchief and glassed the meadow.

"I wonder if the new owner lets anybody on," Frank said. "I mean, if a guy bothered to ask."

"I called the ranch manager yesterday. 'No,' is the answer."

"Sounds like he needs to make up his mind," Frank said, peeling an orange.

"What?" Benny said, still watching the meadow. "I can't hear you."

Frank threw the peel at Benny.

"Well," Benny said, picking up the peel, "I know a little spring where the bluebird sings."

Benny and Frank followed the tracks uphill. Near the top of the ridge the larger set of tracks cut off. The men followed them along a sidehill, the wind in their faces as they crept up through the trees.

At the top of the ridge Benny stopped to give his heart a minute to slow down. He always lost his breath coming up on the spring. He wondered if they had taken good care of his father at the veteran's hospital. Benny hoped that he hadn't been thirsty when he died.

Veteran's Affairs had sent Benny's mother the effects. Apparently, he had listed her as next of kin. She and Benny went through the small box of things together: Navy discharge papers, union card, insurance forms, a ring that neither of them recognized.

"He left us again without saying good-bye," she had said, getting up from the kitchen table to make coffee.

Benny was tossing the papers back in the box when a folded magazine page fell out of the sheaf of insurance papers. The paper cracked when Benny unfolded it. It was a real estate ad folded around a bloodstained deer tag. The tag was notched 18 November 1977. Benny's first deer. The ad was from Paradise Realty. "Hunter's Getaway," one caption read. Another ad, "Sportsman's Dream," was circled. Benny recognized his father's scribbled handwriting in the margins: Creek. Forest access.

Frank touched Benny's arm and they sank to their knees. Frank pointed through the trees. A large mule deer stood in thick timber two hundred yards out, facing away from them. Its ears flicked under a broad, heavy-beamed rack.

"I'm just the accessory," Frank whispered to Benny. "Go for it."

Benny circled off, wind masking the soft rustle of his movement. It would be tricky getting a clear line of sight through the timber. He worked his way to within a hundred yards and still couldn't find a clear shot. Benny was sweating, even though his hands were cold. He crawled another twenty yards and eased the .243 onto a fallen log. The deer was behind a pile of deadfall, but it was looking in the direction Benny wanted it to go. Suddenly Benny detected movement and jerked out of his reverie.

As Benny watched the deer, part of his mind was still on his father. "I hope you never see another big old buck in your life without thinking of your old man," his father had said, laughing, the day he had shot the big muley by the spring. Benny had carried the deer's liver and heart home in his backpack. They might still be in the freezer.

The deer stepped out from behind the deadfall. Benny found it in his scope, steadied the cross hairs over the deer's heart, and took a breath.

"Bang," he said. He lowered his rifle as the startled deer crashed away.

Benny was thirsty. He could taste the water in the spring, a cold crush of watercress and juniper berries.

He heard rocks clattering on the ridge behind him and turned to see two men scrambling down. Benny started to run toward the spring, but one of the men yelled, "Stop! Game warden!"

The warden drew his pistol, and the other man had his rifle at the ready.

Frank'll be pissed, Benny thought. *He'll have to hitchhike back to town.*

The ranch manager carried Benny's rifle and pack on the way out. He had seen the truck, seen the tracks. The game warden juggled pistol and radio as he called for the sheriff.

"Like the sign says," the ranch manager said, walking behind Benny, "trespassers will be prosecuted."

The sheriff was waiting on the other side of the fence. He made Benny empty his pockets before locking him into the back of the patrol car.

"Can't these sons-a-b—— read?" the ranch manager asked the sheriff. "Am I responsible for the idiot still up there hiding behind some tree? Son-of-a-b— will probably want to sue me for not carrying his pack out too."

"We'll cruise the road," the sheriff said. "Probably pick him up near the Dodge."

"This one's lucky that deer moved off before he could shoot," said the game warden, nodding toward Benny in the back of the car. "The new judge is coming down pretty hard on game violations."

"Anything interesting?" the warden asked the sheriff, who was shuffling through the stuff Benny had pulled out of his pockets.

"Just snoose," the sheriff said. He pulled the lid off the Skoal can. Wind swirled gritty ashes out of the can and scattered Benny's father over the fence.

LIONS IN WINTER

BY

E. DONNALL THOMAS JR.

*Don Thomas is not one for doing things by halves. When he hunts it is
with a bow, and the bow won't have cams or wheels or a release or a
little peep sight but is going to be made of wood. And while he hunts
nearly all the species of big game across North America with that bow,
his unquestioned favorite is the continent's most elusive animal, the
cougar, which he pursues not from the seat of a snowmobile or even on
horseback, but on foot. It is almost always the case that many long
miles and longer days pass before a cat trees; but sometimes, as in this
story, you get lucky—if you work hard enough.*

The transition from deer to cougar took place with
remarkable speed that year, hurried along, perhaps, by the
impulse to distraction that always attends the death of a friend.

The Sunday after Thanksgiving, the last day of deer season, I
sat in a favorite stand below the house until dark, cradling my
recurve bow, tinkling occasionally on my rattling horns and
waiting for a big buck that never appeared. Since I'd passed up
shooting opportunities at several dozen deer in the preceding
weeks, I had nothing but my own hubris to blame for the fact
that I was eating my deer tag instead of venison. When the last
shooting light finally drained from the western sky, I trudged up
the hill empty-handed and began to prepare for the opening
morning of lion season, organizing my pack, locating winter
survival gear, and loading chains, scoop shovels, and dog box
into the back of the truck. As I worked, I thought about the
companionship so central to the pursuit of cougars and the friends
with whom I had shared so many tracks: Rosey Roseland and

Mike Bentler, who would be waiting for me the following morning, and Larry Schweitzer, whom I would never see again. Finally, I set the alarm for 3:00 A.M. and tumbled into bed.

I awoke to a pleasant surprise. A skiff of fresh snow carpeted the ground outside the house, the first to fall in weeks. Nature seemed to be making amends for my unfilled deer tag, since tracking conditions couldn't have been better. The hounds greeted me enthusiastically at the kennel, as if they knew their time had finally come, while my Labs howled plaintively when they realized I meant to leave them behind. As I wound down the hill toward town to pick up Rosey and Mike, a wide, heavy 5x5 whitetail materialized from the gloom and crossed the drive in front of me. I hadn't seen that buck all year. I offered it my silent congratulations for surviving another season and hoped we'd meet again.

An hour later, the lights of town lay far behind. Plainly visible beyond the headlights, Jupiter glowed like a beacon in the darkness, beckoning us forward into the hills. As we entered cat country at last, my eyes surrendered to the Morse code of tracks flashing past beneath the truck. Like spotting bonefish on a saltwater flat, identifying lion tracks takes place at a nearly subliminal level, and my instincts felt dull after the long layoff since the end of the previous season.

I wanted a fresh track for reasons more complicated than the usual excitement of opening day, the opening day of anything. Mike had hosted Rosey and me during a week of whitetail hunting at his Iowa home earlier in the year, and Rosey and I, who have taken our own share of cougars, were eager to express our appreciation for his hospitality. Mike had hunted cougar with us the year before, only to be undone by a frustrating series of lion chases that all fizzled after long, lonely miles through the hills on foot. That week we'd refined the concept of snatching defeat from the jaws of victory. Mike is too philosophical a hunter to care, or at least to express any disappointment. But he deserved an honest lion as much as anyone we'd ever hunted with, and we badly wanted to provide him with an encounter with one in the special way in which you sometimes want things for your family and friends even more than you do for yourself.

Then there was the matter of the dogs. For a houndsman, there is no source of pride like a strong kennel. In the days when my bluetick Drive, and Rosey's black-and-tan Moose, led the youngsters out of the dog box at the beginning of a chase, we inevitably set off uphill, confident that only the luckiest of cougars could evade our determined pursuit. But the passage of time had taken its inevitable toll. A victim of premature heart disease, Drive lay buried in the coulee behind my house, and Moose had retired to the rug in front of Rosey's wood stove. At one point the previous season, we'd been down to his Harley and my Beau, two young blueticks with lots of potential but little else.

Then disaster shuffled the deck. Early that season, our old friend Larry Schweitzer experienced a bout of chest pain while chasing cats. Despite a clean health history, one thing quickly led to another. A few days after his last hunt, he underwent cardiac surgery; a few days after that, he was dead. Once the shock had settled, his widow, Kathy, asked Rosey and me to take his two young Walkers, Zeke and Little Joe, and treat them as Larry would have wanted.

By reputation, Joe barked in his kennel and Zeke didn't, and since I live in the country, where yapping hounds don't matter much (not that my wife, Lori, always agrees), Little Joe went home with me. An early bad experience with a Walker (a dog named Dan, acquired from Larry, which discourteously tried to seize people by the throat and rip out their windpipe) had left me with a preference for other breeds, but out of respect for Larry's memory I meant to make this new canine relationship work. Whether the quarry is lions or pheasants, the process (if not the tally) goes better if you get to know your hunting dogs and treat them as friends. Little Joe proved easy enough to like, and a summer's worth of training left me happy with his place in the kennel and confident of his ability at the tree—if a bit uncertain of his nose. All we needed were a few good cougars to help sort out the rest.

Our kind of hunter, Mike expressed more interest in the beauty of the mountains in winter and the excitement of the chase than in skull sizes, and he made it clear that he'd be happy to take any mature cougar. Rosey and I appreciated his enthusiasm. Our young pack desperately needed the experience of a chase, and neither of us felt like turning down fresh tracks because of someone's preoccupation with the record book. When the first set of round prints emerged from the background chatter of deer tracks, I stood on the brakes and we all piled out eagerly. The track belonged to a mature female, by our reckoning, which was not a problem; the trace of fallen snow the prints contained, however, confirmed that they had been left early the previous night. After a brief discussion, we decided to forge on in search of something fresher.

We left the hills several hours later without finding what we sought, teetering on the edge of defeat for the day. As I fumbled with a cup of lukewarm coffee and a box of Pop Tarts—the official breakfast of lion hunters—something caught my attention in the snow beside the county road. The message passed straight from my eye to my brake foot without ever passing through my brain, a silent testimonial to years of tracking. At first I wasn't even sure what I'd seen, but as I backed down the road the story became clear. A lion had crossed the road in the middle of a jumbled deer trail, and the track hadn't been there on our way in.

At this point the county road ran through posted ranch property, and I didn't relish wasting valuable hours trying to run down the landowner. Then Rosey remembered that a mutual friend had recently purchased a piece of ground that bordered the large BLM tract above the road. From the top of the hill, I contacted him by cell phone and obtained his enthusiastic permission to set off from his place. That may be the only time in my life that I've found such modern means of communications useful.

An hour later we were hiking through the big woods in search of the track, and I couldn't have been happier. Thanks to the light snow cover we'd been able to leave our snowshoes behind in the truck, and the hounds were minding their manners on their leashes. Being just below freezing, the temperature made possible comfortable hiking without compromising the scent. (Warm winds can destroy the scent from a lion track like an eraser cleaning a blackboard.) The deep expanse of ponderosa pine stretching away up the mountainside felt delightfully empty: a playing field constructed just for us. Above all, I was glad to

leave the truck. The combination of hunting and vehicles goes against my grain, and I always appreciate the discovery of a fresh track if only to get out onto my feet. For us, the truck is nothing more than a means to the beginning of the hunt. Corrupted, lion "hunting"—in quotation marks—can devolve into little more than a video game played out with snow machines and tracking collars. We prefer to take what lions we do the old-fashioned way: We earn them.

This cougar might have done any number of things after crossing the road, but I felt confident that we'd cut the track again somewhere beneath the ridgetop. By the time we finally did, I was sweating pleasantly, despite the chill. We introduced Harley and Joe to the track, and when they set off up the hill in full cry we released Zeke and Beau and stood back to listen.

Bowhunting is ordinarily a silent affair, all about stealth. I know more than a few seasoned bow hunters who disdain the racket made by hounds. Sympathetic as I may be to their point of view, I find something primal in the chorus. That sound, tumbling downhill through the pines, reminds me of the ancient relationship between early hunters and their dogs. Also, there's an element of pride involved: I raised Beau and trained him, and I befriended Little Joe when he had no one left. With or without justification, all houndsmen assume a measure of credit for their dogs' accomplishments, even though a good lion dog is little more than a nose on legs (brains being optional).

The corollary, of course, is an equivalent measure of responsibility for the dogs' failures. It wasn't long until we began to dislike what we heard, which suggested disorganization rather than focus, flavored, perhaps, by guilty pleasure. Rosey and Mike set off on the cat track while I followed the dogs. Hounds on a chase can commit only one cardinal sin, and several hundred yards of tracking confirmed our worst suspicions: my partners stood on a solitary cat track, while I followed a riot of footprints left by dogs and running deer. I could feel the outrage in Rosey's voice; my own reaction tended toward embarrassment. "I can't believe you drove twelve hundred miles to help us train these boneheads," I said to Mike as we churned through the snow behind the worst looking set of tracks imaginable.

But, as always in the field, there is no substitute for a positive attitude in the face of adversity. Sometimes a breakdown like this spells the end of the day (or the end of the week, for that matter), but all four dogs eventually circled back and let us catch them. After a brief but intense discussion of their evil ways, we led them back uphill until we cut lion tracks again. This time we walked the trail for a mile with the dogs straining wildly against their leashes. Only those who have experienced the dubious pleasure of leading eager hounds through thick cover in steep terrain will know how our rumps felt by the time we finally decided to let them run the track again.

The dogs seemed to know they had one chance for redemption, and they made the most of it. Two hours later, we stood beneath a towering ponderosa. All four dogs were treeing strongly, and Mike had his cat. Those who dismiss cougar hunting as too easy might have had a case if they'd seen nothing but the shot and the dead cougar in the snow.

But that's never the whole story ...

Rosey and I had taken the entire first week of lion season off from work, and Mike isn't the kind of hunter who gets lazy just because he's filled his own tag. So the following morning, the alarm exploded at 3:00 A.M. all over again.

By unstated agreement, I was due up at the plate. Rosey and I have hunted together for decades without ever having to discuss—let alone argue over—such matters. Personally, I hadn't killed a cat in years, despite treeing dozens. Some of the rest fell to friends who had never hunted lions before, while others lived to hunt again, beneficiaries of our enthusiasm for catch-and-release cougar hunting. During that period, Rosey had killed two good toms. I'd been there for one of them and had provided a crucial bit of intelligence for the second when I relayed in a tip from a rancher on a day that I couldn't hunt myself. Now my time had come around again, and after countless miles focused on the chase rather than the kill, I felt ready to string my own bow and kill a cat again, for reasons that are difficult to articulate even to myself.

But not just any cat. Unlike Mike, I enjoy abundant opportunity to hunt cougars and can almost certainly fill a lion tag every year if I wish. Under such circumstances, selectivity makes sense for reasons that have nothing to do with skull measurements—or lion steaks, for that matter. Waiting for a good tom heightens the challenge and prolongs a process I happen to love. And with a whole season ahead of us, I didn't feel like ending matters prematurely.

So that explains our reaction to the first two sets of tracks we cut that morning. Both looked fresh enough to chase, but after following them out under the evergreen canopy and studying their toe pads in the crisp layer of new snow, we just couldn't make either of them belong to a big tom. Once again, we headed down out of the mountains around midday, nearly ready to concede.

As we crossed the corner of an old friend's ranch, my foot was halfway to the brake when Rosey's shout filled the cab and we slid to a stop in another clatter of coffee cups. This time the track looked plenty big enough, but it appeared to have been left early the night before. Studying the open terrain below us, we saw an even set of tracks crossing a field a mile away, and through Mike's binocular we convinced ourselves that they belonged to what had suddenly become our lion.

The track headed toward a thick, timbered basin on a ranch whose owners I did not know. With the sun beating down relentlessly—threatening to make the track's scent evaporate with every degree that the temperature rose—we drove through the hills toward the ranch house while I tried to make myself presentable—no easy task according to those who know me.

Finally, I pulled a wool cap down over my unkempt hair, strode bravely up the steps to the front door, and introduced myself to the ranch wife, hoping I'd once done some member of her family a favor in our local hospital. "You want to hunt *lions?*" she asked when I stated our predicament. I braced for the worst. "We've been waiting *five years* for someone to show up and do something about those cats!" A few minutes later, we had written permission to hunt the place all season and directions through a series of pastures to the ridge we wanted to reach. "And don't forget to come back this spring and kill the bears up there!" she said in parting. Some days it really does pay to get out of bed in the morning.

We planned to run the two-track along the ridge and hope that the cat had traveled all the way through the basin. If we didn't cut its track, we would split up and work our way down through the timber until we found it and hope that we made contact before we ran out of light, snow, or both. But three miles above the ranch house, we spotted a huge, fluffy set of tracks ahead, and Rosey had Harley and Joe out of the dog box before the motor stopped running. By the time I had my pack on, we could hear the sound of the dogs barking treed in the timber on the far side of the ridge.

Lion chases seldom turn out as simple as they first appear. Despite the dogs' enthusiasm, the first tree looked as barren as a telephone pole. After leashing the hounds, we set out in a series of widening circles until we saw fresh, bounding cat tracks headed back across the ridge. When we released the dogs again, our ears soon lost the sound of the chase to the sigh of the freshening wind, and we set off after the track through a nasty tangle of thornbrush in the bottom of the basin.

My face and hands were soon scratched and bleeding, but when the sound of dogs at the tree rose to greet us once more, I knew they had the cat. With the promise of the chase's end ahead, I forged through the brush and old snow until I found myself staring up through a canopy of pine boughs at a long, tawny form surrounded by a corona of dappled light. In contrast to antlered game, cougars, like bears, are particularly difficult to evaluate, even at close range. But good toms are like good art: you know them when you see them. And there he stood on the branch, head like a jack o' lantern, muscles advertising his ability to break a bull elk's neck with a single snap, clearly contemptuous of the dogs and men below. I knew that it could kill us all in seconds if it chose to, and with no firearm among us we would have been powerless to stop such an assault. Nothing but decades worth of experience with cougars suggested any degree of personal safety, but for the moment that would have to do.

Years ago I carried my longbow when I hunted cougar, but I found myself in too many situations that demanded both hands for climbing or catching dogs. For the past several years, I've carried a three-piece takedown recurve on lion hunts. Buried out of the way in my pack, it works splendidly on the trail in rough country—but I hadn't had to assemble my bow quickly for several seasons.

And nothing makes an argument for simple bow design like a nervous cat in a tree. As I fumbled with the bow, Mike and Rosey threw together a pair of our takedown wooden arrows. (Fitting easily inside a backpack where they won't snag on brush, these arrows, designed especially for lion hunting on foot, contain a male-female ferrule midshaft, just like a fly rod, reducing their overall length by half.) As we wrestled with our tackle, the big cat grew increasingly nervous. "He's going to bail!" Rosey shouted as I tightened the last bolt, and then a shower of snow hit me as the tom exploded from the branches overhead. Suddenly, our uncharacteristically easy chase didn't look so easy anymore.

But at this point, the dogs refused to be denied. The cat led us through another mile of thorn and rocks before he treed again, but this time I reached the towering ponderosa with my bow strung and ready. Making a clean shot on a lion in a tree can be more difficult than it sounds, as a lot of our friends have learned the hard way, but when the bottom of the cat's chest appeared through a window in the branches directly overhead, I drew quickly and released. Although I was completely confident of the hit, a wounded cougar in the middle of eager hounds can be dangerous to all, and I quickly followed up with a second arrow through the cat's chest. It was completely unnecessary, as it happened: The big tom was dead before it hit the ground, and not even the work of skinning the hide and boning the meat and getting everything back up the hill before dark could compromise our exhilaration.

Some people are surprised when they hear about packing out cougar meat, assuming that it is fit just for the dogs. Lucky dogs! As only lion hunters or their friends can know, the stuff is delicious, light, and delicate—a treat on any table, once the diners have surmounted inevitable cultural biases against eating cat (or, if they don't know what's on the plate, "mountain veal"). On our hunts lion meat receives as much attention as skulls and hides, and I feel confident that our hunting is the better for it.

Many people, including bow hunters I respect, have reservations about hunting cougars with dogs. Almost always these skeptics have never experienced a lion hunt themselves. Granted, the first week of last year's season—two days of hunting, two chases, two dead cats—made it look easy. But that's the abridged version of the story. Among other things, I've left out seasons full of miles without a track, long trips down through cliffs in the dark, the way your hands feel when you're skinning a cat at twenty-five below, high-centered rigs followed by hours of work with scoop shovels and jack, the heartache of lost hounds, and several tons of dog food going into the kennel and processed dog food coming out. Until you've known all that, you haven't really known lion hunting.

Larry Schweitzer knew all that and more. He understood the magic of hound music and the odd serenity of the high country in winter. When I finally rolled back into my own driveway at the end of our second long day in the field, I hung the lion meat in the barn and tended to the dogs. I spent some extra time with Little Joe, scratching his ears a bit longer than necessary and offering him a second piece of jerky, our traditional reward to the hounds at the end of an especially demanding day. When our retinue of hunters, spouses, and friends all got together for dinner at my house the following evening, we served a traditional two-course tribute to the fallen quarry—cougar Parmesan and sweet-and-sour mountain lion—and raised a glass to Larry's memory.

He would have understood all the effort, triumph, and reward, and our celebration only made us realize how much we missed him.

NIGHT OF THE LIVING ALLIGATORS

BY

JIM ZUMBO

If this is a story by Jim Zumbo, where are the elk, where are the mountains? As anyone who knows him can tell you, though, Jim never met a wild animal or a stretch of wild ground he didn't like, and he has encountered almost every kind of both there is. As improbable as Jim Zumbo as a swamp-rat Ahab, harpoon in hand, searching through the darkness for his own private Moby Dick, may be, I believe that what he learned about alligators, a strange new country, and himself didn't surprise as much as captivate him.

The horrible sound still echoed in my head. Just minutes before, somewhere in the night, a gator had caught a crane, and we had to listen to the screams of the dying bird. As peaceful as this alligator swamp had seemed at first, it had become clear that there was more than enough death in it to go around.

Now ahead of us in the faint beam of the guide's headlamp loomed the menacing apparition of a gator. Our boat glided toward it, and I tightened my sweaty grip on the harpoon. As we closed in, the dim light showed more of the gator, and I was struck by the weirdness of all that was about to occur.

In a few moments I would try to drive a harpoon into an ancient reptile, which now looked to be longer than our sixteen-foot boat. In all of the perilous situations in which I had found myself, my heart never pounded harder. Each of the elements of dread was here—danger, the unknown, the feeling of total inadequacy. Mostly danger.

When the harpoon struck that huge creature, an instant explosion was inevitable. A quarter-ton or more of gator would be whipped into a frenzy, with a slashing tail, popping jaws, and unbridled power. Our boat, which now seemed woefully unsuited to the task, offered little protection.

What made all this even more disturbing was the premeditated nature of the deed. I've been chased by grizzly bears, rhinoceroses, and had several other close calls; but those harrowing moments didn't allow time to think. On this hunt, I had all the time in the world to worry about what was about to happen. And the screaming of that crane had not helped.

The giant gator was now five feet away. I held tightly to the harpoon, leaned over the rail, and summoned every cell in my body to provide the strength I'd need to drive it home. I can remember asking myself, "What, in God's name, am I doing here?"

The outdoors has been the focus of my life, and I have always found adventure there, wherever "there" might be. When I was a city kid growing up in New York State, I lay on the sidewalk and fed the ants in the cracks of the cement. With tweezers, I'd drop a tiny crumb of bread and watch the ants drag it into their hole until it was time for me to go inside to eat, or play stickball with my buddies. I knew where every major spider web was in the hedges in front of the house, and each day I fed the spiders the ants I had fed. As the spiders grew I switched to bigger prey, such as flies, until finally the predators were large enough to take down a grasshopper. I kept a big preying mantis in a large cage I had built out of hardware cloth, and I fattened it with insects, letting the mantis go after I had observed it for a few weeks. But it was snakes that intrigued me most.

Along the east wall of the church across the street from my house, a natural phenomenon occurred every year. As the wall heated up from the sun's spring rays, dozens of garter snakes crawled along its base. I'd catch a bunch and put them in my empty mantis cage and feed them for a while, usually letting them go after a few days. I wouldn't be caught dead trying to catch a rattler, though, and I was always at high alert when I hiked a hill near my house where copperheads had been seen. When I went fishing every snake in the water was a potential moccasin, and I gave it a wide berth. I didn't really fear snakes; I simply respected them with a peculiar fascination and kept them at a distance. I was also fond of watching turtles and had a number of them as temporary pets. Later in life, when I worked for the U.S. Military Academy at West Point as post forester and wildlife manager, I trapped snapping turtles from the many lakes and ponds on the military installation.

Using Bailey beaver traps, which are made of heavy-duty chain-link material and resemble a giant clam when open, I tended the traps before and after work hours. The idea was to catch the turtles alive, keep them in good health until I acquired at least a dozen, and sell them at Fulton's Fish Market in New York City. The trapping involved tying a dead sunfish or perch to the trigger, which normally activated the trap and caused it to slam shut when a beaver brushed the trigger with its belly. But I had it rigged so that a turtle would jab at the bait with its beak, closing the trap. I would set my trap near a small stream or creek where the scent of the bait would be carried into the pond, always in water shallow enough so that part of the closed trap would be above the surface, enabling the turtle to breathe air. I didn't want any of my valuable turtles drowning.

After trapping the turtles, the next step was to keep them in a safe place, where they wouldn't be discovered by the military personnel who were always about. I found the perfect spot. I would take the turtles in my truck and drive into the artillery impact area where the cadets trained with 105mm howitzers. The place, of course, was absolutely off-limits because of the obvious danger, but I carried a badge and was also the post game warden, having total access to the 16,000-acre reservation. There was a swamp off an old woods road that was ideal. I put a couple of big wooden boxes in the swamp, sinking them with enough rocks so that they weren't completely submerged. In them went my turtles, some of them being thirty pounds or more. I kept them alive by tossing in roadkills, usually woodchucks, foxes, and other stuff I found along the highways. The only danger I faced was being in the area into which very large explosives would be hurled. I checked the artillery schedule whenever I needed to tend to my turtles and timed my visits accordingly. One day, however, I read the schedule wrong, and I heard the big guns pounding away from a hill a half-mile away. I got the hell out.

NIGHT OF THE LIVING ALLIGATORS

When I had enough turtles in the boxes, I would remove them carefully: One careless mistake would cause a serious injury if a reptile nailed me with its powerful beak. I took the turtles to Talbot's Fish Market in the city where I lived, and they would make the delivery to Fulton's, sixty miles away. The local fish market would take a small commission, and I received a nice check, most of which went to buying Christmas presents for my kids.

I guess you might say I just liked reptiles. When I moved West, I always had a horned toad as a pet, feeding it insects with my children. One of these days I'm going to a rattlesnake roundup, though I haven't decided, yet, if I'll try to catch one by myself.

Among reptiles, the alligator is certainly king. A couple months before that night in the swamp, my friend Linda invited me to hunt alligators in Florida. Right away she had my interest, but I had some questions. I assumed that we would hunt them in the routine way, which is to toss out a huge baited hook, wait until a gator chomps down, then haul the beast in and dispatch it with a gun. Not exactly my cup of tea, but I was nevertheless curious.

"How do we hunt them?" I asked on the phone.

"With harpoons," Linda responded.

"You mean, up close and personal?"

"Yep, we just sneak up to them in the dark and let fly."

"Count me in."

It was dark when we made our way from the lodge on the plantation, where we were staying, to the dock. Prior to departing, DeWitt, our guide, showed us the skull of a gator and explained the vulnerable spots. Unless the harpoon hits the right area, he told us, which is right behind the eyes, it will skid harmlessly away. The detachable harpoon head resembles a frog gig. One end of a stout thirty-foot string is tied to the head, and the other to a large, empty propane tank. When a gator is struck the hunter lets go of the harpoon, and the head separates from the eight-foot pole. The gator will dive with the hook embedded just under its leathery hide, but it won't be mortally wounded—simply attached to the float. The hunters watch the float, and when it is still, the cord is pulled up with a tired but very angry gator at the other end. The next step is to draw the furious creature close

enough to the boat that it can be quickly dispatched with a "bang stick." The stick looks like a six-foot broom handle with a .357 magnum cartridge inserted into the end. The head is driven toward the gator's (tiny) brain and the cartridge discharged. The expired gator is then hauled out of the water headfirst and the jaws are quickly wrapped shut with duct tape. That done, the animal is deposited in the boat.

Now then, all of the above is what is supposed to happen. Reality may differ.

We weren't ten minutes from the dock when I witnessed an incredible display of outdoor skill. DeWitt shone a powerful flashlight beam far out into the water and spotted two gators. He turned off the light, and I watched amazed as he and Sid—DeWitt's assistant, who ran the outboard and electric trolling motor—guided the boat toward one of the gators, using only the stars to light the way.

Linda had insisted that I be up first, so I stood at the bow with DeWitt, trying in vain to make out the alligator.

"Can you see the gator?" I whispered to DeWitt.

"Yessir," he responded. "Comin' up on the left, about a hundred yards out."

I saw nothing but the surface of a very dark lake.

DeWitt turned on his headlamp, which cast a light so dim that it hardly seemed worth it. I saw nothing but flat, black water. Then an object materialized in the darkness. The form took shape, and there was an alligator floating ten yards off the bow.

I grasped the harpoon tightly, positioned it about twenty inches over the water, and drove it down when the alligator was within range. The animal lunged, sending water flying over the boat, but the harpoon had missed its mark.

"Too far back," DeWitt said. "You just tickled him."

Now I was rattled. This was going to be more than I had bargained for.

For the next half-hour DeWitt and Sid spotted gators in the dark that, as far as I was concerned, were nonexistent. These men had the kind of night vision you acquire only by being born and reared in the Florida swamps. Even more astounding was their uncanny ability to tell the size of a gator by the reflection of its eyes at distances of several hundred yards. A big gator has bigger eyes and a wider space between them. How these men could evaluate a gator that far away I don't know.

Presently DeWitt located one that interested him.

"Big gator," he said simply. "He's a good 'un."

DeWitt turned off his lamp, and using hand signals in the starlight, once more he and Sid teamed to guide the boat straight to the reptile.

The boat eased forward, propelled by the small electric motor. I was ready this time, but when the alligator appeared in the diffused light, I was suddenly intimidated. This was far bigger than the one I'd missed.

Again I gripped the harpoon tightly and waited until the very last moment. The animal was facing away, at an angle, and I plunged the harpoon downward with a swift thrust.

All hell broke loose. As instructed by DeWitt, I let go of the harpoon as soon as I had rammed it home and let the gear do its work. The harpoon head disengaged from the pole as it hit. Struck, the gator slammed the boat with its huge tail and disappeared into the depths amid a colossal plume of water that sprayed high into the night air. The empty propane tank tore from the side of the boat and skidded swiftly across the surface of the water, cutting an eerie sound as it sped through the darkness.

"Gotta get another harpoon in that big boy," DeWitt said. He and Sid rigged up a second point attached to another buoy, and I got set to do it all over again. They caught up to the propane tank, and by pure brute strength DeWitt and Sid slowly hauled in the big gator, retrieving the rope hand over hand. It was a colossal struggle, with the men pulling for all they were worth. Finally the gator hove-to in the beam of light, and I stood at the rail with the harpoon. The animal I was looking down on had jaws that seemed to be two feet long. It twisted and lunged beside the boat, banging its lethal tail in a furious struggle that showered water everywhere.

"Damn big gator," DeWitt said flatly. "Probably go close to twelve feet."

I held the pole ready, but the giant crocodilian sounded in another slashing explosion that churned the water to froth. I watched stunned as the buoy sliced across the surface.

After another titanic battle the gator was once again alongside the boat, thrashing, twisting, and slapping the hull with its impossibly long tail. I saw an opportunity and jammed the harpoon home. This time the alligator rolled violently before I could let go of the pole. Pain shot through my upper shoulder as the muscles tore, and I saw more than just the stars in the sky.

The reptile was well struck, though, with a pair of harpoons and two huge floats slowing it down and tiring it out.

Now the gator could be pulled alongside the boat and killed with the bang stick. DeWitt had been casual about pretty much everything so far, including the dangers associated with close encounters with gators, but he was concerned about the handling of the bang stick.

"Be real careful," he said. "That thing will go off if anything touches it. Keep it pointed way up in the air, and tap it hard behind the gator's eyes so the bullet goes into his brain."

With the harpooned alligator brought alongside the boat, I aimed the crude weapon precisely behind the eyes and thrust down hard. The cartridge fired and the gator gave a huge shudder, then lay still.

"Give him one more," DeWitt said. "We can't take no chances."

Sid loaded another cartridge, and I administered a final shot. The gator, we hoped, was finished. But DeWitt severed the spinal cord behind the head with a knife and taped shut the jaws before he and Sid hauled the heavy carcass in over the gunwale.

"I'm glad we got this critter," DeWitt said. "A big one like this kills plenty of deer every year."

Now it was Linda's turn.

Once more we searched the darkness. Soon DeWitt spotted an alligator, and we moved in. As before, the two men eased the boat toward the reptile. There wasn't a sound—no water slapping the hull, no conversation, no animal noises from the swamp.

In the starlight I could see Linda's fingers tightening and loosening on the pole, and I knew that she must be feeling some of what I had—apprehension, intimidation, and self-doubt. Added to her feelings, though, was the knowledge that DeWitt had never had a woman try to harpoon an alligator from his boat before.

We glided forward, and I saw Linda lean toward the rail and position herself. She jammed the harpoon down, the water boiled, but the point merely bounced off the gator's thick hide.

"Don't feel bad," DeWitt whispered. "Lots of folks don't get it right the first try. It might take another try or two."

"We might see that gator again," Sid said. "He's so tough he don't know what hurt is. All that harpoon point did was graze his hide. He'll get over it in a minute."

Suddenly DeWitt came to life. "Big gator," he exclaimed. "Over yonder, across the lake." For the first time there was genuine excitement in the guide's voice.

The light went off, and we cruised in the dark. We were nearing the gator when I felt something scrape my leg. My dead gator was moving! I didn't want to say anything to distract Linda and the two men from the stalk, and I resisted the urge to turn on my tiny flashlight.

It couldn't be alive! I had sent two bullets into its brain, and I watched DeWitt sever its spinal cord. But those thoughts offered no comfort when the gator's feet started moving slowly back and forth.

Jim Carmichel, I recalled, had once shot a tremendous African crocodile in the brain with a .338. The "dead" crocodile was then lashed head to tail in a small boat. As the boat traveled across the lake, Carmichel saw one of the croc's eyes open. Moments later the entire animal came alive, roaring and twisting. The tail broke free, and the boat almost capsized in the croc-infested waters as the big reptile thrashed wildly. Luckily, they got the croc "quieted," and Carmichel's party made it to shore with no injuries.

So now here I was, with a huge gator apparently returning from the dead at my feet. I fully expected the tail to come whipping around, knocking us all into the water—into a lake full of prowling alligators.

But that didn't happen, though the legs continued to move in a bizarre and threatening fashion that made me wonder if my minutes on earth were numbered. I took a bit of solace in the knowledge that with reptiles, a dead one doesn't always lie still. I remembered completely beheaded snappers—ones I had dispatched for dinner—walking around in the bed of my truck.

The movement is a mere reflexive action, the brain having ceased to function. That's how I tried to reassure myself, anyhow.

Soon we were upon Linda's alligator. I could barely see it as we approached, but I could see Linda's fingers tightening and loosening, tightening and loosening.

At the last moment, the gator turned and began to submerge. Linda's thrust would have been perfectly on target, but the angle was slightly off. The harpoon missed.

"Didn't want to get you excited," DeWitt whispered, "so I didn't tell you how big it was. That gator was easy twelve feet, probably bigger than Jim's."

More troubles haunted us. Linda nicely drove the harpoon into another big gator, but when it was pulled alongside the boat, the bang stick didn't fire, even though it was driven perfectly. The gator made a terrific lunge and the harpoon pulled free.

"He's barely scratched," DeWitt said. "He'll be good as new tomorrow."

As the night wore on the air and water cooled, and the reptiles were harder to locate. At last, at 2:00 A.M., Linda scored on an eight-footer. The harpoon struck fairly, and this time the bang stick fired. It was with a great deal of relief that De Witt hauled the alligator into the boat.

"Are you ever going to try this again?" I asked Linda.

"Absolutely," she said. "There's a twelve-foot gator out there with my initials on it."

That's how the night of the living alligators ended, and it had been one of the strangest, most primeval experiences I had ever known. When, before, had I ever hunted a beast as old as the dinosaurs with a hand weapon as old, in design, as the human species? If I had asked myself the question I had put to Linda, what would my answer have been?

The only one I could think of was that, as much as I would forever love chasing elk in the Rockies, there are no monstrous gators—biggest of all the reptiles—on those snowcapped peaks. So there would always be a reason for me to return to the dark swamps of Florida.

THE HELLPIG HUNT

BY

HUMBERTO FONTOVA

When was it decreed that hunting demands decorum? Pick up the latest issue of almost any hunting periodical and you will see exemplified a mode of personal deportment that would make Steve Douglas, the somnambulistic patriarch of the 1960s television show My Three Sons, *look like an East African* shifta *bandit high on* qat. *Today, no outdoor magazine art editor would dare to run a picture of Douglas without photoshopping out his tobacco pipe, lest a ruinous example be set. Humberto Fontova, south Louisiana Cuban conservative polemicist, is under no such restraint. He's got a wild hair somewhere that will undoubtedly, and regrettably, be underappreciated by more than a few hidebound hunters. His wildness is on open display in this epic hog-hunt story, with a lagniappe of deer. As you read it, recall that not once did Thoreau say, "In mannerliness is the preservation of the world."*

Normally I'd be half-crazy with restlessness by now. An hour on a deer stand and my eyes usually start begging for different scenery. My muscles yearn activity. My nervous system pleads for stimulation. My buttocks itch for a softer seat.

None of that on this early January day, because I'm perched in a scraggly willow on a mushy spoilbank in the Mississippi Delta. Hence, I'm in bliss. I had decided to sneak in a quickie morning deer hunt before the hog hunt with the neighbors. They said we wouldn't be heading out till 9:00 or so. I had plenty of time.

For a lover of wetlands there's nothing quite like this place. To my left: a canopy of lush green willows contrasts against a lightening sky, under them a thick mat of elephant ears, glistening with dew. To my right: a vast shallow bay, lightly rippled by the breeze, stretches for a quarter-mile until it meets a wall of Roseau cane that wraps around its eastern edge. At an opening with the pass, duck potato, three square grass, and knee-high willows sprout from a network of sandbars left by the high river last spring.

Since daybreak I've been watching pintail and gadwall dropping into the bay. Sometimes they circle to within a hundred yards of my perch on the way down; the sun, just topping the treetops, makes their late winter plumage glisten gorgeously.

The delightful racket of pintail whistling and gadwall gabbling isn't a sound normally associated with deer hunting. Neither is the banter of a few hundred geese conversing on their flight overhead. But down here you learn to expect it—indeed to yearn for it. It's part of the reason for going through the trouble of getting down here. Add the sights associated with those sounds—the bays shimmering in the sun, the willows and elephant ears still green in January, the rafts and flights of ducks, the osprey crashing into the pond and struggling off with a mullet in its talons, the raccoon groping for a meal along the mudbank, the roseate spoonbills winging overhead, the deer ambling—THE DEER?

It's a deer! A buck, no less! It's ambling along between the marsh alders and elephant ears, about a hundred yards down the shoreline, and heading my way. It's probably making for that thick stand of Roseau cane just behind me, to bed down for the day. If so, and if it stays on the trail, I'll get a twenty-yard broadside shot. Good God, the shakes are starting.

Deer stick out in this habitat. This far south, they never get that gray winter coat. This one's still reddish-brown. And it's not a wallhanger; looks like spindly forks on his head. But so what? It looks fat and healthy, as befits this Delta habitat and its year-round buffet. I can't make out the ribs. That's the best sign of succulent venison—if I get a shot.

My bow was hanging from a branch, and I reached for it—but s-l-o-w-l-y. There, got it. Now clamp the release on the string—but s-l-o-w-l-y. No jerky movements. There, did it. Now turn slightly to get the perfect angle when it walks by—but again, s-l-o-w-l-y . . . *PLENK!*

Now I've done it! The damn fiberglass bow taps the deer stand as I try to bring it into position. The deer stops. It's looking this way. It's rock still. Don't move, Humberto. Don't even *breathe*, for God's sake. Now it's bobbing its head. Looks like I've blown it.

Wait a minute. Now it takes another step. It stops and looks behind it, then nips at a bush. Hummmm. Looks like it's calming down.

VRRRRRMMMMMMMM! What's that?! Don't tell me! Yes, it's a boat coming down the pass. Probably Louisiana Department of Wildlife and Fish Senior Agent Nicholas "Ratso" Rizzo. The jerk will probably stop when he sees my pirogue on the bank and walk up to spoil my hunt. The buck's looking toward the pass now. Its ears are up and pointed toward the noise.

I look over and see the boat. But it's not Ratso. It's my friends Chris, Tom, and On-the-Ball, heading out for their duck hunt. Hope they don't . . .

Ah, the deer has turned back now. It's nipping the bush again. Shoulda known. These deer live with dozens of blazing boats every day of their lives. They don't associate an outboard's racket with danger, much as their upland cousins don't associate cars and trucks with danger—until they stop, that is. Especially in Louisiana.

A recent incident explains why no deer "infestations" bedevil Louisiana motorists and yardkeepers. The Louisiana Department of Wildlife put out a plastic deer with luminous eyes beside a well-traveled bayou highway, planning to stake out the place that night and nab some poachers.

When they came back a little later for the stakeout, that deer was already . . . remember Bonnie and Clyde at the end of the movie? Remember Sonny Corleone when they trapped him in that tollbooth?

Well, they got off easy compared with that deer. Plastic deer confetti is what the agents found. The thing had been blasted to smithereens by every caliber bullet and conceivable projectile. A few recognizable pieces of plastic even had arrows sticking out of them. We take our cuisine seriously down here.

So the game agents came back with another plastic deer, put it out, and stayed. If I recall from the news story, about half the vehicles—everything from pickups to limousines—stopped and had a go at the deer with armaments ranging from rifles to shotguns to pistols to crossbows. One guy charged it with a pocketknife, cheered on by his wife. Another guy was observed belly-crawling toward the deer clenching a tire iron! The game agents said they almost needed respirators on this fascinating assignment. Their stomachs ached for days.

Anyway, this ain't no plastic deer still walking toward me. Its ears are down, and now it's back on the trail, about sixty yards out. At twenty, I'll take it. Just a few seconds to go . . . my knees are starting to knock. I'm a basket case. Always happens when I see a deer.

At twenty-five yards I finally raise the bow—and D-R-A-W! There, perfect to the corner of the mouth. The sight-pin dances over its chest, just behind the shoulder, as I take a deep breath. I'm breathing in gasps. *Calm down, for heaven's sake; you'll blow it, I say to myself.* Another deep breath. The sight-pin finally stops jerking . . . stops wobbling . . . steadies. Right behind the shoulder now . . . the deer's stopped and is looking straight at me.

Release.

RELEASE for God's sake, Humberto! He'll bolt. . . . *FLUNK!* I squeeze the release, then—*WHACK!!* The arrow hits, and the deer's bolting off. Two bounds and it's lost in the brambles to my right. I'm shaking spastically now, a complete basket case, like David Byrne in that *Once in a Lifetime* video. My knees are almost knocking.

But I didn't like the sound of that arrow hitting. That wasn't the nice wet, hollow *WHUNK* you hear when you slam an arrow through a deer's ribcage. No, it was more like? . . . Is that? . . . Let's see. I peer closer.

YEP! There's my arrow, stuck in that big driftwood log. Looks like I blew it. No way that arrow would embed in hard wood like that, after exiting the deer—not with this sixty-pound bow.

I humped down the tree frantically with the stand, ripping off half the skin on my wrists in the process, and walked over. Sure enough, my arrow was embedded in a huge, brush-covered board that probably floated in with the last hurricane. No blood or hair anywhere. I'd shot over the damn deer. I blew it. But it's only—let's see? Ah! Only 8:15. Got plenty of time to make that hog hunt with the new neighbors.

"That's a *dog!*" I gasped, after returning from my deer hunt.

"And a damn good one," Jesse nodded. "Here, you want to bring him along?" He started handing me the leash. I reacted as if he were trying to hand me a scorpion.

"He's Wally," Jesse said, as I finally grabbed it. "Best hit dog we got. You're gonna be a hit man on this hunt. Did your buddy Pelayo tell ya? Means you're gonna bring along the hit dog."

"Wonderful! But I mean, does he ... can't *you* ...?" I was aghast.

"Don't worry," Jesse said. "He won't go after ya—unless we tell him to."

"AHHAAAA-AHAAA." Ronnie (who was a funhouse-mirror version of Goober, the timeless *Andy Griffith Show* character) got a big kick out of that. He was pouring a little whiskey into his coffee by the fire, the bayonet he used to kill hogs hanging on his belt.

These were our neighbors whose tents were pitched near ours at the Delta campsite during our hunting trip, two of four fanatic hog hunters from up in Mississippi. And we were going hog hunting with these people—Pelayo and I, that is. Chris elected to hunt ducks with On-the-Ball and Tom this morning, as I'd seen from the deer stand. They'd already been gone two hours. No reason to get up with the stars to chase hogs, though. That's one advantage to this sport. Sure came in handy this morning, too. This dog they wanted me to bring on the boat was the most hideous creature I'd ever seen: full-blood pit bull, they explained. He definitely had the jaws and the little pig eyes of one, and the body—low, squat, and powerful. "Pit bull" summed it up perfectly.

It looked like a walking tackling dummy, but with a huge, ugly head. George Lucas couldn't dream up a creature this grotesque for *Star Wars.* I've never seen a dog I didn't want to pet. It's instinctive. I love them, all breeds. But *this* thing. If I saw something like that in my backyard, I'd shoot it on general principles, just to rid the world of something so vile looking.

"I guess you're wondering why Wally don't have any ears," Jesse said, looking over at me.

"Yeah," I replied. "That kinda hit me right off. And no tail either. Don't pit bulls usually have tails?"

"Usually, yes," replied Mark, another of the neighbors, who'd just emerged from his tent right behind me. "But you don't want anything on a hit dog for the hog to grab." Mark made a snapping motion with his hands around his ears for effect. "Any little thing that sticks out of his body, a hog will try to grab with his snout to get the dog close to him, so he can slit his throat with his tusks. We've seen it happen too many times. So we figured we'd rather have an earless dog than a dead one. I'm sure Wally there agrees. Don't you, little feller?" And he bent down to pet and nuzzle the hideous thing. The creature licked his face and wiggled its butt like a cute little beagle puppy.

I was laughing at the sight when a thundering yell from our campsite jerked my head around. *"Well I got up this morning— and I got my self a BE-er!"* Pelayo was doing his Jim Morrison again—"Roadhouse Blues," to be precise. He ambled down the trail, bobbing his head, singing between swigs, acting out the song. He stopped short when he saw Wally. "What the—?" He looked over, laughing, beer spurting from his mouth. "Well, makes sense," Pelayo snorted, after I'd explained. "What the hell," he said after a hearty chug. "My wife would freak out if she saw that dog."

"Mine, too," I said, nodding.

"She'd probably call that *cruel*. Yeah, right. But she had our Pekinese 'neutered.'" He mock-smiled and made little quote marks in the air and scissor motions near his groin. "But man, if I was a dog," he roared suddenly, "I'd rather have my ears cut off than my balls!"

Ah yes, nothing like an early morning beer to make a man philosophical. Bud and venison sausage—can't beat it for breakfast. I grew up in south Louisiana, so I'd been in some pretty weird hunting groups in my time, believe me. But here I look one way and see an earless pit bull nuzzling Mark, who now, without his hat, looks like Seinfeld's neighbor Kramer. And there's Jesse, who I can't look at without thinking of Mr. Ziffel on *Green Acres*. He's even got denim overalls on this morning, just like Arnold the pig's owner. Goober and the fourth Mississippian hunter, "Mongo" (a hideous-toothed lummox who reminds me of Alex Karras in *Blazing Saddles*), provide the backdrop.

Jesse's getting the strike, or track, dogs in the boat with him. Those are a sight, too—Airedale, pit bull, Catahoula mutants, the craziest looking things you ever saw. They have the long hair of

the Airedale around the face, the head of the pit bull, and the body size, long legs, and coloration of the Catahoula. They look like four-footed Chewbaccas that had been sprayed-painted camouflage by graffiti artists.

Mongo, wearing a battered straw cowboy hat this morning, is doing a little pigeon-toed shuffle toward the boat, looking sharp with a bulldog collar tattooed around his neck. He passes on the way but makes no eye contact.

Pelayo and I get in the hit boat with Jesse and the hit dogs. Chases down here usually aren't long—not nearly as long as in the pine uplands or even the hardwood swamps. Because of the nature of the terrain, hogs usually come to bay fairly quickly in this Delta. There's not much high ground down here: the natural ridges alongside the main passes, the spoilbanks created when canals are dug or the passes are dredged for navigation, that's about it. These all sprout in veritable jungle.

The mild climate and fertility of the soil mean that any little tuft of ground down here sprouts in lush tangles of elderberry, willow, briars, Roseau cane, elephant ears, pea vine, marsh alders, and wild millet. You almost have to hack your way through with a machete, except for the deer and hog trails. Just hacking out a campsite takes some doing; fortunately, they last the whole season.

All the rest of the terrain in the Delta is water—shallow water, usually. These shallows convert to mudflats on the low tide. So a hog chase is usually short down here, but messy and brutal: slogging through the slop, sinking to your knees, hacking and trampling through the thickets, sweating, panting, dodging cottonmouths. If the chase were any longer, you'd never bay a hog. You'd never get to it in time to save any dogs.

We'd gone about ten minutes down the pass when Mongo, Goober, and Mark started dropping off the strike dogs ahead of us. "You pretty much know they're gonna strike in just a few minutes on this ridge." Jesse pointed ahead with one hand and edged the throttle up with the other. "We'll motor out ahead of them a bit now. Usually, we just follow along in the boat. Most times you'll see the hog rumbling along the top of the ridge as soon as you hear the dogs barking a strike. Then we'll try to follow as far as we can by boat, and get out when we hear the dogs barking bay."

Sounded like a cinch. We were actually on private land here, Jesse explained. "There are a few patches of it mixed up with the state and federal land. We've already had a few run-ins with that game warden, that Rizzo."

"Ratso!" Pelayo yelled as he handed me a brewski. "Oh, yeah! We know Ratso, don't worry!" Just then an osprey flapped overhead. Jesse looked up and pointed with his chin. The osprey had a mullet in its talons; they hold them parallel to their body, the way a torpedo plane carries its torpedo. It was only about fifty yards overhead, and we could see the mullet wiggling, dripping water. It would be ripped apart and eaten alive in a few seconds.

Ain't nature grand? Just as I said, nothing like an early morning beer for a clear view of the Big Picture. A flock of pintail over the osprey distracted us as they cut up and started circling down. "We oughta hear Chris and them shoot any minute now," smirked Pelayo.

But the next sound was barks. The strike dogs erupted in howls. "There's ole Rocky!" Jesse's eyes lit up. "Just like him to strike first!" Then the two other hounds joined the chorus. "They got his trail now!" Jesse looked behind him, doing a thumbs up to Mark, Mongo, and Goober, who followed in the other boat.

Mongo returned the gesture and actually seemed to smile. Goober whipped out his bayonet and held it aloft with a two-handed grip like a samurai, like King Arthur hoisting Excalibur, grinning crazily with that mangled face of his. Everyone nodded excitedly. "They got him now!" yelled Mark.

"There!" Jesse grabbed my shoulder just as I turned back and pointed. "See him!" Ah yes, a huge black blob was plowing through the brambles like a tank. But it looked like it had a tail, a straight tail. "Sure that's a hog?"

"A big one—a *boar!*" Jesse roared back. His face was aglow. "Whatsa matter with you, boy? Ain't never seen a wild hog before?" Actually I had, and plenty, but usually from a deer stand. This offered a different profile. That's the first thing that hits you about truly wild pigs: the straight tail. When chased, they often hold it straight up, too, like this one.

It topped the ridge and disappeared over the backside. The dogs loped by a few seconds later, howling crazily, literally hot on its tail. Wally was going crazy on the end of the leash, yelping, tugging, shaking, and dying to get in on the action. I was holding that leash. Pelayo was holding the one with Huck, the other strike dog. He also lugged the little beer cooler in a backpack. Huck was going nuts, too. I looked down at the dogs and thought: *I've seen these same excited faces, heard this same panting, observed this same spastic trembling, this drooling—on friends as we entered the Gold Club "gentlemen's lounge."*

"Looks like here's where we get out, boys." Suddenly Jesse rammed the boat up on the muddy bank. Mark did the same behind us. They hopped out, stumbling up the ridge, and headed for the action. Another canal turned off at a right angle here, but it was silted up. No navigating it. The hog must have known that, because it took off along its spoilbank, headed away from us now, headed for the thickest and wettest and remotest stuff around. We knew the area well. Deer like the area, too, especially late in the season after the pressure's on. We'd hunted deer there once before. We entered in pirogues during a high tide, then the tide fell. Getting out was a major hassle; especially with the spike and doe we'd arrowed. Never again, we said. Now we were being led back into it by a wily wild hog.

YOW—YOW! came the yelps from over the ridge. "Bay!" yelled Jesse. "Sounds like they got him!" Goober was just topping the ridge. He looked back at Jesse and held up both fists, then he started waving us in.

"Let's go, guys!" Jesse was yelling as he grabbed Huck's leash from Pelayo and pushed me off the bow. "Let's go!" We started clambering up the spoilbank. I still had the leash with Wally, and the ugly little bastard was actually pulling me along, like a little tank, when: *YEE-YEE-YOW!*

"God—, that dog's been cut!" Jesse cursed. "Hurry!"

"Rocky! Rocky! Get out of there!" Mongo was yelling. "Get out of there, boy! Git!"

YEE-YEE-YOW! A helluva battle was raging. Wally was barking up a storm. Huck, too. Then the barking changed. "He broke bay!" grimaced Jesse next to me, as he tugged back on Huck's leash. "Hell, shoulda known! Couldn't be *this* easy! Let's go!" And we stumbled forward.

We got to a little clearing surrounded by willows, and Mongo waved us over. "Over here!" He was holding Rocky by the neck as Goober worked on him with a surgical staple gun and some iodine. The dog was frantic, shaking its head, whining, trying to slip from Mongo's grip. It had a six-inch gash along its ribcage yet was frantic to get back into the fight. "Told you, guys," Jesse said, looking over at Pelayo and me. "Dem dogs live for this stuff!" Then he looked down at the dog. "Ain't that right, Rocky?"

Rocky looked over, whining, barking, drooling, squirming. The dog could hear its buddies yapping in the distance and was desperate to join in. Goober snapped the last staple, and the dog was off like a rocket, yapping away, as if yelling: "Wait for me, gang! Don't hog all the fun!"

"Here!" Mongo suddenly grabbed the leash roughly from my hand. He turned to Jesse. "Whattya say, Jesse? Let Huck and Wally go now?"

"Yeah, guess so," Jesse replied, while bending down to unsnap from Huck's collar. "We'll all go faster that way." *YOW-YOW-YOW!* The hit dogs scrambled off instantly, their stubby legs going a mile a minute.

A crazed, sweaty, mud-splatter scramble through stinking slop and brambles lasted another half-hour. We'd traveled maybe a quarter-mile, then the barking changed again. "Got him bayed!" panted Jesse, as he pulled his boot out of the mud next to a sweating, panting Pelayo. "Got him bayed *again!*"

It sounded no more than a hundred yards away. *YOW-YOW! YEEE-YEE!*

"God— it!" yelled Jesse, as he took off again. "Another one's cut!" Mongo, Mark, and Goober sounded like they were already at the bay. Pelayo and I raced after Jesse, the racket increasing in volume and ferocity with every step.

"Outta there, Rocky!" Mongo was yelling. "Outta there, boy!" *YOW-YOW!*

We hopped over a little slough, clearing another ridgetop, and finally got to the action, and what action! That Rocky hadn't had enough. It was lunging into the fracas like a maniac. The hog was surrounded, huffing and snorting, spinning around as a dog grabbed its butt, never letting one get behind it. Amazing how agile the big bastard was. They'd nip its butt and it would spin around like a rabbit, lunging with its big head, swiping with its tusks, but fast, *lightning* fast.

WHACK! YEE-YEE! It got one that time. "Huck!" yelled Mongo. "Get outta there, boy!" Huck came in fast for the hog's head, but the hog had just spun around. The hog jerked its massive snout, and Huck sailed through the air, legs spread. *Christ,* I thought. *That dog's gotta be dead!*

Instead, it hit the ground, spun around, and charged again, just as Wally moved in from the other side and *CHOMP!* Wally got hold of an ear. The hog snorted and started shaking its huge head like a terrier with a rat. Wally was lifted into the air, but its jaws hung on like a snapping turtle's. It flopped back and forth in the air like a stuffed animal toy.

Now Huck made a hit from the other side and grabbed an ear. Rocky and another track dog came up from behind and started nipping. I couldn't believe what I was seeing. It was horrible! It was brutal! It was cruel! It was crazy! Let's admit it: It was—thrilling as hell!

Suddenly, the hog lunged, jerked violently, and Wally flew off its snout. Then the boar made a mad dash, with Huck still hanging onto its ear. Huck bounced alongside the boar as it rumbled past a willow and—*SMACK!* Huck hit the tree with a blow like from a baseball bat. It fell off and sat there for a second. *That freakin' dog is dead,* I thought.

Then, *YOW-YOW!* It was back up and giving chase right behind ugly Wally.

The hog ran thirty yards and turned around again, but now it had a huge driftwood log behind it. No dogs could blindside it now. "This here's a smart one!" Jesse gasped from next to me, smiling, panting, and wiping his muddy brow. "Think we'll catch him live. Bring him back home to release, huh, Ronnie?" He looked over and Ronnie nodded assent.

"Hail yeah!" Goober whooped. "We could use some of this kind up at home! Looks pure Russian!"

Like a brave *toro* that gives a magnificent account of itself, a brave boar often gains a pardon from execution. Sympathy has nothing to do with it. The boar hunters, like the prancing matador, simply want the privilege of challenging and tormenting the magnificent animal again—and to let it spread its valuable seed. This calls for one guy coming up behind the hog as the dogs distract it by gripping its face in their trip-hammer jaws, grabbing its hind legs, and flipping it, then quickly tying its legs. They release it elsewhere to sire more broods and to spread its valiant genes to another herd in another swamp.

A thumbs-down for the hog means close-quarters stuff, no rifles, pistols, or even bows. In diehard boar hunting circles, those qualify as the long-distance weapons of pansies and faggots. Purists, true aficionados, like the dirty business at intimate quarters, the full fury of the desperate prey erupting in their face, its crazed squeals and popping tusks, the ghastly musk from its inflamed glands, its blood and possibly theirs gushing in crimson splendor.

"Blood has an unequaled orgiastic power," writes José Ortega y Gasset in his classic *Meditations on Hunting*. "When it is spilled, it intoxicates, excites, and maddens both man and beast. . . . [T]he Romans went to the Coliseum as they did to a tavern, and the public bullfight does the same. . . . [B]lood operates as a stupefying drug."

Not exactly fodder for the Oprah Book Club, but perfectly true. With a death sentence for the hog, the hunter rushes in from behind and flips the boar by its legs or stabs it as it stands, low behind the shoulder, where it erupts in a geyser of blood, drenching the hunter and anointing him into this barbarous brotherhood—assuming that the hit dogs hold fast on its head with their trip-hammer jaws and keep the hog from jerking around and slashing its executioner across the face or neck, using its tusks as daggers.

"Hell, Humberto," said Jesse, turning to me. "We was gonna let you do the honors with the bayonet. Remember drawing straws last night? But you don't mind if Jake [Mongo to Pelayo and me] catches him, do you?"

"No problema!" I shout, elated. "None at all! Y'all go right ahead and catch him!"

Now, with its rear covered, the big boar had a little breathing room. It even looked more relaxed. No more huffing or squealing as it turned around to face its tormentors. The dogs barked mechanically all around it, but the boar was silent. It just stood there, glowering at its barking captors.

No bluffing by this animal. That's what worried us. It was coal black with a silver sheen to its coat. "Gotta go three hundred pounds!" Goober yelled. He grabbed a beer from his pocket and gulped a foamy swig. I was parched myself and motioned Pelayo over for one.

This pig was a veteran, definitely keeping its cool even as canine bedlam erupted. The dogs seemed to sense it, too. None rushed it now. They were content to stand ten feet away and bark like banshees.

Finally, Huck, Jesse's prize dog, made its move. Unlike Wally, it had ears ("My wife grew attached to Huck," Jesse explained. "She wouldn't let me.") It rushed in and tried to grab an ear. The boar made a lightning swipe, so quick you could barely catch it.

YEEEH-YEEH-YOW!—YOW!—YEEEH! Huck got ripped good this time. It hit the ground, rolled, and we immediately saw the crimson gash running clear from neck to haunch.

"HUCK!" Mongo growled. "You stupid little bastard!" Mongo was yelling as he ran over with the staple gun.

"Get him!" Jesse yelled. "Get him outta there!" Huck wasn't back up and jumping into the fight this time. It was moving slow. If the hog caught it again, it would be dead for sure. But the plucky little bastard ran in and clamped down on the hog's snout, up close to the nose—too far up, too close to those tusks. The hog swung its head, and this time, Wally swung off, rolling in a flurry of brush and mud twenty feet away. The track dogs barked but kept their distance. They couldn't get behind this hog.

"Huck!" Jesse was roaring mad, too. "You stupid son-of-a-b—! Come here, boy!" First Rocky gets his flank ripped, now Huck gets mangled. This was getting expensive.

"The truly brave bull gives no warning before he charges," Hemingway wrote, "except the fixing of his eye on his enemy."

Yes, it was the hog's beady little eyes that were starting to worry me. They'd turned from the dogs, and they were focused on us.

The boar was looking past the maniacally barking dogs to the upright creatures that chugged beer while pondering its fate like Roman emperors at the Coliseum. We were no more than sixty feet away, in an area pretty much cleared of brush by the spoil deposit from some recent dredging. This hog was a smart one. You could almost see the words turning in its big, ugly head. "They're the instigators of this whole mess," it seemed to say with its beady eyes and twitching snout.

We were just starting to relax when it bolted—at us! "Pelayo!" Jesse yelled, but Pelayo hardly needed the warning. He saw the boar: How could he not? It was thirty feet in front of him and closing fast, heading straight at him in a mad rush.

Pelayo sprang into action. As I said before, there were not many trees down here. Next to a sawed-off shotgun loaded with double-aught buck, a sturdy tree with low branches is a hog hunter's best friend. Pelayo had a lean willow just to his left, and he sprang for it like a gazelle. I'd never seen the boy move like that. He jumped, grabbed a low branch, and lifted himself up like a monkey, just ahead of the hog. I was stunned by his agility. Sometimes it takes him five minutes just to move from his La-Z-Boy to the refrigerator.

The dogs closed in on the hog again. Rocky grabbed it by the butt, and the hog spun around quick as a cat, swiping with that wicked snout but missing this time, thank God. The hog made another swipe at Wally, missed, then stopped and backed up to the willow—Pelayo's willow. It stood there, glowering again at the canine bedlam around it. Looked like it had picked the willow trunk as its back guard this time.

Pelayo was clutching frantically at the branches above him now. The damn hog was less than three feet below him. Luckily, that's one thing hogs aren't good at: looking up. Their bone structure doesn't permit them to lift their heads very high. Pelayo appeared to want a little more elevation, though.

"Shoot the god— thing!" Pelayo yelled between gasps. "Shoot him! Stab him! Take him out!" At first I thought Pelayo was laughing; then I looked closer. No, that crimson tone to his face was not from laughing. Those cue-ball eyes did not denote mirth. Those desperate screams were not of hilarity. "Shoot him!" Pelayo's voice was cracking. "*Shooooot* the god— thing!"

"We wanna take him alive!" yelled Mongo, who quickly looked over at Goober. Were they smiling at each other? Sure looked like it.

"Bullshit!" Pelayo raved. He was gasping and grunting, clutching maniacally at branches still higher above him, breaking them off in his frenzy, slipping, grunting, wheezing. "Shoot him! Blast him!"

Goober and Mongo appeared in no hurry. Hell, we had no guns, anyway. Then the distance between Pelayo's ass and the hog's snout started shrinking. What are willows famous for? Bending? Well, this willow was true to form. The branch that Pelayo had his legs wrapped around was about wrist size. He weighed 160, easy. Now he was bringing the whole top of the tree down with him ... down ... down ... down. The higher he climbed, the lower he got. He looked down and saw that he was about a foot above those tusks. "Shoot him!" he raved.

If he grabbed the trunk a little lower it would start straightening up, away from the hog's tusks, but no more than a couple of feet above its snout. "On the tusks of a dilemma," you might say.

Suddenly Wally rushed in out of nowhere and made a hit, chomping an ear. It must have hit a sensitive spot this time. The hog bawled like a banshee, kicked, and started snapping its tusks in rage, but Wally hung on, growling like a chainsaw, tightening its muscle-bound jaws on that big, black head. That set off the other dogs; they closed in, barking and nipping. "Now we got him!" Jesse roared. "That's it! Git 'im! Git 'im!"

"Wonder if they hear this in Venice?" I looked over at Jesse.

"They can probably hear Pelayo," Jesse said, laughing.

It was a hellish racket—mangled dogs, blood-lusting dogs, furious dogs, terrified Pelayo—a din straight from Dante's third circle of hell. The boar jerked its huge head savagely from side to side, desperate to shake off the pit bull fangs that gripped and ripped its face.

It turned with little Wally still attached, slashed, and the yelps erupted. *YEEH! YEEH! YOW-YOW!*

"God— it!" Ronnie yelled. "We're gonna lose half the pack! Knew we shoulda brought the damn gun!" Now a track dog made a hit on the other ear, and Mongo rushed in without a word of warning. I couldn't believe it. He grabbed the hog's hind legs and flipped. Ronnie was right behind him. Boy, were they fast, like those rodeo riders who rope and tie up the calf. I was stunned. The whole thing was a blur. They had the damn thing trussed up in seconds. *YEEEE-HAAA!* They stood and raised their arms in triumph.

Jesse whooped and then moved over, pulling out the oyster knife he kept in his pocket, ready to start prying the dogs' jaws loose. Pelayo slid down from his precarious perch, almost on top of the newly trussed boar, looked at it for a second, then staggered over. "Brewski time?" he gasped, while nodding at me. I stifled a laugh. I could only nod. We popped open the Buds and toasted. They were hot and well agitated. They foamed all over us. No matter. They tasted superb. Unreal. The whole thing had been unreal. I patted Pelayo's shoulder and guffawed. He doubled over himself, cackling crazily. He couldn't help it.

A camera crew from a local TV station went out on a hog hunt with our friend Johnny last year but shucked it after the first chase. "This is barbarous!" blubbered the yuppie producer, who'd had sausage biscuit for breakfast. "You people are *sick*. And *crazy!*"

"Perhaps," Johnny answered, "but seems to us, these hunts pay a boar the tribute he deserves."

Chill out and think for a second. Which swine exits more nobly? The poor sap in the slaughter pen? Or the one battling a pack of blood-lusting dogs and a gaggle of drunken whooping yahoos after a two-hour chase? To ask the question is to answer it.

These Delta boars go out like a bull in a ring. Like the fighting *toro*, they die violently but nobly, face to face with a foe who chooses weapons that shrink his odds. The boar's miserable domesticated cousin dies at a meat factory—anonymously, horribly, obscenely. Its death is ordered by a fat-assed bureaucrat from afar and carried out mechanically by a weary and joyless dolt.

The gloriously wild pig of the Mississippi Delta exits in a blast of trumpets and blaze of glory like the defenders of Bastogne and Stalingrad, its death inflicted on the spot by visible adversaries in the heat of battle. This boar becomes Davy Crockett at the Alamo or Tom Hanks in the rubble of that Normandy village, or a gladiator, dead in the end, but—what a grand finale! Brave, defiant, glowering at the enemy and lunging with its last blood-choked gasp, maybe taking a few down with it.

I'm sure the boars would agree. With us, not only does it go out in a blaze of martial glory but it also gets its picture taken. Then its carcass, lovingly marinated and draped over open coals, inspires a south Louisiana outburst of revelry and gluttony, another occasion to gather and imbibe. Long after any memory of its domesticated cousins has gone out with the garbage, its mounted head, adorning a den or hunting camp, provokes no end of convivial yarns and banter—and all in its honor.

Yes, compare this life and fate to that of the fat, feeble porker incarcerated for its short life in a stinking pen, castrated without anesthesia, whomped on the head by a bored drone, then churned into plastic-wrapped sausage so that you, dear readers, can eat it for breakfast. No contest. And anyway, this one lived to do battle another day.

As for the dogs, they loved every action-packed second; they reveled in the primal battle. That gelded and perfumed little poodle with the diamond collar on Malibu Beach will never know the thrill, will never be as true to its canine ancestry, either. That's the dog I feel sorry for. Its claws are clipped so it won't rip the sofa; its hair is cut so it will look cute; its testicles are removed to curb its natural exuberance. It will use its teeth and jaws for that mush they give it in a bowl. That's not what they're for. Ask Rocky, Wally, and Huck. They'd sooner walk into the ASPCA's gas chamber voluntarily than trade places with that poodle.

A FRIEND OF THE DEVIL

BY
STEPHEN J. BODIO

Controversy surrounds the question of whether the jaguar was truly native to North America above Mexico. Like too many matters these days, it is as much, or more, a question of politics as a question of natural science: A certain brand of command-and-control environmentalist virtually salivates at the thought of the extra ace he would have up his sleeve if the jaguar could be added to the list of U.S. endangered species. His rugged wise-use counterpart, understanding the ramifications of such a classification as unmistakably as his green brother, swears 'tweren't never so. In this excerpt from his novel Tiger Country—*about a quixotic quest to reintroduce big, dangerous predators to the land—my friend Steve Bodio envisions a Southwest in which the jaguar without question belongs—whether or not that was ever a verifiable zoological fact.*

"So, what kind of a thing is a jaguar?"
Juan Aragon looks at Shelagh Donovan. "It's the Aztec god of the underworld. I think it's the finest damn predator on the continent. It's a big cat, stocky, muscles all over. Low, big head, eyes like headlights. Club tail. Not pretty like a lion—cougar, that is. Ted Hughes in England wrote a poem about him—'Like a thick Aztec disemboweler.... Carrying his head like a brazier of spilling embers.' I love that. Mostly they got big circles of spots, rosettes. The Spanish called him el tigre, *the tiger. Not real accurate. This one is* black. *If you get him crossways in the light you can still see the spots, matte black on oily shiny black. Green eyes on that. He's an eerie son-of-a-b— for sure." He sits forward, waves one finger. "Wait a minute. Close your eyes. I'll show you."*

He reaches into his pocket. She makes herself still. Closes her eyes. Opens them. When she does he is holding an object, yellow and black-and-white, inches from her face. She pulls back and focuses. It is a head, a face, a fanged mouth, yellow with black spots and cat's eyes and whiskers. In the mouth, like a jawbreaker, is a grinning human skull. The skull looks far happier than its tormentor.

She puts out her hand. The head is no bigger than a golf ball, the skull like a marble. It is hard and rough and light: papier-mache or some kind of plaster. She raises an eyebrow.

"Day-of-the-Dead figure. Viejo México. That's 'what kind of a thing is a jaguar.'" The mockery is light, Juan's accent switching effortlessly as always.

"Cool."

"Ain't it?" Now they are both grinning, inches from each other's face.

Pause and regroup. Juan is sitting pensively staring into space, smoking a joint, his hawk's profile turned toward Shelagh. He is wearing a black baseball cap, a threadbare pearl-button cowboy shirt, salmon-pink cotton hiking shorts, bare feet. His shaggy hair sticks out the hole in the back of the cap, and there's an earring in his left ear. He passes the joint to Shelagh, wordlessly, absently. She inhales deeply, lets her mind drift. It fastens on his earring. "You don't look very cowboy today."

"I could say the cliche. I don't want nobody mistaking me for a truck driver. Or an Albuquerque lounge lizard."

They smoke companionably for a few moments. He stubs the butt out like a cigarette in the full ashtray, pulls a long thin cigar from his pocket, rolls it between his fingers, then takes out another and offers it to Shelagh. She accepts, and he lights it with a quick flick of a disposable lighter in a heavy turquoise-and-real-silver holder.

She puffs. "And what is the story with *this* particular jaguar?"

"Well, you know what the plan was—first wolves, then bears, then jaguars. Government shocked the s-- out of me when they started the wolf program, though it's still too wimpy—I'll put some in White Sands yet. How do you think they'll do against oryx?"

"*Jaguar*, Johnny . . ."

"I do have a tranq gun but—it's the s–ts—I think we might just have to kill this guy. Even if we get him alive he's a problem. He was a bright idea of Trigg's, who keeps telling me it was a favor. You know what the deal was? He was a cattle-killer from down south where Trigg knows the dope aristocracy, and the peons were getting tired of him. They let ol' Bilious trap him, he sets it up for an illegal rent-a-hunt on his uncle's near Patagonia, Arizona, and the sumbitch runs right over the dentist, who then pees his pants and has a heart attack. So Trigg's uncle gets all bent out of shape and wants to kill it. But it goes up a tree and Trigg figures he can just trank it out and sell it to me for another thousand bucks."

"He sounds like an enterprising gent."

"*He* thinks he's a genius. But anyway: This cat lives on cows, and apparently isn't too afraid of folks, either. There's some stories about kids. . . . He's not a good choice—I never should have started with him. Big animals are like a drug I can't resist. Besides, if we don't do him, somebody else will—he's too imprinted on cows, and he'll jeopardize the whole deal. And conscientious old Nick is already freaked by everything. . . ."

Nicholas Sharpe returned to a scene of activity. Juan was pacing back and forth, talking on his cell. "Yeah, well, for the dogs I guess. I guess you're in it as deep as we are. But I want to try calling first." He listened a while, then exploded. "Why the f–k don't you tell me the important things first?" He put a hand over the receiver and said, "Two more calves. They picked up the first one. Or maybe it's just smart enough to eat and move on." He removed his hand. "Yeah, yeah, OK, OK. We'll stake one out on your place if we've got to. But what makes you think it'll go there? . . . You *heard* it? Are you sure? I think you'd lie because I don't think you know the difference, that's why. OK, OK. Seven, right." He clicked the button off with one hand and tossed the phone to a couch covered with calfskins. "Trigg claims it's been walking around the back of his place, calling. Hard to believe, except he's right in a good place—good for the jaguar anyway. South of the refuge, canals and mosquitoes and tamarisk and lots of cows nobody sees except when they're gathering. It's a jungle."

"Where have the kills been?"

"All down the bottom. The first one in somebody's backyard, right north of the refuge. They picked it up. Then a big one, a yearling, above the trees in the greasewood, and then one on the riverbank road a quarter-mile away. A fisherman found it."

"Do they know what it is?"

Juan shook his head. "How could they? The Socorro papers are calling it the 'Bosque Bigfoot.' There ain't no tracks yet. Game and Fish thinks it's a bear. Like a black bear would break the neck of a yearling steer. I love it."

"So what're we going to do?"

"I'm gonna put some gas in the truck. Why don't you and Shelagh get some food and guns and maybe some camping stuff, and meet me back here in a couple of hours? This might be over tonight, or it might go on for days."

Back in the truck, headed for his house at Ultima Esperanza, Nick handed his silver flask to Shelagh, who took it, then hesitated. "Maybe we should stay alert, huh?"

He was mildly surprised. "Sure."

He paused, wondering what went on in there. Then dismissed the thought; she was not as much enigmatic as living right at the edge of action, like Juan. He often knew exactly what each would do, but shied off from admitting it. They scared him. Still ... "Penny for your thoughts, love."

"Not many. I want to see this jaguar."

"And then?"

She stared at him coolly. "And then write about it. What could be more at the heart of the West than Johnny and the predators?"

"Sounds like a band. No, no, really. But you know if he gets all his animals in, even if they can't prove it, they're not real endangered species. They couldn't have just held out since the '30s."

She began to smile, staring straight through the windshield, as though coming to understanding of a difficult mathematical theorem. "I think, sir, you underestimate the power of the press." She turned toward him. "Seriously, Nick. You think if I do a big national piece on this that there'll be any choice? If anybody kills these animals they'll be *lynched* by the time I'm through."

"You think that's the way to do it?"

"It's the way it's doing." She bent to light a cigarette. "And, I think you're jealous."

Does she expect me to deny it? thought Nick. "Watch out for Johnny. He's too much like you."

What to pack? He grabbed bread from the freezer, cheese, fruit, chocolate, the old Zeiss binocular, two down sleeping bags, all into a large backpack. What gun? Mostly he used well-worn old deer guns, small caliber; a 6.5 Mannlicher from the '30s, a Savage .250-3000 with a tang peep sight even older than that. Though cats were notoriously soft-skinned game, Nick figured that he needed more power for a jaguar.

At last he picked from the rack a gun he had not fired in years and had never needed: a bolt-action .416 Rigby, a heavy thing capable of killing a Cape buffalo. This one had been used as an Alaska brown bear gun by an eccentric plastic surgeon from Boston. It had a barrel twenty inches long, for handiness in heavy brush. He popped open a little trapdoor in the rifle's grip with his thumbnail to remove a rectangular bar of ivory, pulled off the iron sight on the end of the gun's barrel and replaced it with the white bar, grinning with satisfaction at its neatness. "I never thought I'd have a chance to use this in real life."

"What is it?"

"It's a night sight. See, it's visible 'cause it's white. They used it to shoot cattle-killing leopards at night, over bait. This is too weird to be true."

"This belonged to, like, a white hunter?"

"No, actually it belonged to a doctor from Boston. I bought it at an estate sale after he got killed in his house by a burglar. I guess he was thinking about shooting the wrong bad guys."

"Big hole in the barrel there." She pressed her finger to the tip. "Can I shoot it?"

"Not today. You can't learn to shoot an elephant rifle without trying something smaller first." He blushed at his own condescension. "I assume you haven't shot anything."

She smiled, seeing right through him. "Just .22 target pistols in a college course. I'll wait. What can I take?" He pointed at a duffel containing the overflow, picked up a box of 400-grain heavy handloads for the gun, and followed her out the door.

A FRIEND OF THE DEVIL

The sunset had been lurid, volcanic bands of red burning up the sky behind the mountains, but now the swamp under the desert was surrounded by shadow. The faint glow over the mountains did not illuminate the riverbank. The evening chorus of birds and bugs and God-knows-what-else had resembled the soundtrack of a jungle movie, but now the loudest sound was the whine of the mosquitoes. It was an unusual place, thought Nick. Even in daylight it seemed to repel the humans who had fashioned it from the sifting braided sandbars and gnarled spreading cottonwoods of the old river flood plain. Once it had been cool and shady, a legendary haunt of cat and bear and a shelter for the raiders who had given their name to one portion of it—*Bosque del Apache*, the Apaches' grove. Now flood control channels divided it into straight lines of dike and ditch, vanishing into perfect perspective points in the distance, eerie and geometrical like a de Chirico print of railway stations.

There were a few big cottonwoods shading the permanent banks, full of herons and warblers and butterflies. But cottonwoods are a short-lived tree, dependent on seasonal flooding for their reseeding, and now the dominant growth was the tamarisk, the salt cedar. It grew in dense groves twenty and thirty feet high and appeared to be made of coarse green feathers. You couldn't walk in it, or see more than five feet; it looked, and grew, like an invader from another planet. Little lived under its shade but half-wild black cattle and diamondback "coontail" rattlesnakes as big around as a fat man's thigh. Right now, after the spring runoff had risen and retreated, the smell of the salt cedar flowers, like pungent orange blossoms, mingled in Nick's nostrils with the reek of rotting carp and the odor of insect repellent.

And, to complete the oddity, they were below the desert. The valley above the flood plain was thinly covered by tarry dark-green creosote bush. Higher up was a roll of hard-bitten semi-grassland; above that, a peppering of juniper bushes freckled the barren hills. You couldn't see an individual tree anywhere above the drying remnants of the spring puddles, though Nick knew that the blue cutouts to the west that had blocked the sun's last rays were covered with cold forest. This is no place for humans, he thought, for not the first time.

"Listening? You won't hear a thing this early." Juan had come up behind him as he stood on the little sand ridge above the trailer in the hollow, looking west.

Nick turned to him. "Not really. Just looking and wondering if we know what we're after."

"Are you faggots gonna knock off the love feast up there and give us a f–kin' hand?"

Billy Trigg. The poacher stood below with his hands on his hips, grinning. He had a tractor cap, a long, thin red beard, glasses, and a broken tooth. Over his shoulder, on a carry strap, was a Third World knock-off version of an AK-47 military rifle. Behind him was a little old Airstream trailer, settled into the sand after its last journey. It was surrounded by the world's smallest slum—a backhoe, two dead trucks, more cans of more kinds than he had ever seen outside a municipal dump.

But it wasn't the mess that made him shudder at Trigg. He knew many poor people back in the mountain towns above who kept yard cars for parts, and chicken coops and storage for cans or just because it cost money to tow them to a junkyard thirty miles away. It was the other stuff that made him sick. The bones, garbage, dog droppings, cowhides with the hair rotting off (he wondered whether the local ranchers ever lost cattle nearby); the skulls stuck up on poles like Satanic icons, the chains clanking around dogs' necks. And the noise of twenty chained hounds. With that many frustrated dogs, one or two were always snarling, whining, or barking. Nick felt that anyone apparently sane who could sleep amid that much noise and stink was really deeply twisted.

"What with, Bilious?" said Juan with a genial grin.

"Y'all could help me put these dogs on the truck. We're gonna take four of these Plotts if I can get 'em into two boxes without them killin' each other. And Julie and the Airedale and old Boney." He turned and walked back to where a squat '50s truck stood, surrounded by Shelagh, Juan, and now another, silent man. He was very dark and had a perfect silver-belly Stetson pulled down over his face so that even in the light from the trailer doorway his upper face appeared black. He also wore a silk bandanna knotted tight around his throat.

They moved out of the way as Trigg boosted a thin dark-striped hound with short ears up and through the doors of one of four aluminum boxes belted to the truck bed. "Stay there, you," he said, without a trace of the surliness that seemed to underlie all of his human conversations. The dog stayed, sitting, until he put a similar dog in with it. The first muttered, but moved out of the way. He loaded a second box with two more of the tigerish beasts, but these disagreed until Trigg thumped the box with the heel of his hand and glared darkly at them. He put a huge male Airedale with the fuzz and shoebutton eyes of a hypertrophied teddy bear into the third, with a beautiful doe-eyed, velvety-eared black-and-tan bitch that licked him on the face as he patted its neck. He then disappeared behind the trailer to return with a huge scarred white dog in his arms. It had a head like a pit bull's but even more so, deep and square, jawed like a hyena, with bulges of muscle above its jaws. He kissed it on the mouth as he told it to stay, and turned to his audience. "Know what he is?"

Shelagh, Nick, and Juan all shook their heads. "That's a genuine American bulldog. The dog of the pioneers, the bravest, stoutest, gamest dog in the world. Old Boney would eat one of them Meskin pit bulls for breakfast. Look out Mister Jag–you–ar." With that he seemed to have exhausted his store of civility. He turned to the dark man. "Come on, Manuel, let's get this f–kin' show on the road." They climbed into the truck with no further ceremony and backed around. The rest of them boarded Juan's big ranch diesel and pulled out after.

"Don't know what it is about them. Trigg hates everything but his dogs, curses Meskins and greasers and spics and beaners, can't even say his name right. And Manuel is one of God's own gentlemen. But they work together on a hunt like they were born brothers. Natural houndsmen, I guess." Juan turned to Shelagh, who had taken the front seat. "You're going to see something special now, Shelagh. Trigg is worthless, but Manuel is one of the honest-to-God last great jaguar callers in Mexico. There's not much call for 'em anymore. Even where they haven't killed all the cats out they can use electronics—you know, jaguars recorded in zoos. But Manuel still does it with a horn made of bark."

She said nothing but cut her eyes back to Nick, grinning around her cigarette.

They ground south along the edge between creosote desert and bosque. The darkness seemed total now, accentuated rather than diminished by the hot white glow of the headlights. After a half-hour of low-gear travel, Trigg's truck cut left and bounced along a narrow track between the salt cedars. They followed, down a path so narrow that the feathery branches whipped in through the windows, and stopped at a clearing. His lights flicked off, and Juan cut the engine. The houndsman was in the window.

"Leave the dogs here," he said in a whisper. "A little bit of luck and we'll never even need 'em."

They walked single file down a still narrower track, Trigg shining a light directly on the ground no more than five feet ahead. In a moment they emerged into ghostly light and a horrible stench. On the white-gravel road that glowed dimly in the starlight were the disassembled pieces of a black calf. In front of them, paralleling the road, was a ditch full of shining black water, fifteen feet wide, stretching left and right as far as the eye could see; beyond that, another gravel track, backed by another feathery black mass of tamarisk. Beyond *that*, Nick knew, was the Big River itself, but at this time of the year most of its water flowed through the ditches. Just a little downstream a narrow bridge, suspended from cables, crossed the flow; it was just wide enough for a single person to pass at a time. Light reflected off its cables, picking it out.

Manuel spoke in a low Spanish whisper to Juan, who replied in kind. He came back. "Manuel wants to stay out here by the carcass—he'll call up and down, and the sound should travel a long way up the ditch here. He wants us back by the trees. Nick, why don't you go downstream a bit, across from the bridge. Bilious will go up. That way we'll have a clean field. . . ."

Trigg started out, but Juan made an impatient motion.

"Not so fast. First of all, if the cat comes out down here, Billy, damn well better not shoot toward us. This ain't no trophy hunt. Second, the cat's probably behind us. What if it jumps out and decides to eat Manuel before it figures out he's a Mexican and not a trespasser? We can't shoot toward each other."

Trigg gestured. "Manuel can take care of that just fine. *Mostralo tu pistola, hombre.*"

The flash of white teeth in the starlight: Manuel was grinning. He said in English, "Colt single-action Army .45," and waved an old cowboy six-gun at the others in a way that could be considered reckless north of the border.

"I load it up with handloads you wouldn't believe—don't know why he hasn't blown it up yet. It's a long-range paper-punch. Probably drop that cat in his tracks faster than that elephant gun of yours, Nicky," he added.

Nicky, thought Sharpe. *It'd drop you, you arrogant son-of-a-b—.*

But Juan just worked the action on his old pump shotgun, took his elbow, and moved with him downstream.

Shelagh watched with her journalist's eye. The Mexican was bending over, tossing dry chips of cow aside. After a moment he sat down cross-legged amid the remains. He was holding a pale object about 18 inches long that Sharpe hadn't seen clearly yet but that looked like a megaphone.

He bent over, and from him issued a sound that was not human. It was a bit like a repeated cough, but deep and hollow with a resonance like a drum's. He stayed absolutely motionless after it ended. There was no other sound on the riverbank but the muted gurgle of the water in the ditch, heading for the Gulf. There was no breeze, and the smells barely touched her nostrils. She swore that if she listened just a little harder she would hear the blazing stars sing.

Ruuuagh, rurgh, rurgh, rurgh . . .

"Listen." Juan. Manuel had not called for ten minutes—his rhythms were his own, not apparent to the others. They both breathed consciously, delicately, through their mouths, trying to deaden the small sounds of their bodies. After a moment he shook his head. "I thought . . . *nada.*"

"*Shhh.*"

This time they all heard it. From out of the darkness all around them it came, from the river and the trees, upstream and down, from inside their chests and between their ears, humming and ticking. The rhythm was exactly like Manuel's, cough, *cuff, cuff,*

cuff. But no human lungs, even amplified, ever resonated like that. It was omnidirectional, and as it died they all looked wildly around, hair standing on end on every neck. It was an old sound, a sound from before fire and security, a sound from when all the forests of the earth still held beings to whom humans were no more than another kind of tasty prey. Before their scalps had stopped prickling it came again, louder: *RUUUUAGH, rurghh, rurrrgh, rurr, rurr ...*

"Where is it?"

"WHERE IS IT?"

"Where is it???"

"Holy s—."

Juan to Nick: "I always heard you couldn't tell where it was coming from. Oh, *man*, this is amazing."

"SHHH!"

Rurghh, rurgh ... Manuel.

And then absolute silence again. Nick raised his rifle barrel to see if he could make out the vertical ivory bar. He could, just barely.

"I know you like that rifle, Nick, but I'll stick by this." Juan wiggled the old Winchester Model 12. Nick noticed for the first time that there was a strip of white tape around the barrel's end. A good sensible solution, he thought, not some damn romantic's toy. . . .

Juan was kneeling, peering forward. "I thought ... no ..."

Ruuuargh, crrruff, cuff. . . . This time it definitely sounded closer, as if they were inside the sound itself. But there was still no direction. . . .

The movement at the bridge took Nick by surprise. A piece of the shadows from the wall across the creek had detached and was drifting in front of the paler shadows of the bridge's planks. He touched Juan's arm, swung his rifle toward the darkness. He could see his sight, but nothing behind it. . . .

And a solid beam of white light stabbed at the bridge, lit it up against the darkness beyond, lit up a hunk of night with sudden white fangs standing stock still as Trigg opened up with the AK on full automatic, cutting a string of splashes four feet under the cat and climbing. Nick had a sense of its rushing forward, toward him, then lost it entirely as Juan, who had fired once, knocked him sprawling just as Trigg's gun stitched the foliage where he had been sitting a moment before. He heard Juan shout, "You *a–hole*, Billy," and then the noise shut off.

Manuel ran toward them, speaking in rapid Spanish. Juan shoved past him to where the other three stood and grabbed Trigg by the shirt. "You're off this as of right now. Who told you to use the light? And why the *f–* did you use that machine gun?"

"I don't have to answer to you, boy. Who the hell do you think you are? You're just a Goddamn wetback with an attitude! I can use any damn gun I want. And if I'm off, so are my dogs, got it?" He was pounding on Juan's breastbone with his index finger now. "I don't want to risk my damn dogs is why I used a damn light! You wanna do anything about it, BEANER?"

This last was shouted, sprayed, three inches from Juan's face, who reversed his shotgun and shoved its butt into the screaming poacher's belly, then knocked him sideways as he doubled over, grabbing the AK-47 from his hand as he fell. "And I don't have time for this *s–*. Get the dogs."

The dogs had milled around for a few moments, bristling. Then little Julie had thrown back her silky head and bawled, and they had disappeared into the blackness. Juan was fooling around awkwardly with the receiver for the dogs' radio-collar transmitters when Trigg lurched up out of the darkness, breathing heavily, and wordlessly shoved him aside to flip three switches, then put on a pair of headphones.

For a while the signals came from south of them. Then, before dawn, they began moving west. The trucks followed a good dirt track under the interstate on a strong signal, then a worse one that meandered back and forth across a scrub-filled arroyo with walls a hundred feet high, due west toward the castellated ramparts of the San Mateo Range.

"He's going up Black Springs Canyon." Nick looked up at the sheer vertical profile of Vittorio's Peak, rose-gold in the dawn, which guarded the edge of the Apache Kid Wilderness. The canyon ran below it, carved by rushing water in the spring runoff and the summer rains, with miles of walls too steep to climb.

"Great. Just the ruggedest piece of land in the Lower Forty-eight."

"Sure is pretty, though." Juan seemed serene; since he had knocked Trigg down he hadn't said a tense word. Shelagh slept like a baby in the backseat, face crushed up against the seat, rolling a bit but not waking.

They found the first two dogs, Plotts, in the gravel of an arroyo bottom, under a shining live oak tree. One's head was crushed, and the other was disemboweled. They were dead, sightless, but not yet stiff. Trigg picked each up and talked to it as he laid it out in the back of his pickup. As he lifted the second, he stared deliberately at Juan.

"I'd hate to have anybody look at me like that."

"His problem."

"Well, he is good to his dogs."

"If he hadn't jumped the gun, all his dogs would be alive."

The cat left a trail of dogs. The next, as though to defy Trigg's belief in its invincibility, was the great bulldog. Its sides were flayed as though by skinning knives, but it had died with its jaws full of black fur. "Marked the bitch," muttered Trigg. Then the third Plott, looking unhurt but stone dead, then the Airedale, then the fourth Plott, almost decapitated. By then they had abandoned the cars and were struggling along a ledge cut decades before by miners, high above the bottom. Below, far below, were hundred-foot spikes of ponderosa and a silver streak of water that glittered but did not seem to move. Above them was red rock, and in their path, rooted in the cobbles of the miners' track, were hundreds of stubby live oaks, yuccas, and junipers. When they had struggled through a last grove of them the road simply ended in a little platform above the valley, overlooking only air. Lying on its lip, groaning, was the last dog, soft little Julie. One taloned mitt had laid the little dog open all along her ribs, but it struggled to its feet to send one more howl after its assailant as Trigg stooped. He stared at Juan. "We stop here."

Juan looked back at him levelly, then walked forward to the edge to look over the country. The only sound was the jeering of the Steller's jays in the brush below and, more distantly, the drumming of a woodpecker. The cat had gone as certainly and instantly as it had appeared, gone where the light goes when you flip off the switch. After a moment he turned and walked back down the way he had come. Nick looked at Trigg. "Looks like she'll make it. They were good dogs." But Trigg just gave him the same stare he had given Juan, and walked back down after him, carrying his only friend.

THE PLASTIC DEER

BY

SAM FADALA

Records, rankings, G-2s, ⅝ᵗʰˢ as an irreducible fraction, deductions (how do you accurately calculate a deer's deductions any more than a desert's, a canyon's, or a mesa's?)—that entire numerological ball of wax can be the dark side to which the "book" may lead an otherwise perfectly sensible hunter. Call it a "condition" (digititis) that too many hunters suffer from, and one that Sam Fadala addresses head on, as it were, in this memoir of being drawn to the verge of obsession.

Four years of high school lasted twenty; it was so bloody boring, and though I read voraciously, I had no interest in poring through the pages of the books laid upon me in subjects like math, history, social studies, and Spanish. The only good I got out of four years at Yuma Union High School in Yuma, Arizona, was the Spanish—I somehow picked up enough to get me by on hunts years later in Mexico. And so I was a D pupil, except for a B in biology, once, thanks to a wonderful teacher who made me class curator of wild animals.

At the close of my senior year I, along with every other departing student, was brought into the counselor's office. I cannot recall her name. She was also the teacher of my social studies class, in which I paid more attention to Jackie, the prettiest girl in the school, than to class lectures. The counselor told me that she had excellent news. The city of Yuma was hiring, and since I was a pretty good boy, I could work up from being on the garbage truck to driving it.

I had no business attending college, least of all the University of Arizona, which was academically ranked number twenty-five by North Central Accreditation—quite lofty, considering that there are hundreds of institutions of higher learning in the United States. But enroll I did. And flunk out I did. In the course of two and a half almost totally wasted years, however, during which I never cracked a book, one good thing happened: I met Robert Bradsher. Robert was from the little town of Patagonia, on the Mexican border. He was a fiend for hunting Coues deer, the diminutive whitetail of northern Mexico, Arizona, and New Mexico.

"Come and try it," Robert offered, and I did. I hit it off with his parents, who were a retired couple living on social security, and the game was afoot. That first season I carried a Winchester Model 94 carbine, a .30-30. I did well with that little shooter on everything *but* Coues deer.

For some reason, I never settled down to draw a fine bead. I just up and fired—snapshooting, some call it. I did not get a deer. The following summer I went to work at the Saddle & Sirloin Restaurant in Tucson as a pearl diver, a quaint title for dishwasher. I earned enough to purchase a brand-new Model 70 Winchester .270; that was Jack O'Connor's favorite, and Jack was the king of outdoor writers. Topped off with a Kollmorgan Bear Cub 4X scope, my outfit was deadly indeed. The scope forced me to take aim, rather than spilling out a volley of rounds just to hear the rattling echo in the canyons. My confidence in my new rifle ran so high, in fact, that I vowed to hunt only bucks that would make "the book."

From then on I passed up buck after buck. I had the time. Attending university was of no importance compared with hiking the Patagonia hills. But as that second season rolled on, I found no buck that would qualify for the Boone and Crockett ego trip.

"You boys ought to go to the Town Mill," Mr. Bradsher said one day. "Sam has only a couple of days left on the season, and he's hell-bent to take a big buck. This time of the year, big bucks have been chased out of the high country, and they're hiding in the grass breaks just out of town." We'd try it.

On the first day there was nothing—well, bucks, but not what I wanted. And then, up it came. There was no doubt in my mind. I had latched onto a batch of loads sold through Jensen's Sporting Goods in Tucson. They were built on necked-down .30-06 brass loaded with 140-grain MGS 2-D bullets. The 2-D stood for two-diameter, which they were. They were also tough as tungsten and wouldn't open up on an elephant, as I was about to find out. The buck ran straight away. If it topped the rise, I'd never see it again. I took a well-aimed, if hastily fired, shot. The deer showed no reaction.

My mother hated cussing, and I never did any around her. But what foul words I knew blurted out in between the next three shots. And then, miraculously, the buck crumpled, just before it topped the rise. All four bullets had connected. It was mine, and its rack did make the book. I found that out by taking it to an official measurer in Tucson, the gifted taxidermist and dedicated hunter John Doyle. John said that the buck was record class, and if I wanted to enter it, he would take care of the paperwork. I said I did.

And then I got a flow of counseling.

"Nothing wrong with the book," John said, "but this buck will go in near the bottom, and the scores are going up soon anyway. Why not try for a bigger one next year? There's a new club forming. We're going to call it the Record Desert Whitetail Club. It's for hunters dedicated to trophy Coues. If you shoot one that does not make the book, you're out." It sounded OK to me, and so I became a charter member. At the first meeting, the trophy was presented. It was a wooden column with a whitetail buck on top. The buck was a bronze color but looked as plastic as a water gun. I didn't care. I wanted someday to sit at the head of the banquet table after the season, having taken first place, my name engraved on the brass plate beneath the plastic deer. If I could do that three times, the trophy would be mine forever.

My quest for the plastic deer lasted for the next ten years. I met a friend, Señor Victor Ruiz of Nogales, Sonora, Mexico. He and his partners had developed a new shooting game across the border they called *Silueta*. Would I like to come and shoot? The idea was offhand firing, with a hunting rifle, at metallic cutouts at various distances, up to five hundred meters on the *borego*, or ram. I said I'd show up and I did, but I was not much interested in throwing bullets at make-believe animals. *Silueta* failed to hold my interest, but my new friend had another passion—Coues deer. Would I like to join him on private ranches in Sonora to hunt the wily *cola blanca*. You bet.

I was invited at that time to leave college, a nice way of saying that I was kicked out. My name was prominent on the dean's list, which was not an honor then. The dean's list was for those students who were flunking out. As I stood on a street corner in Tucson one day, a fire engine screamed by. That looked exciting. I learned that the city of Tucson was hiring. I took the written test and passed it—not many did, and I was surprised that I was one of them. The physical test was punishing, but I was in decent shape, always being in the mountains—if not hunting, then scouting. I found that I could do the one-man-fold-and-carry, 78 pounds with 50 feet of 2½-inch hose, plus 22-pound nozzle, in the Arizona sun on a dead run fully around the block. The aerial ladder was pure excitement, and only a few could whip me going up.

I loved the job, but a strange desire to take another jab at college pulled me away three years later. Eventually, the school that booted me out presented me with a doctoral fellowship, graduation with full honors, and an earned doctorate in research. But that was later.

In the meanwhile, I continued my quest for the plastic deer. I now had three more teachers. Jim and Seymour Levy showed me the true meaning of tough hunting, and it was biologist Jerry Day who taught all of us how to use a binocular for finding—not simply for magnifying something we had already seen. I found myself spending a full week at a time in the mountains either hunting or scouting, often with nothing to eat for the final three days or so. I knew where the water holes were, however, and ended up drinking from potholes that today would make me recoil in disgust. But you can ignore green slime when you're as dry as popcorn in the summer sun.

Over a ten-year period I took fourteen Coues bucks that qualified for the record book at the time they were taken—witnessed, but not entered into the records. As the minimum-points requirement rose, several of my deer would have been out, anyway, had I sent the papers on to New York. I also learned something about myself. I had become a zealot, a person bent on an unholy quest.

"Where did you get that fine buck?" a fellow asked one day as I stood in John Doyle's taxidermy shop with another big deer. In smartass fashion, I responded, "Right through the heart."

John looked at me and said, "Sam, tell the man where you got the buck." I was embarrassed, realizing what a chicken answer I had given.

"I got the buck in the Canelo Hills," I said. John nodded his head approvingly. I resolved to change, after that.

Of course, the route to noble-mindedness did not always run true. One day John and I were slowly descending a steep grade in the mountains when we encountered a truck coming up. It turned out that we knew the hunters, two men from Tucson who had been in the shop. They had asked where John and I were going to hunt that season, and we told them—the truth.

"Well," they said, as we got out to talk, "we're surprised to see you two up here. We thought you had given us a bum steer. This damn place never had a big buck in it and never will. The only reason we came back is that we didn't scout anyplace else and are stuck here."

Uncharacteristically, John said, "You might want to take a look at the buck Sam got this morning. It's in the back of the truck." The men walked around, and I lifted the protecting tarp from my trophy, an impressive, shoo-in B&C 4x4.

"Oh," the guys said in unison. "Oh." They couldn't seem to find many more words. I gloated.

I still hadn't shown the worst of myself, though, in my quest for that plastic deer. That happened when my good friend Max Wilson asked if I could, just once, allow his son Beryl to tag along with me. Just once.

"You're a hero to the boy," he told me.

I said all right, and Max, his son, and I found ourselves in a steep canyon. Normally I hunt from high points, but this was different. I had located a couple of big bucks by walking in the bottom of this deep cut while looking up onto the sides. I had taken to using a Moses stick, as we called it—a staff built of a light but strong dead agave stalk topped with a leather handle and a crutch bumper bottom. The walking stick was also great for glassing. I looked up the side of the canyon, and there, quietly

reposing by the side of a huge boulder in the shade of an oak, lay a record-class Coues buck. By then I was able to judge a buck very accurately, and this one would fall sturdily into the upper third of the book.

"OK, guys," I said. "Stand still. I've got one."

I could not sit to get a rest and still see the buck. So I used the Moses stick to steady my shot. My first bullet flew just over the buck's back. It got up and took off, but lots of practice on jack rabbits came through, and my next shot dropped it on the run.

The three of us labored up the side of the canyon to the buck. And there it lay. What a prize! Coues bucks typically are what we Westerners call three-pointers—a main beam, two main points off the main beam, plus an eye guard—an eight-pointer for other hunters. But when I turned the head over, what I had was, in Eastern-Northern-Southern lingo, a nine-pointer. There was no match for the final beam point on one side.

"Blast it!" I yelled.

The buck would still crack 110 B&C points after deductions, but the lack of that point moved it down several notches on the scale. "I'd like to kick this thing down the canyon," I blurted out.

Max looked at me with a pained expression. Here was his young son listening to his hero tarnish what was otherwise a shining moment. Later on, Max said, "Sam, I've known you since you were sixteen years old, and this is the first time I've been ashamed of you."

I got the picture real fast. Although I continued to hunt trophy Coues, I did so with a revised attitude. Later on, I altered that attitude even more.

I did end up taking the Record Desert Whitetail Club trophy three times, with dozens of interesting experiences for each buck. Then I quit the game. I simply hunted Coues deer for the sake of hunting. Sure, I would be happy with a big one, but when I introduced two sons to hunting, I told them both that we were putting trophy, trophy, trophy on the back burner. We learned just to enjoy the experience.

And when I look back on my quest for that plastic deer, the finest memories have no blood on them at all—at least, not Coues blood. My best day ever saw no bullet leaving the muzzle of my rifle. John Doyle was a powerful walker. It was our normal pattern to hike in the dark to begin the day and return in the dark, as late as midnight, to our camp. But John was plagued with asthma. I was our scout. I was also our pack mule. I had located a special deer while scouting in the preseason, and I felt that the buck would challenge the world's record. I told John so. "We're going for that one, and only that one," John declared.

The first day of the season found us in a spot we called the Honeycombs. I was first to locate a buck. I told my partner that he could have the shot, and if he didn't shoot I was going to. The buck was coming toward us, undoubtedly seeking a cool spot in the rocks to rest out the day. As it got closer, it became clear that this buck would go well over 120 points, and we both decided that 125 was a conservative estimate. John said that he didn't want the buck. I got ready. I flipped the safety off and took aim.

"Is this the buck you saw when you were scouting?" John asked. I said no.

"Was the other one bigger?" he slyly queried. I said yes.

"Then why are you going to shoot this one?"

I lowered my rifle, and the big boy walked by within a hundred yards, never knowing we were there.

By midafternoon we had seen several fine Coues bucks, a red-letter day to be sure. High in the Honeycombs we climbed to a ledge where we could eat lunch and rest. We sat for a full hour, continuing to hunt by glassing between bites for a bedded buck. Suddenly, another clearly record-class Coues buck leaped out from below us no more than fifty yards away—typical of that clan's ability to stay as still as a stone seemingly endlessly. I'm not now sure why, but neither of us went for our nearby rifles. We just watched as the buck, tail high, leaped away. Then it was time to get at it again.

"Be careful," I told John as he got to his feet. He had been having a little trouble breathing, and I could see that he was not entirely steady.

"Sam," he instructed me, "I'm not going to fall off the face of this bluff. You don't fall *away* from the side of a mountain. You fall *into* the mountain. Gravity man, gravity."

And with that, he stood up and fell headlong from the face of the bluff, at least ten feet down to the next ledge. Later, we would laugh about it. But it wasn't funny that day. Blood began to seep over the top of his boot. He had ripped a strip of flesh completely away from his shinbone. I helped him off the ledge. He said he could carry on and that we could go on hunting, but I knew better.

We headed for the truck.

I never again saw that huge buck I'd spotted. But it's still alive in my memory. I'd been glassing from the top of a draw and there it came. It moved slowly, remaining in my view for a half-hour, my final look at a mere twenty yards, with a breeze coming up the draw from the buck to me. It had six points to the side, counting the eye guard. Four points met at the tip of the beams, sort of like holding your hand out with fingers extended. Weight was neither pencil-horn nor heavy. The rack was "Coues-deer" symmetrical. I added up the score in my mind.

The inside spread was about fourteen inches, maybe a bit more. The beams were easily twenty inches. I had taken a buck with such beams before, and I knew what twenty inches looked like. The back point had to extend fifteen inches in order to meet the tip of the beam. That was thirty points all by itself. I whispered to myself, *This buck will go 150 points* as it disappeared upward into a jumble of rock and brush.

The funny thing about Coues deer is that they never seem to be quite as real as when they aren't there anymore. Even today, that buck may have been the most real one I ever saw—more than all the deer made of plastic, anyway.

BROTHERS OF THE WOLF

BY
ROBERT F. JONES

*We are not without our lone wolves, but, on the whole, humans are by
nature pack hunters. (At our Paleolithic beginnings, armed with
sharpened sticks and chipped stones, we had no option but to band
together in order to bring down large mammals.) The deer camps we
gather in every fall are a clear expression of that essentially evolutionary
characteristic. One of the qualities that distinguish our packs from the
wolves', though, as the late and much-missed Bob Jones tells us, is that
we don't drive away our old ones, but instead often give them the seats,
or stands, of honor.*

> It's da second week of deer camp and all da boys are here.
> We drink, play cards, and shoot da bull, but never shoot no deer.
> The only time we go to town is when we're outta beer.
> Oh, da second week of deer camp is da greatest time of year.
> —*Da Yoopers*

Deer camps run the gamut from bare-bones scruff to the
ultimate in luxury.

As a kid growing up in the 1940s, I hunted out of a dilapidated
bunkhouse on a lake near Rhinelander, Wisconsin, that once
belonged to a logging company. The outfit had gone under in
1917, after a disastrous 20,000-acre forest fire wiped out all the
harvestable timber on its land. But the bunkhouse survived: Its
mossy, cedar-shingled roof leaked even when it wasn't raining;
the rotting white pine logs of its walls glowed at night with fungus;
wood rats and cooties shared our bed ticking. The cast-iron
cookstove snorted fire through its rust holes like a demented
dragon but generated heat enough to warm cans of Hormel chili,

or fry eggs and deer liver for breakfast. Why would anyone choose to live that way, even for a few days? For us, the abundance of burly, tall-racked whitetails in the swamps nearby was all the comfort we teenagers needed.

By contrast I once hunted big bucks out of a truly elegant camp. My late good friend Joe Judge's Twin Ponds Duck Club was a 1,643-acre sprawl of dove fields, waterfowl marshes, and deer woods near Centreville on Maryland's Eastern Shore. Contoured to the gentle landscape of the Eastern Shore, and surrounded by sunflower, soybean, feed-corn fields, and acres of acorn-rich oak woods, it sat on a low bluff above the tidal waters of the Corsica River near Chesapeake Bay. The silvery cedar-shake roof and slate-blue siding blended nicely with the wraparound topography. A weathered wooden deck ran the length of the lodge overlooking the river, with a battery of foot-traps mounted along its railings. Boxes of clay pigeons and shotgun ammunition in all gauges stood ready at hand for any and all. Pine-paneled walls sloped airily upward to a skylit cathedral ceiling where big fans slowly stirred the air. A sunken lounge with a huge stone fireplace centered the long, burgundy-carpeted main room of the lodge. The west end of the room was the dining area, replete with long pine tables, comfortable easy-chairs, and a kitchen dominated by a gleaming, industrial-strength Vulcan gas range. The cuisine at Joe's was, in a word, *haute*: oysters on the half shell, freshly caught blue crabs, homegrown turkey or beef or honey-cured ham. Game in season: black ducks, whole sides of corn-and-nut-fed venison, and the best roasts of Canada goose I've ever sunk my teeth into. At the far end of the main room was an amply stocked bar with Harp beer on tap. On the walls of the lodge hung mount after mount of flighted waterfowl—Canadas, snows, blues, canvasbacks, and redheads circled the interior walls in a seemingly nonstop skein. But what endeared me to the place were the mounts of colossal white-tailed deer.

No matter how well or poorly they're appointed, all deer camps have this in common: They're not just a home away from home. In their essence they're far more exciting than any home can ever be. At least for the few weeks that the season might last, a deer camp is where we belong. It's where we shed the thin veneer of civilization, drop the uncomfortable masks of dutiful husbands, stalwart job holders, sensitive fathers, and go back to being what evolution bred us to be: members of a hunting pack, brothers of the wolf.

Both literally and figuratively, deer camp is our place to howl. The area where I live in southwestern Vermont is studded with hunting camps. They vary in scale from one-room tarpaper shacks to elegant, slate-roofed log cabins; but drive past any one of them on a night during deer season and you'll hear what I mean: From each and every camp comes the high-decibel roar of men having fun. Guys laughing in full bellow at one raucous joke after another, or whooping with delight at a good poker hand, or moaning with mock sorrow as someone recounts a muffed shot at what had to be the biggest buck in North America. The deer that are missed, of course, are inevitably Boone and Crockett monsters, 12 points by 250 pounds at least. Moderation and understatement have no place in deer camp. A whole school of folk literature, our best and most distinctively American fiction, derives from the hunting camp experience: the tall tale. Think Mike Fink, Mark Twain, even Moby Dick.

The meat pole in most camps, on the other hand, tells a different story. There we see what the woods really hold. Increasingly over the years that I've lived and hunted in New England, the deer that dangle each fall from the meat pole have been getting smaller. A 10-point buck I dragged from Bear Mountain eight years ago dressed out at 175 pounds. Last season I helped another hunter with what at first glance could have been that earlier buck's twin. Yet at the check-in station, it tipped the scales at a scant 127. Compare photographs of hanging deer taken at the same camp over a period of two or three decades and you'll see the difference. "In the old days," says my craggy Vermont neighbor Eldon Rogers, "say the 1950s and earlier, if you dropped a buck you had something to chew on all winter. Nowadays you're lucky to get a month's worth of stew meat and deerburger." The same principle holds true, in my experience, in camps from Maine through Michigan to Wisconsin. Where are the bucks of yesteryear?

They're not getting a chance to grow up. Older hunters in all the camps I know sing the same lament. Today's young Nimrods are trigger-happy, far too eager to have something—*anything*—with horns, hanging from the meat pole. With whitetail numbers increasing every year as deer grow more and more habituated to the proximity of people, this killing of small bucks—spikes and forkhorns that no hunter of the old school would have wasted a bullet on—is arguably doing no ecological harm. But it is eroding the whole value and tradition of trophy hunting. Call me an old coot, but I have to agree with the graybeards: The neurotic need for instant gratification is debasing our sport.

End of sermon.

For all that, a well-run deer camp is still the best place I know to get away from the tribulations of everyday life. I hate any camp with television. The happiest camps, I've found, have no electricity at all—thus no TV, though nowadays with the advent of cheap, miniaturized, battery-powered sets and satellite receivers they're getting harder and harder to find. I also find boom boxes, and even portable radios, objectionable in any self-respecting deer camp. The excuse for radios is usually to get the weather report, but most of the men I hunt with can predict the weather more accurately by a quick glance at the sky than can all the satellites beaming down to the Weather Channel. Once a radio is in camp, you're doomed to hear music. But we get enough of that—especially the opprobrious and ubiquitous noise called hip-hop—at every turn in the soi-disant Real World. In the camps of my youth, the only music we heard at night emanated from the rattling nostrils and soft palates of our fellow hunters, as they snored up the moon. Often it was counterpointed by the hoot of hunting owls or the melodious yipping of coyotes as they sang the moon down again.

The best camps are lit by firelight and kerosene lanterns or, conceding something to modernity, Coleman lamps. At the end of the hunting day, boots are arrayed just inside the door, capturing the dance of the warm light and adding the rich aroma of oil-soaked leather and the faint hint of bipedal Limburger to an atmosphere already tinged with the scents of woodsmoke, Hoppe's Nitro Powder Solvent, pipe tobacco, and wet wool.

Sometimes during the doldrums of midsummer, when it seems that November will never arrive, I find myself wishing that some canny *parfumeur* could bottle that aromatic essence: Eau de Deer Camp. Not a chance ...

You can tell a lot about a man's character by the way he treats his rifle. The best I've ever known in that respect have been World War II infantry veterans, men to whom a gummed-up firing pin, a jammed cartridge, or a misaligned sight could mean no tomorrow. I love the ritual of gun care after a hard day's hunt: The harsh whisper of brass brushes snaking their way down .30-caliber barrels from which most of the bluing has been worn over a lifetime of strenuous use. The tangy scent of gun oil lovingly applied as men recount the day's adventures. The low, quiet, sensible talk of strategies and schemes for tomorrow. The clatter of bolts socking home. The finality of it. It's even better than the pro forma poker game. It's what we're here for.

Nowhere does the analogy with the wolf pack come into play more significantly than in a deer drive. It's a classic tactic that dates to the days of Cro-Magnon vs. woolly mammoth, Sioux vs. buffalo. Here's where the long-nurtured companionship and cooperation of deer camp, the respect for seniority, and the true appreciation of mature masculine strategy come into play for the payoff. The old guys in camp know the lay of the land. The young guys, with their strong legs and bottomless lungs, do all the walking.

When I was a kid in Wisconsin, we neophytes from the bunkhouse ("Boy's Town," we called it) teamed up with a bunch of old geezers from a nearby camp—elderly gents in their thirties and forties—for some exhausting and highly productive drives: exhausting for us, productive for them. The old guys knew every clearing and muskeg in that patch of the North Woods, and through years of experience had worked out the best way to "push" it. They stationed themselves at the far end of the half-mile-long section we'd be beating, ensuring themselves open lanes of fire, and sat back against some ancient Paul-Bunyan-felled white pine stumps, sipping hot, brandy-spiked coffee from their Thermoses while we worked toward them. We made plenty of noise en route, rifles slung over our shoulders for the most part,

whacking the brush and the tamarack trunks with sticks, hooting back and forth to one another to keep the line straight, occasionally getting bogged to the waist in bottomless sinkholes of icy black muck and having to be winched out by our buddies. We could see the deer spooking ahead of us through the cutover second-growth jungle, bounding high with their long white tails flagging like shaggy metronomes, but of course we dared not shoot with our elders out there in the line of fire. Now and then a deer would panic and try to break back through our line, usually a young spike or forkhorn, but on a few occasions a decent, sizable six-pointer. Once it was past we were free to blaze away, but we rarely hit anything. Meanwhile, the rest of the deer were racing past the old guys on stand. Their shots always told. "One shot, buck," runs the old Indian saying. "Two shots, maybe buck. Three shots.... *Noooo* buck."

After the drive we'd help the old fellows gut and drag out their deer, then they'd invite us into their far more comfortable camp for a big feed, with plenty of cold, dark amber beer to wash down the steaks and stews and potato salad, and even a schnapps or two after dinner. Good times, good times....

Now, half a century later here in Vermont, I'm one of the old guys, a senior wolf with arthritic legs and a white muzzle. I sit comfortably on my stand sipping coffee and waiting for the buck of my dreams to appear, while the young wolves whoop and beat the bushes. I like it that way. What goes around, comes around. In deer camp, if nowhere else, rank hath its privileges.

DEER HUNTING

BY

DAVID MAMET

One of our great playwrights, David Mamet, presents us with a meditative analysis of what he learned from a full season in the woods. It is clear that he is fascinated by the intricate puzzle of deer and the hunting of them, and has set himself the task of at least attempting to solve it. It is a most lively enterprise, even though there is ultimately no solution to be had. As Mamet and all good hunters know, there is only next season.

It is December 13, and there are six inches of powder snow on the ground. It would be a perfect afternoon for cross-country skiing, and in any previous year I would be thrilled at this first chance to ski. This year, however, it's going to take an adjustment, for if it is a perfect day to ski, must it not also be a perfect day to hunt? And why would one ski in the hunting season?

One would not. The hunting season ended yesterday.

And there, of course, were the fresh tracks of a buck mocking my path from the house to the cabin this morning. I knew they were fresh, as the snow kicked up in front was bright and sharp; I knew they were a buck, as I could see the imprints of the dewclaws behind the main hoofs. Now, I know that opinion is divided on the reliability of the dewclaws as an index of sex, but his was my first serious season of hunting, and so I count myself the heir to any information, any hypothesis, that might aid me in the understanding of the deer.

The dewclaws bit was garnered from several of the many hunting books I read before and during the season. The nineteenth-century hunter-writers endorsed, and then contemporary ones derided, dewclaws as a test. My friend Bagwell informed me to look at the register—that is, the relative position of the front and rear hoofprints. When the rear hoofs print to the inside of the front, you've got a buck, as the buck's shoulders are wider than its hips; with a doe, he said, the opposite is true. This morning's track, by that test, is, again, a buck. And lo, I am on my way to my own mass of fact and misinformation.

My pockets are full of compasses and match-safes improvised from empty shotgun shells thrust one into another. My mudroom is hung with various blaze-orange garments. There is the last of "hunter's soap" by the tub, and phosphorus-killing clothes wash by the washing machine. My hunting licenses (Maine, New Hampshire, and Vermont) are in their little blue folder, and up on my desk. They've ridden in my pocket for the last two months. I suppose I should give them a Viking's funeral and toss them into the cabin stove, and perhaps I will. After this short review.

Bow season started in October. Jimmy at the River Run Cafe told me that there were deer down by the bottom of his land, and he would put me on a stand. So I went out with him.

I was dressed in about fifteen layers of clothes. My army surplus pants were crammed with extra knives and hones, with candy bars, and rope. I carried a belt pack that had a camera and film, and a small daypack in which was I cannot remember what.

We went down to the stand, and I somehow got up it. I belted myself to the tree and hauled my bow and then my various packs up, and hung them in the tree.

There I was, a lovely autumn day, Camel's Hump off in the distance, the tyro, attired in camouflage, my face obscured with burnt cork, up in the air, waiting for a deer.

What did I expect? It took all of five minutes, and there they came.

Suddenly, from God-knows-where, there were two deer in the small clearing beneath me: a doe, and what looked to be a spike-horn buck. Now, the season, at this time, was "any deer," and I could have shot either as they walked up to my stand. But I would have much preferred to shoot a buck, and I could not make out for certain, at the distance, if the second was a buck or not. So I waited for them to get closer to me, which they did.

They walked right underneath my stand. Sure enough, it was a buck. And he was standing there, grazing, swishing his tail side to side in what some authorities say is the "all clear" signal.

Heh-heh. I had him. What was this nonsense about the trials of deer hunting?

Then I realized that I was on the wrong side of the tree. To shoot the buck, I'd have to maneuver my arrow and bow out from the right side of the tree, lean back, and bring them to bear on the left side, without disturbing the deer.

Ever so quietly, I did so. And I did not disturb them, for they walked quite peacefully off, and back into the woods.

It seemed quite a while before my heart stopped pounding.

It had been thrilling to see them appear out of nothing. And they were so beautiful, walking up the hill. Well, it was four o'clock, and the deer tend to move at sundown, so there I was, up in the tree, and I settled down.

I think that if you'd like to renew your acquaintance with yourself, you could do worse than spend time on a deer stand. Sometimes the hours go quickly, and you become part of the scene. Sometimes each half-minute is torture, as you strive to settle down. On the stand last year, I had a bird land on my bow and start to hop to my glasses, when his eyes flashed, "What in the *hell* . . .," for all the world like a vaudeville comic doing his turn. Up in Maine, I had another bird land on my rifle.

I got to see the sun come up and go down in the woods many times, and the various squirrels and chipmunks. I heard a lot, and began to understand what some of it meant. I heard deer several times. I saw only the two, but I saw them repeatedly.

There I was, up there in the tree. As the sun started coming down around seven, there were two deer, coming back. It was fairly dark, and I was not certain that they were the same I'd seen before. By the time I was certain, I had missed my chance, and they were too far in the shadow for me to risk a shot.

I was back the next afternoon, carrying a third of the equipment of the day before. I was up in the tree at 3:00. At 4:00, here they came, up through the same clearing. But this

time they were out of range. And I stayed in the tree till 7:00, when, again, back they came, again out of range.

And so *that* story went. Several nights, the deer just out of range, and me thinking: *If this were rifle season, we would tell a different tale.* And Jimmy got his doe, and hung her up at his house, and she looked real pretty. I regretted not taking my shot, but I consoled myself that several weeks of deer hunting lay ahead. Then I went up to New Hampshire, for the beginning of the muzzleloading season.

My friend Bob put me onto what seemed a superb site. There, in a small group of apple trees, was some deer sign. They were eating and defecating there. And there was a scrape. During the rut, bucks paw the ground, urinate in the scrape, and draw a hoof through it to advertise, to mark their territory. A buck was coming through here, and he meant to come back. So I got out my bow saw and cut down some branches, put up the stand, and sat up there afternoons, and I saw the sun go down in New Hampshire a bit.

Now, what was going wrong? I knew I could sit still; hell, the bird landed on my bow. I knew my camouflage was good; the deer had not seen me. I knew the wind was right to keep my scent from the deer, and I knew there were deer. Why didn't I see them?

I puzzled that one out for a while, until I came across a tip in a contemporary book. The hunter-writer had been approached by a friend who had a question similar to my own. The writer had reviewed his friend's apparatus and behavior, and his prescription was: "Paint the bottom of your tree stand." The top of this man's stand was brown, but the deer saw only the bottom, and the bottom was white.

Now, I remember reading that book before the season and thinking, *What an idiot.* And so I thought until I left the stand the last day in New Hampshire, and looked back at what had been the position of my stand, shaking my head, and saw the bright white stumps of the boughs I had sawn off demarking my position in the tree.

Was that what kept the deer off? I think so. In any case, it was a lesson.

Bob invited me to Maine. That's where the big bucks are.

And we got up at 4:00 and were out in the woods by 5:30 or so. We'd split up and meet to have lunch. I was Up There in Maine. I liked the sound of it.

Again I started off carrying too much gear. But I began to emulate Bob and by the third morning was down to a wool shirt and vest, and moving pretty quickly through the woods. I was looking for tracks. The second morning I found those of a doe and thought, *If I can figure out this is a doe, perhaps a buck can, too,* so I tracked it.

It was as beautiful a morning as I've ever seen. I tracked her for several hours up a mountain. At one point I could see that she had started running, and I wondered why she would. Then, fifty yards up, a coyote's tracks came in, and the coyote and doe continued up the mountain.

It was getting to be about time to turn back for lunch, and I was sorry to do so. I would have been happy tracking that doe forever.

I made a fire, brewed a cup of tea, and sat there in the snow, by a brook, up on the mountain.

Afternoons, I'd generally sit on a stand, over sign; then, in the evenings, we'd repair to one of the cafes and check the logbook to see who had brought in what; and check at the reporting stations to look with envy at some rather large bucks (180 pounds is big for Vermont; in Maine we were seeing 260-pound deer). Now, each day, at the end of the day, I'd sigh, get up from my stand, and start down the mountain, trying to determine how I had erred and castigating myself for those errors: "You were not sufficiently still, you did not accurately gauge the wind, you were not acute enough to observe movement. . . ."

Then I would remind myself that I'd just had about as good a day as anyone is entitled to have—which was true—and that I was learning, and those things were the whole point of the exercise.

So I would stoically return with Bob to the cafe. There I'd see the other men, who had taken deer, beautiful deer, and I would be washed by envy and the wish to "get out there" the next day.

And then one afternoon we saw the monster track.

This was a big buck. His hoof was more than five inches long, wide, and rounded at the tip. His shoulders were set wide, and if you followed those tracks, they must lead to a deer. We lit out after him.

After a bit, the deer's ambling gait quickened. He knew he was being followed. Bob had spotted the tracks first, so it was "his" deer, and he took off after him. I took a course out to the right in case the deer circled—not a bad bet.

At nightfall—no deer. We met back at the road.

The next morning Bob was back on the south side of the road, where he had lost the deer, and I went up to the north. I came across the monster tracks and followed them up the mountain, and lost him up there.

But I'd come across a game thoroughfare, new and older sign of moose and deer, and I inferred from it the deer's daily pattern. So the next day at dawn, I was back on my track, on the thoroughfare.

There were no fresh tracks of the buck, but I crossed those of a sow and cub bear, fairly fresh—I'd missed them by as few minutes as will make the story acceptably dramatic—and fresh tracks of moose. I took a stand, that day and the next, in a high position over the game trail, but I saw nothing.

And that was Maine.

I was flighty, and unscientific, and not sufficiently perseverant, but I'd gotten out there and learned a very small bit about tracking. And I'd sat in the snow and the rain and the dark and was having a superb time.

It was now centerfire rifle season in New Hampshire.

I took a Mauser .308 and sat on the ground, up the hill from the scrape I'd found there earlier. I thought that perhaps the deer had had time to forget and/or forgive my solecism with the naked stumps, and sure enough, there was fresh sign.

On the second afternoon I was sitting, quiet as the bored dead, when I heard *snuffing* off to my right and behind me—this was not a drill—and I thought I would turn ever so slowly, and all that I saw was the bush whipping in the wind and the hindquarters of the deer, bounding into the dark.

He'd (I afforded him the courtesy designation of "buck"—it was too dark and much too sudden to make out what surely were horns) come down the hill and would have walked right past me. It was three and one half paces from me to the bush. And *what* was I hoping to accomplish? I knew that I could not beat him. I *knew* that he had to see me coming around, and I knew that my only chance was an excellent chance: that he would continue down, positioning himself perfectly, quartering away, close enough to throw the rifle at him, and the wind still in my favor. And yet I found it good to turn around, and there was that deer. . . .

And it was also centerfire season in Vermont.

Now, I knew where the deer were around my house. Didn't I see their sign there every morning? And I knew they went up the hill in the morning, right up from the apple trees. I tracked them back there, just behind a given-up apple orchard and right beside an open field, a textbook-perfect location for deer. In support of which theory, in a small clearing in the woods, there was the first sign and scrape, and the deer were there.

And opening morning, I was there, and went out of my house to see a couple of trucks parked up the road. Hunters other than myself had sussed them out, too, and were back in my woods.

I stayed home.

My third great-disappointment-lesson of the season happened in a field not far from my house. I knew there were apple trees back there, and I'd seen a rub—a mark on a small tree made by a buck rubbing its antlers. There are two sorts of rubs. One is made in the summer, by the buck rubbing the "velvet" off; the other is made in the fall, as he prepares for the rut. This was a fresh "rut rub," and he was out there.

I tracked him evening after evening and saw his path, down through the field, over the rise, down into the knoll, and into the woods where he'd made his rub.

It was all right but the wind.

The prevailing, fairly invariable wind blew such that it would be impossible to take a stand above the knoll without also taking my scent to him.

Yes, you have it, until the afternoon.

Well, the wind was correct. I put some "doe-in-heat" buck lure down in the woods, by the rub.

The buck would come down, and the wind would take the lure to him and keep my scent off. The buck would come down the knoll, and I would have an easy shot before he made the woods.

I sat against a tree, just under the crest of the knoll. I practiced mounting my rifle. If he came down, well, then, I had him. He could not see me; he could not smell me. I was quiet, so he could not hear me.

The sun started to go down, and I heard the buck walking just above the knoll. He snorted twice. He'd gotten the lure. He was saying, clear as day, "Grace, is that you ...?"

And everything was just the way I had planned. I covered the safety with my left hand and eased it off with my right, and it went *click* loud enough to wake the dead, and he snorted again, in transit, and was heard lighting off for somewhere else.

I would have given, at that moment, much to have an anvil and a maul. For my beautiful Mauser rifle was a worthless traitor, and I was a fool. I fumed.

My last adventures came in the last week, during Vermont muzzleloading season. My friend Bill Bagwell, a skilled hunter, had come up from Texas. I showed him the stands, and we sat.

It was late season now. The rut was over, the food source, apples, was exhausted, the deer had been hunted heavily for a month, and they'd abandoned their usual patterns.

The stands proved dry. We walked a path, hoping to cut a track, and we found the track of a buck and followed it into the woods.

We saw him go from a browsing, meandering walk to a determined stride, and then to bounding, as he heard us behind him. We saw an eighteen-foot leap, on a slight downward slope, as he cleared a deadfall that held us up for several minutes, and we tracked him to a brook.

Now, this was a real obstacle. He cleared it in one bound, but it was partly iced, and we did not know which ice covered a rock, and which a drop into the water. As we cast up the bank for a crossing, we heard him up there, looking at us. And when we got across, we saw where he'd stood as we floundered on the bank.

We tracked him till the sun went down.

Bill went back to Texas, and I played out the season on various stands, and as of sundown yesterday, that was it.

What is the clue? Start early, get serious, learn from your mistakes, give them respect. Lord, they are smart.

I played high-stakes poker at casinos in Nevada for a while, and for a while, I did fairly well. But I will not forget those players with knowledge, character, and experience, the true professionals. One could not trap them, as they were more wily; one could play ploddingly heads-up, and they, being more skillful, would prevail. One could hope to get lucky, but their character and skill would get one broke before that occurred— there *was*, in fact, no "getting lucky"; if one wanted to beat them, one would have to study them, get serious, and give them respect.

What an education one can get out in the woods. The wind, the weather, the food sources, the phases of the moon, the habits of the deer and of the other animals—they can alert the deer to you, and vice versa—are all part of the study.

I saw the ground breathing, on a New Hampshire hillside.

There was a very high wind, and the treetops were whipping. I was on the ground, looking at sign, and I saw what appeared to be the ground heaving up. I blinked, but it continued. I saw it was a regular movement. Up and down. Regular, rhythmic movement. Perhaps there was a bear hidden under the leaves. I stood up and saw that it was a large area, some four or five feet on a side, that "breathed." I stepped back and saw that the area was double that size, and the breathing continued. It was no bear. It was no animal at all. Either I was hallucinating or I'd stumbled upon some unknown natural phenomenon.

My heart raced.

I tried to manufacture an explanation. Then I heard the creak and saw that it was caused by a tree. A birch tree had spread its roots wide over a little gully. The gully had washed out, leaving the roots exposed. They had been blanketed by leaves, and the high wind was swaying the tree. As the top swayed, the roots answered, and raised the carpet of leaves to resemble the process of breathing.

I remember a story by James M. Cain. On sentry duty in France during World War I, he had felt the earth "breathe" and had noted it in his sentry log. He felt it, and I felt it out there, too; not at the birch tree, but at that time just before dark when it, if you will bear with me, "decides" that the day is done.

If you are sitting still, you see the gradual dimming and the change of the woods. It progresses, and then there is one moment, as if a ratchet had slipped, when it is something new; it is not day, but night.

It is as if the woods breathed.

I saw that many times this fall, and got my heart fluttered by what could only be the white tail flickering in the woods up ahead. It was a snowflake, two feet from my eye, at the end of a spiderweb, and as I watched, a second slid down the web to join it.

Now, at the end of the season, as at the end of the day's hunt, a review seems to banish remorse and to goad information into knowledge, and to gently counsel thanks.

THE INDIAN GIVER

BY

BILL WISE

Bill Wise lived a great life. Now, what is supposed to be said is, "in spite of being confined to a wheelchair for forty years." But that wheelchair was simply another fact of that life, and Bill seemed hardly confined at all. Surfing put him in a wheelchair, but he still returned to the ocean and even found ways to ride the waves. Bill and his wife raised their children, and he taught them all he knew about firearms and shooting. And with the help of a true friend he found his way back to the hunting he had never stopped loving. So Bill had a great life because he lived it never less than greatly, which ought to be the measure of all our lives.

The wind, stiff off Delaware Bay, was perfect for hunting deer along the adjoining marsh edge. Greenhead flies, mosquitoes, and more important, human scent were swept inland, away from both hunter and hunted. A mule-faced doe stuck its head and shoulders from thick switchgrass and tall phragmites. It cautiously surveyed fifty yards of open grassland to the sorghum plot beyond. There it would feed on succulent grain heads.

Sitting in a wheelchair behind a blind at the edge of the sorghum, a middle-aged man shook with deer hunter's fever. It was the same excitement he had felt forty years before, when in his early teens, shotgun in hand, he saw his first whitetail.

This marshland adventure was one of his first deer hunts in twenty-seven years. When he was twenty-six a surfing accident changed his life. The wave he was riding crested steeply over an offshore bar. His surfboard slipped from under his feet, and a flat dive with outstretched arms did not protect him. The impact of his head hitting the sandy bar fractured three cervical vertebrae and crushed his spinal cord. In the time it takes for a seagull to flap its wings, his strength and athletic grace were forever stripped away.

From armpits down he was totally paralyzed. His arms were weak and his hands immobile. For decades he stubbornly resisted suggestions to try to fire a gun. He couldn't pull on his pants, wipe his butt, or flex his trigger finger, let alone hold a shotgun.

Yet there he was, watching a deer scarcely forty yards away. He needed help turning the wheelchair for a shot. His guide and companion lay curled on the ground at his feet, snoring gently, warmed by an autumn afternoon sun. The sleeping man and the man in the wheelchair had traveled together on hunting expeditions for twenty years. Although paralyzed, the man in the wheelchair drove a car with hand controls. On solitary patrols he covered the countryside looking for deer, geese in fields, or ducks resting on small streams. When he located game, he would alert his pal. In those days only one of the pair could handle a shotgun. The ambulatory man with the gun would be dropped off in places where game could be ambushed. The paralyzed man was called "Scout" by his friend. In turn, his friend became "Indian."

"Psssst. *Pssst!*" Scout hissed. "Indian. Hey!"

Breaking cover, the deer swiftly crossed open ground and entered the food patch fifteen yards from where the two men were hiding. It wore stockings of black mud up to its belly from traversing the marshy tidal guts where this deer, and others of its kind, found sanctuary.

Stirring, Indian blinked inquisitively.

Pointing with his arm, Scout implored, "There's a deer, close."

Indian rose to his knees and peered into the dense sorghum stand into which the doe had disappeared. Scout shook his head. Indian took position behind the wheelchair, where he could rotate the hunter. It was necessary to line up the chair, with weapon fixed in the gun mount, somewhere near the quarry. The paralyzed man could do the rest from there.

For the remainder of the afternoon Indian sat at the ready, out of sight, behind the wheelchair. Before sunset a dozen deer crossed open ground between marsh and feeding area. None were close enough for Scout to try.

THE INDIAN GIVER

On the way home the pair stopped at the Coral Reef Restaurant. They bought crab cake sandwiches and clam chowder in plastic cups to go. The crab cakes were quickly devoured in the van. Indian wedged a cup into Scout's hand.

"Are you all right? I'll be glad to help."

"I'm OK," Scout nodded. "Drive on!"

Indian placed the van in gear, and it rolled across the parking lot. Just as Scout lifted his cup to his lips, the van lurched into a pothole. Steaming clam chowder flew up and over Scout's face, covering the lenses of his glasses so he could not see. Thick liquid dribbled down his camouflage shirt.

"Damn! I'm sorry," Indian said with remorse.

He turned on the dome light. When he saw his companion covered in milky chowder, he burst out laughing.

"I can't help it. You're a fright." Chortling, he added, "We'll get you cleaned up soon enough."

Indian opened both van doors, lowered the wheelchair lift gate, and stepped in beside his friend. He stripped Scout to the waist. Then Indian, with his own T-shirt dampened in a nearby puddle, mopped Scout clean. A dry shirt followed. They looked at each other and grinned. It had been a good day.

Indian had been Scout's sidekick for more than twenty years. After Scout's paralysis, they had found each other at the fox hunter's club grounds. There was a rifle range at the club, with a high earthen backstop. Scout and his young sons visited to test-fire shotgun slugs. The boys were firing, their father looking on from behind the wheel of the family station wagon, when a battered Ford pickup slowed and turned in. Getting out of the truck, a bearded man sized up the three youngsters with guns in their hands. The oldest boy was no more than twelve. When they walked toward the target, the bearded man silently accompanied the boys. Scout wondered what he was thinking.

Scout's sons ran back to the station wagon, holding the target for their father to inspect. The stranger stood back a few steps and said, "I sort of keep an eye on this place for the club, seeing as how I live just down the road. Kids with guns sometimes means trouble."

Squinting, the man looked into the rear of the station wagon. He spotted Scout's wheelchair. "I've heard about you and your boys. From the looks of that target, they're pretty good shots." He added, "If you need help out here, or anyplace else, just stop by my house." He pointed in the direction of a tired gray farmhouse. The man, who looked vaguely like Charles Manson, extended his hand. As time went by, Indian helped fine-tune the boys' firearms, helped them build tree stands, and helped them track deer when their father could not.

For years, Scout's sons, friends, and Indian had all insisted that there must be a way Scout could shoot. Scout had long believed that a shooting man's identity was strongly tied to his firearms pursuits, but he had drawn the line at his own physical involvement. Indian, not philosophically but perhaps on a more basic level, felt that Scout was incomplete without the gun he had incomprehensibly swept aside. The persistence of Indian and Scout's sons was based on the belief that Scout might be more "whole" if he could once again shoot and hunt.

Relentlessly they designed gun mounts and conjured up triggers, from complex to simple. It all came together in a rush when someone discovered a swivel wheelchair gun mount made by a man in Texas. The mount soon arrived, and Indian brazed a trigger shoe with a length of key stock that offset and extended below Scout's autoloader trigger guard.

The initial trial with this rig occurred in an Eastern Shore Maryland cornfield. Indian tacked a paper plate to a wooden post twenty long strides from Scout's wheelchair. Scout's backers cheered when a pattern of lead 8s smothered the paper.

Indian suggested that Scout activate the trigger with his left wrist. That proved easier for the paralyzed shooter. Ammunition changed to Foster slugs, the accepted prescription for deer in that part of the country. Four rounds fired to the mark all touched. Warmed by the results, Scout called for greater challenge. The target was moved to thirty yards. Two shots later, with both cutting a ragged hole, possibilities became reality.

On the target was written, "Sept. 2, 1991 . . . first slug shots since 1964—27 years. Witnessed by . . ." Names and signatures of six men, including Scout's son and Indian, followed. The paper plate found its way into a file marked "Important Papers," where it was stored with the paralyzed man's birth certificate, military discharge, marriage papers, and other significant documents.

From that day forward, from the first of September until the last of January, Scout desired to be afield with crossbow, muzzleloader, or shotgun as many days as he could find someone to assist. Indian felt a sense of missionary zeal, since he had fanned the glowing embers into a blaze.

Indian had been a full-time hunting guide for more than ten years after he retired from shift work as a mechanic in the local DuPont nylon plant. Waterfowl were his hunting passion. When setting decoys he was fastidious about wind direction and the placement of blocks. If the outfitter asked him to guide deer hunters, he would do it grudgingly, and only as a favor. Indian was not a buck hunter. He liked eating venison, though, and would shoot whatever presented itself in gun range. To that end he was not particular about wind direction and didn't really take pains to cover his scent. Indian didn't believe the lengths that some people went to take whitetails. That was before Indian convinced Scout he could shoot and provided him with the equipment to do it.

"Scout," he proclaimed, "this witchcraft about deer smelling you is nothing but bull crap. Deer are dumb as posts."

From the beginning Scout's penchant for detail was opposite that of Indian's deer-hunting philosophy. Scout employed deer decoys to distract attention from his exposed torso above portable blinds. During the rut, decoys occasionally attracted bucks close enough for a shot. As many as five full-bodies, which could be handled only if his helper wore rubber gloves, would be placed just so.

One day, when setting the spread, Indian wryly observed, "I'm damned glad we aren't hunting elephants!"

Scout purchased various scent killers and insisted that they be sprayed on Indian's footgear and every decoy. Rubber boots were mandatory. The only delight Indian found in this was when he turned the bottle of spray on Scout.

Estrus-doe scent lines were trailed with a drag rag by Indian at Scout's direction. Like a field-trial retriever handler, Scout awkwardly waved his arms, attempting to correct any path

perceived as errant. Indian carried out Scout's obsessions in stoic silence. It must have crossed Indian's mind more than once that his friend was "one crazy s-o-b."

Indian filled the role of Scout's big game collaborator for ten years. When the power wheelchair was deep in the muck, or when the batteries died, he bulled five hundred pounds of chair with occupant in and out of places most men would not walk. Indian fed his companion sandwiches with muddy thumb prints, wrapped him up when he was cold, and emptied his pee bag when it was full. His was an exercise in loyalty beyond imagination.

Indian would tell his companion after a killing shot, "That was damn good." Indian didn't elaborate. But everyone in the local barbershop and greasy spoon knew that the man in the wheelchair was considered exceptional by his companion. That was as close to bragging as Indian ever got.

Scout and Indian never came close to taking a record-book whitetail. They never saw one on the hoof, even though Scout dreamed about bucks with Canadian-dimensioned antlers. Indian, on the other hand, couldn't have cared less. Scout's partner felt that huge old does were worthy of attention. He once bagged a doe that field dressed 146 pounds using his preferred magnum load of double-aught buckshot in a 10-gauge side-by-side.

"Now that is a trophy," proclaimed the triumphant venison hunter.

It was the attraction of antlers, though, that made 15 November the day when Scout most desired to be behind his scoped shotgun. The magic of the rut would be in full swing then.

One year a storm swept through on 14 November. Rain and sleet kept Scout and Indian out of the field. That night a front dropped temperatures into the thirties with winds gusting to 30 mph. Some authorities who wrote books and authored magazine articles claimed that deer do not move in winds like that. Scout believed otherwise. Thirty years before he had taken his largest buck ever during a day of strong northwest winds. On that day three other rack bucks had paraded past his stand before he took the 12-point. Over the years his sons had been equally successful on windy days. They had each taken bucks of more than 200 pounds, field dressed.

Before Indian went to bed, he called Scout and confirmed that they would be set up by late morning. After breakfast Indian arrived at Scout's house, where he gathered him up with all his paraphernalia. There were two olive drab duffels the size of small body bags stuffed with odiferous concoctions in jars, spray containers of scent killer, a sledgehammer with iron decoy stakes, assorted antlers, deer tails, grunt calls, camouflage nets, and mysterious objects from Scout's imagination. Already in the vehicle were several life-size decoys and materials for a blind big enough to conceal a sports car. Indian wedged Scout in his chair amid the equipment.

They would hunt a twenty-acre field surrounded by a thousand acres of cutover timber, the surrounding undergrowth so thick that it was difficult to see thirty yards.

Indian warned: "The ground is soaked. I don't think we can drive just anywhere."

A road through the middle of the field was slippery. Near a lone, winter-bare walnut, they stopped. Indian said, "This is it. If we go any farther we'll get stuck."

Indian set about laying two sheets of plywood near the base of the tree. He then set up a blind that would completely encircle his companion. The blind was made of tree pattern cardboard staked up with metal posts, then covered with surplus military netting and finished off with small cedar trees and pine branches.

Indian dragged Scout in his wheelchair onto the plywood. Battery power could spin the wheelchair in any direction. The blind concealed Scout up to his armpits, with only his camouflaged gun and head showing over the top. More than an hour of work went into the effort. Indian slipped a pair of woolen World War II GI mittens on Scout's hands and wrapped a scarf around his neck. After loading his gun, Indian asked, "Are you ready?"

"You forgot my decoy."

"No," Indian grunted. "But I hoped you would. Where do you want it?"

"Eighty-five yards toward the island stand."

"I suppose you want that huge 'Gadget' decoy," Indian shouted against the wind.

"Get the big antlers too, and make certain you stake him down good."

When he had finished staking down the decoy, Indian backed the van down the road until it disappeared into the woods. Scout, alone with his back to the chill west wind, surveyed the surrounding wood's lines for deer. Indian had taken a stand hidden from view. Nearly two hours passed, with nothing moving on the ground. Overhead, endless flocks of snow geese labored in unsettled skies toward inland fields.

Then Scout spotted a deer 250 yards away, staring at his decoy. It broke into a trot and headed in the right direction. Dark brown in color, the two-and-a-half-year-old buck carried a spindly 8-point rack. Scout judged the buck at 150 pounds. It circled ten yards downwind of the decoy and stopped, broadside. With cross hairs behind the front leg, Scout whispered to himself, *"Bang!* You're dead." Then he picked his head off the stock, leaned back in his chair, and shivered. The young buck remained standing 70 yards away for several minutes. A gust of wind suddenly blew the decoy over. Spooked, Scout's 8-pointer bounded tail-high across the field and out of sight.

Scout's heart sank. There wasn't much hope, sitting in the middle of the field without a decoy to draw a buck within range. Forty-five minutes passed. Five does entered the field at the far end but stayed close to cover before they disappeared. Temperatures dropped, and the wind picked up. Scout became more depressed, withdrawing his head into the protective shield of his hood. It would be foolhardy to leave the blind. He doubted that he could make the road without getting stuck. And even if he did, he questioned whether he could get close enough to where Indian could hear him.

Another thirty minutes went by.

"Scout." From behind, a voice startled him.

Scout spun around into the wind to see Indian entering the hide from his blind side.

"I figured you'd be cold." Indian knelt down and opened a canvas bag, extracting a thermos. "You look like you could use some hot tea."

"To hell with the tea! Get that decoy back up and anchored down." Despair quickly changed to agitation.

"Easy. Drink this."

The warm liquid in his gullet and belly felt good. Indian went to the downed decoy and repositioned it. Without asking, Indian knew that Scout preferred a solitary vigil in which the only luck, or lack of it, was his own. He picked up his 10-gauge side-by-side and headed away, leaving Scout to his own devices.

As the afternoon light faded toward darkness, deer filtered out of the brush into open corn stubble. Scout moved his head slowly from left to right, observing animals by themselves or in small groups. Some 150 yards downwind a doe suddenly bolted from cover, followed by two bucks, one behind the other. The front buck had a deep chest and sag belly. Its antlers were wide and heavy. It was the biggest whitetail Scout had ever seen. This was a dream buck.

The hot doe headed swiftly toward Scout's decoy with her entourage not far behind. Suddenly the lead buck whirled and faced its somewhat smaller adversary. Horns rattling, the two battled briefly then backed away, facing each other. They were only sixty short yards from the paralyzed man.

When a quadriplegic remains in one position for a long time, any movement of voluntary muscles often results in spasms. And so it was for Scout at the moment of truth. He leaned forward, extending his left arm to engage the trigger extension with his wrist. Quite suddenly his arms flailed uncontrollably, and the unthinkable happened. A single shot accidentally fired, high over the treetops. In a blink, every deer exited from view.

From his own stand, Indian had heard Scout's shot and came to see if help was needed.

"Well?" inquired Indian, not seeing anything on the ground, "I suppose you wounded him?"

Scout stammered out what had happened.

"Where were they?" Indian strode off in the direction Scout indicated. He stopped and shouted back, "Fifty-nine yards. I never thought someone as precise as you could blow an easy shot like this." He bent over and measured one of the tracks, using his index finger. Scout cursed softly to himself.

Indian prodded. "Big deer, Scout. Buck fever, I'd say."

"That's not all," Scout jibed back. "I think I crapped my pants."

"From the size of that track, I guess you probably did. You are going to have to sit in it until I pick up all your stuff. It's getting dark."

In the gloom and bluster of an oncoming winter night, the man collapsing the blind told Scout, "Be looking for a mud puddle. Tonight we are using your T-shirt to clean up."

In 1999, Indian learned that he had cancer in his liver, and the doctors told him he had two months to live. Defying their predictions, he vowed to hunt with Scout again. And they did, for two more glorious autumns, each man taking deer. One weekend in May, Indian entered the hospital for the last time.

Scout had not seen him in the last few months of decline, because he could not access Indian's house in his wheelchair. And when he visited him in the hospital, he was warned that Indian might not recognize him. When he rolled to the bedside, though, Indian looked up and said, "Scout," then weakly reached for his hand. Scout took it and told him how much he meant to him. He was thankful for that time.

For two hours Scout sat with Indian, unsure if Indian knew he was there. In a way, Scout wasn't there, but out again with Indian, traveling together to find deer. Memories floated through Scout's mind. From a bloated buck carcass that Indian discovered, Scout had watched his partner fall back in a tangle of briars when a possum scurried from its meal. Scout thought of the advice Indian had given: "Drop them where they stand. I don't like to track." Scout could see Indian's smile when it worked out that way. They had shared woodcock in stuttering flight against the afterglow of sunsets, owls hooting in the winter dark, and red fox mousing in the fields. He remembered Indian cocking his crossbow for him in the September woods. For an hour they sat side by side, watching a spider spin what could have been its last web of the season. Mesmerized, neither had uttered a word.

Scout left the hospital. In the darkest hours of the next morning, Indian died.

Big-game hunters sometimes hang trophies for display. If they are really fortunate, they carry trophies in their hearts or dreams. Success can be measured in record books—or on a paper plate with holes in it. It can be the sound of a friend snoring as a trophy doe sneaks away, or thoughts of what might have been....

WILD AND FAIR

This is a story of what was. It is remembered because, years ago, one man cared much about providing hunting opportunities for his friend. I know this to be true because I was called Scout by a man I knew as Indian. Together we hunted whitetails.

BLIND FAITH: THE DARK CHRONICLE OF A LONE STAR INSTITUTION

BY

THOMAS MCINTYRE

The secret, dirty or otherwise, of big-game hunting in North America is that it is big business, billions-of-dollars big, with nothing bigger than white-tailed-deer hunting. Not counting firearms and clothing, there is a cornucopia of gadgets and gizmos designed almost exclusively to divest whitetail hunters of their disposable incomes. Then there are large-ticket items like ATVs, shooting houses, and closed-circuit surveillance systems, closely followed by hunting leases and land purchases. One cannot help but wonder where all such commerce threatens to lead. In South Texas, the wonder ends.

> At La Ciotat, near Marseilles, a large body of men armed with swords and pistols used to hunt the wren every year [in the early winter]. When a wren was caught it was hung on the middle of a pole which two men carried, as if it were a heavy burden. Thus they paraded round the town; the bird was weighed in a great pair of scales; and then the company sat down to table and made merry.
>
> —James G. Frazer, *The Golden Bough*

If anything bears responsibility for South Texas deer hunting—where the whitetail is king, and its hunters fanatically regicidal—it is the devil of January. When that wintry month has the North in a frigid figure-four leg lock, there appears to be nothing else to do, some argue, but to head for a ranch on the South Texas Plains and offer sacrifice. Down that way the bunchgrass will be filled with bobwhites, and mourning doves perch in the branches of the mesquite and huisache. Large white blooms droop from the *anacahuita* (Mexican olive) trees; and the prickly pears swell with vaguely lascivious purple fruit. Ducks and herons come to water; and javelina, their bodies half head, scurry about in the brush. Turkeys, coyotes, and roadrunners occupy the places in between; but deer are why you go, and deer remain the incontrovertible meaning of "hunting" there.

More to the point, deer are the incontrovertible raison d'etre for any of that other wild stuff's existing at all in South Texas. There's a joke that explains the echelon that whitetail occupy in that neck of the woods:

Seems that when Hank and Jimmy weren't back to the ranch house on the deer lease by nightfall, the other hunters were going to go for the sheriff. Then Jimmy staggered out of the dark with a buck slung over his shoulder. Laying the deer on the ground, he fished a beer out of the cooler and squatted by the fire.

"Where's Hank?" the others asked.

"Well," Jimmy said after three swallows from the can, "I killed this eight-point late afternoon out by the old windmill, and Hank and I headed in. Then the sumbitch Ford quit, and we started packing the deer. Got about a mile from here when Hank just fell down. Stroke, I figure."

"You left Hank and carried in the *deer*?" they asked.

Jimmy took one more sip of beer.

"Nobody's going to steal Hank."

As pretty a picture as any South Texas ranch might be, whitetail are increasingly the only reason for *its* existing, too. Take the Guajolota ("wild turkey," but don't let that fool you— Rios are not what the ranch is about), an hour out of McAllen, whose 6,125 acres have progressively become more about deer, and less about cows, over the past thirty-five years. And if you hunt it, as I did at the start of one January with a young guide named J. D., you will see that what you are engaged in is not so much about the allure of the chase as about a surgical strike to make the ranch even better for whitetail.

In most if not all of South Texas, and not just on the Guajolota, the bettering of whitetail is conducted in this fashion: While his dad drove, J. D. and I sat in the high bench seat in the chopped-out back of the windowless Blazer, looking for a deer of a certain age. This was a "ranch choice" hunt; somewhere in the thick head-tall brush was a buck in his dotage at six and a half years of age, but carrying no more than eight total points. That sort of buck brought nothing to the party in terms of genetic excellence, and so when we saw it, it would become my obligatory buck of choice.

What whitetails are to hunting in South Texas, vehicles are (about everything) to whitetail hunting. From midmorning to late afternoon, the high seat of a hunting rig is more like the dryland version of the flying bridge of a marlin boat as the dense cover is sailed past and scoured for antlers the way a compass of blue water is cruised in hopes of spotting dorsal and tail fin scything the surface. And while elsewhere it is at the very least heretical, in South Texas being able on a private road on private property to shoot a suitable buck *from* a vehicle is nearly doctrinal.

Looking around at the dense cover, I could not deny the method in the madness, though thankfully it wasn't the only method. In the first and last hours of light there were box blinds to sit in and wait for the deer to drift from their daytime beds to their nighttime feeding, and back. Hunting on stand seemed somewhat less iniquitous than a drive-by shooting—even when, as J. D. and I squeezed into the kiosk-shaped blind, his dad drove up and down the dirt road the stand sat on, pressing the camo-painted Blazer's horn button (wired to the feeder mounted on the front bumper), broadcasting shelled corn as he went. Within minutes of J. D.'s dad's driving off, does and forkhorns left the brush to answer the call, and we were, as they say, hunting with the kernel. The deer fed to within a chain's length, but they seemed notably imperturbable. I carefully raised one of the Plexiglas windows to let out some of the accumulated heat of the day, while J. D. used his folding knife to lance an enormous hornet that had crawled inside to join us. The deer went on feeding.

The genuine bucks came after sundown. A 4x5 appeared up the road, and other bucks moved in the high grass and brush in front of us. J. D. studied the buck on the road, trying to make sure it was old enough. The deer would have been a good "ranch choice," with a little crab claw at the end of one main beam, but J. D. couldn't verify the minimum age. Another, larger deer was in front of us in the grass. But it was too dark to make out its antlers when the lights of the Blazer appeared, and we returned to the lodge for supper and sleep.

In the morning, back in the box blind before any light, fresh corn scattered and deer moving to feed, I considered how South Texas had once meant big deer in uncorrupted terms. Three centuries before, when wildfires kept the brush thinned on the plains, Spanish explorers observed hundreds of head of deer at a time, along with buffalo and antelope. Americans in the nineteenth century saw deer in like numbers. Then cattle and, especially, sheep grazed the land until the grass gave out, ending the grazing. With the wildfires put out, the brush grew up as it never had before. Devoid of roads, the country, up until World War II, was a sanctuary for *muy grande* whitetail. Although in the midst of the grinding poverty of the period, and the general impenetrability of the habitat, no one paid undue attention to antlers; other qualities (such as protein) held everybody's attention. Then came oil and gas exploration and Caterpillar tractors and more open access, and deer, which had once been thought of fundamentally as cheap meat for hard times, gathered to themselves an entirely new cachet.

Antlers were elevated to objects of veneration, and counties such as Dimmit and Webb, or whole regions, such as the Edwards Plateau, became legendary for bucks growing into serious "South Texas deer"—not because it was planned, but simply because it seemed ordained. Landowners, though, began to get an inkling that if there was money to be had in leasing their properties to deer hunters, then *serious* money was to be had in tending the land specifically for deer, rather than crops or livestock. A reliable harvest of large-antlered bucks every season became the production target, leading in short order to game-proof fencing, selective brush clearing (or "sculpting"), intensive culling, introduced forage, supplemental feeding (not coincidentally conditioning the deer to respond positively to the whir and clatter of a feeder), and enhancing the bloodline with Northern deer until a buck could be as pedigreed as the Best of Show at the Westminster Kennel Club. And the name for this became "quality deer management."

This business model—like stock swindles, oil scams, and real estate fraud—was not for long confined to South Texas. As the concept spread north of the Rio Grande Valley, every year the estimated whitetail population in the state seemed to record a new high: a million head, over a million, 3.1 million, 4 million—with half a million hunters and as many or more deer taken each season. By the end of the millennium there was money—and then there was *deer* money, verging on the unconscionable. Guided hunts ran into the middle to high four figures; leases in the fives; sale prices on fully stocked, turnkey deer ranches in the seven- to eight-figure range, accessible only to class-action-suit attorneys. Whitetail hunting was a bona fide billions-of-dollars-per-annum industry. Along the way a sense of place no doubt got vitiated, until all of Texas had become South Texas, cosseted deer (at least until shot) growing big statewide, and the boot taps of trophy deer hunters no longer echoing exclusively on the streets of Laredo.

It was South Texas that I was in this morning, though, foresworn to hunt whitetail the traditional South Texas way. There was some consolation in the thought that such a tradition had not been imposed but had evolved, maybe even slightly "naturally" in adaptation to the habitat. I could tell myself that it benefited the deer as a whole—like those proverbial fifty million Frenchmen, four million whitetail weren't likely to be wrong—not totally, anyway.

Nonetheless, there was something oddly enervating in the sight, before dawn, of half-a-dozen good bucks, and several times as many does, strung out up the road from us, jockeying for corn. None were better, or older, than the buck we'd turned down the night before, all of them taken together somehow being like the cervid equivalent of a rack of size 42 regular worsteds to be sorted through at the Men's Wearhouse. As the dawn came up like thunder—or more like a slow-rolling tumbleweed under the overcast sky—there was a sort of anxious, rather than frolicsome, deer-park ambiance to the tableau.

A buck emerged from the tall brush at the back of the pack and worked its way deliberately toward us, lesser bucks stepping aside. It caught our eye immediately, and as it progressed its antlers got better and its age greater. It was a heavy 4x4, antlers gnarled and bumpy with a handful of stickers sprouting off the Gs. A 44 long, if ever there was one. Before J. D. gave me the official nod, I had the rifle up and pointing out an open window of the box blind.

"All right," J. D. said, still glassing the buck. At least he didn't ask what I thought of the lapels.

I quietly bolted a .300 round. The buck, gray as a slate roof tile, came down to 75 yards from us and turned broadside. I had to wait for the other deer in back of it to clear; then I put the cross hairs behind its left shoulder.

The 150-grain bullet passed through its heart and broke its off shoulder, so that when it tried to bound at the shot its right leg would not hold. The deer somersaulted to the ground. We took pictures that came out dark, and we dressed the buck while we waited for J. D.'s dad to bring up the Blazer. Then we loaded the deer and took it back to the lodge and to the walk-in refrigerator that was already filling with other hunters' whitetails—all dead in the cause of the betterment of the ranch herd.

Supper was, as always, superb. Afterward, I sat outside beside the coals of the mesquite fire and consumed some considerable quantity of corn liquor, leading to distorted sensory perceptions, an apparent stumbling-and-falling incident, and various discouraging words directed at those gracious enough to assist me to my quarters for the night—words that would be quoted back to me with arched eyebrows and knowing smiles the following day. Awaking to a bleary consciousness sometime late in the morning, with a headache most definitely come up like thunder, I tried to cobble together sufficient coherent thoughts to comprehend what had gotten into me—not the sour mash, that is, but what had precipitated the sour mash.

It seemed to me that what I had reacted to was the grim realization that what whitetail hunting had organically grown into in South Texas—ghastly warts and all—and wanted to be, out of imitative flattery, in the rest of the state, was what whitetail hunting was threatening to metastasize into everywhere, a result of the most premeditated and impenitent calculation. And what was being left out of the equation of quality deer was the fundamental factor of wildness, leaving one to wonder if wildness was doomed in time to be wrung out of all hunting.

South Texas whitetail hunting was what it was, though, and would always be. It was very much like the original Elvis—outsized, vulgar, oleaginous, bizarre, and sweaty. But Elvis was none other than the undisputed king, which made everybody else just a sorry impersonator.

South Texas whitetail hunting—*in* South Texas—was a dogmatic creed, to be accepted or renounced, unconditionally. And if it weren't for January, the decision would be considerably easier. As much as it made my head—and sometimes, not a little, my heart—hurt, I wasn't sure I had the rectitude to renounce it forever. The most I could say for it was that it would always be a decidedly mixed blessing. At best, as long as snow fell and rivers froze, the devil would always be in the details, if not the whitetails.

A MOUNTAIN GOAT HUNT

BY
RON SPOMER

Some years, and rather too many pounds, ago I hunted wild sheep. I remember my young guide advising me that all it took to travel safely at elevation was to watch where and how the sheep walked, and do exactly as they did. He then added with a shrug, "Of course, you try that with goats, you'll die." The thought of rock chutes and talus slides can still cause me to shudder, so I'm glad to be able to experience goat hunting through writer-photographer Ron Spomer's prose. The only troubling aspect is the way the story makes you want to head up a goat mountain to see it for yourself.

It's been said that North America's mountain goat is the poor man's mountain sheep, and I guess that's true. You hunt in mountain habitat and pay outfitters a lot less for the privilege. Gravity extracts about the same price.

While it's true that goats are sometimes shot from the surf along southeast Alaskan cliffs, most climb for their white trophies. From Colorado to Alaska, you hike and gasp and scrabble hand-over-head to reach your dreams. And you see sights to move poets. Peaks standing above peaks, purple to the horizon. Rainbows arcing over tundra basins green as Ireland and just as treeless. Rivers being born from glacial ice, dripping, seeping through talus slides, bubbling up in pools reflecting the royal purple of fringed gentians. You drink freely, knowing you're above pestilence, but slowly, for it is cold as ice. You sweat as your legs tighten, sit on a frozen boulder to rest them, shiver as a glacial gust pushes your wet shirt against your back, duck inside a shallow cave as rain pelts down, half ice. Or all snow.

In goat country you always expect snow. Old patches of it rotting into tarn lakes. Long troughs lying on north slopes perfect for glissading. Delicate new flakes drifting hesitantly like tiny butterflies afraid to land. Determined blizzards flying horizontal across ridges, riding updrafts out of defiles, swirling to rest with you behind sheltering cliff walls.

Then there is the wildlife. Marmots fat as Buddha whistling as you climb. Ground squirrels standing like miniature stumps. Pikas squeaking, their mouths stuffed with hay. Water pipits flitting from rock to rock like windblown leaves. Golden eagles jousting with red foxes. Ptarmigan the shape and color of lichen-covered rocks. Grizzlies standing on their hind legs. Wolves crooning in the distance and leaving tracks the size of your hand.

Surrounding it all is air so pure and vast that you can feel it, a glorified silence, the echo of wilderness. Here you climb. Here you quest for the silent, hump-shoulder white buffalo of the high places, the North American mountain goat.

"We'd better look around the other corner before we drop down," lanky Bryan Martin shouted above the wind. He popped the last chunk of a Snickers bar into his mouth, pointed north into the clouds and snow, pulled up his hood, leaned into the wind, and started hiking. Assistant guide Todd Kelly stood and followed, ducking his head so his cap wouldn't blow off. Aliya Jacob, wrangler turned packer, brushed snow from her legs and tightened her pack strap. "You ready?"

I looked one last time at the incongruous green tundra in the basin below. The three billies we'd been glassing stood out like golf balls. One may have carried 10 inches of horn, but there was no hurry to shoot it. We'd reached the summit and crossed the divide only an hour earlier, and from base camp the previous day we'd seen twenty-two goats on this mountain. I shouldered my pack, picked up my rifle, and turned into the gusts.

"*Whoa, whoa, whoa.* Back up." Bryan crouched and waved us back. "Big billy. Big one."

"Where?"

I found it with my binocular while Bryan was setting up the spotting scope. It was as yellow as old newspaper, lying below snow line on the crest of an outrider ridge, smack on a trail like some territorial marker that wolves had been peeing on for generations. The hoof-packed trail led down from the peak on which we hunkered, tracing the crest of the side-ridge, leaning and bending with it before petering out on lush alpine pastures a mile away. Beyond lay the broad river valley, dark with spruce, fir, and pine.

"Look at the mass on him. That's gotta be an old goat, close to ten inches. Check it out." Bryan leaned away from the spotting scope, and Todd peered through it. He concurred. I took a look. It was the yellowest mountain goat I'd ever seen, and I'd seen more than a few. The lone male I'd watched in Idaho's Frank Church River of No Return Wilderness for a week in 1986 was yellow. So was a rutting billy I'd photographed in Montana in 1989. The young billy I'd shot in southern British Columbia in 1988 had a yellow cast, but it was like cream compared with this pumpkin.

"Looks pretty heavy, but I can't get a read on its length," I said. "Too much of a down angle. Need to get on his level."

"Can I see?" Aliya asked, and she leaned into the spotter.

Then we backed away on our butts, gathered our gear, and hiked back to the saddle to get out of the wind. There was a chimney here leading into a steep chute that opened into a rockslide spilling onto the green tundra a thousand feet down. We could get down here but would be exposed the whole way.

"We'll have to wait," Bryan said.

I ate a granola bar and some nuts. Then a Cliff Bar. Bryan ate his third candy bar of the morning, having already burned the calories in the two dozen pancakes and peanut butter he'd had for breakfast.

"Want some jerky?" he offered.

Todd and Aliya tore off chunks of the dark meat and chewed, while I chipped ice from the neck of the water bottle I'd filled at a spring two hours earlier and eight hundred feet lower.

"Pretty cold for the first week in September," said Bryan.

I dug out my down vest and put it on, then my second stocking cap. I couldn't understand how Todd could sit there in only his baseball cap and buzz cut. He certainly wasn't insulated by body fat. Was I that hot-blooded at nineteen? The snow fell harder.

"Maybe it'll cover us until we get to the bottom?" I suggested.

"More likely it'll stop, and we'll be pinned down in that chute."

"Yeah. I guess."

After an hour Bryan thought someone ought to step out of our protected little grotto and check the flank of the mountain. I was closest.

"We never did see over the top, and there's a major trail comes around there," advised Bryan softly. "Go careful."

I didn't, and by the time I saw the goat it was already running. A billy. It must have been walking toward us just above the grotto wall. It paused a time to stare back as if disbelieving we were there in its stormy fortress. Todd and Bryan got to see it well enough to confirm it was no record. A nine-inch horn, but not heavy. It must have alarmed other goats when it walked over the far ridge, because a pair popped over, heads up, looking for trouble. These were bigger, two veterans that might have gone ten inches. They didn't hang around.

"That makes seven billies already," Bryan pronounced. "In one basin." He was pleased. We wriggled back out of the wind.

"Hey, Old Yeller is up," Aliya said.

We watched the goat on the trail stretch and urinate. From new angles its horns still looked good. Then, like a trucker after his mandatory stop, it pulled out of the parking lot and back onto the trail, walking steadily toward the pastures. We watched until it disappeared around a corner. Then we, too, loaded up and started down, picking our way, testing slippery, black slab boulders before committing our weight, brushing snow away to check handholds before lowering ourselves. Several rocks and two boulders broke free and went crashing and bounding as if to show the way, but there were no sustained rockslides. Halfway down, the gravel lay deep enough that we could stamp little ledges with the outside edges of our boots. Toward the bottom we began bouncing down, riding deep scree until it packed tight, then jumping into loose gravel and sliding again until it settled.

We put up the tents on a bench in the northwest corner of the basin above a brook running over boulders bordered by yellow saxifrage. At nine o'clock it was still light enough to climb the ridge where Old Yeller had lain. We found its bed and its tracks, cut deep in the muddy gravel. On the north side of the

ridge was another basin, deeper than the one we were camped in. It was eroded farther back into the black mountain, its flanks broken and littered with shelves, cliffs, and chutes. A narrow waterfall poured from a tarn through a trench lined with green tundra where a nanny and kid were foraging. Two billies were picking their way along the face of the opposite mountain, nearly at its top. "I think those are the two that popped over the ridge earlier," I said.

"Naw. Too far away."

"I don't know. If they were spooked they could have gotten that far." We glassed until dark, returned to the tents to boil water for cocoa and freeze-dried stew. I ate two handfuls of M&Ms for dessert. It had stopped snowing.

Dawn brought glorious golden light and the hissing of Bryan's mountain stove, instant oatmeal, and coffee. We climbed the ridge to glass. By midmorning snow squalls were sweeping through, and I was hungry again. You could see the snow start over the peaks to the west, deep gray clouds rolling over and down to cover the sunlit rocks in cold shadow, then the highest stringers of green. The distance grew indistinct through the fog of flakes. Then the first ones reached us—innocent, ephemeral things that quickly grew menacing in numbers until you turned your back against them and huddled behind a boulder, wrapped in winter. And then the snow would stop and the sun would shine a golden respite over the mountains until the next squall poured over the peaks. I ate granola and nuts. Aliya offered me sticks of spicy jerky. We waited for the yellow billy to show itself.

"I think he's bedded or feeding just below this ridge," Bryan said as we stood where blocky hoofprints disappeared in the grass. "I think he fed here last night and crossed over to bed this morning. There are a lot of hidden shelves and crannies lower down."

We slipped along the crest, then followed the ridge out as it climbed up and down two minor peaks. We peeked over, stepped up, scanned new terrain that opened, alert for a patch of white, watching for gleaming black horns, finding rocks.

"Did you hear that?"

"Sounded like rocks rolling below."

"That's him. That's the billy," Bryan hissed. "Get ready."

I shucked my pack and sat commanding the defile for hundreds of yards. Anything that broke from a hidden chute below would be in range. Nothing came out. After fifteen minutes, Todd stood.

"I'm going to go around and peek over that knob there. I'll wave if I spot him." He never waved.

"Must have been rocks melted loose by the sun."

We continued hunting along the crest, but there was no yellow goat. In the big green basin below camp three billies walked to an isolated cliff and lay down to ruminate. A nanny in a huff hustled her kid away from those rancid bachelors as if they'd said something indecent, passing below our tents without a glance. By noon we were near the terminus of our ridge, where it broke down toward the valley forest. Bryan didn't think the goats would go that far. He began glassing back into the basin, hunkered against a gale rushing off the mountain. Aliya and I retreated from the wind and ate jerky in the sun.

"Got two billies. Up high. Come see." Todd, coat sleeves flapping, waved us up to the spotting scope. "Take a look."

I could see the pair bedded near the top of the highest peak, specks above the tarn now reflecting deep blue sky. The image vibrated too violently to judge horns.

"Hey, I've got Old Yeller." Bryan pointed up the canyon. "He's bedded in those black benches. See? And there are three nannies and a kid, I think, below him. One might be a young billy."

We hurried back up to our morning's lookout above camp.

"I think we could get to Yeller from there," I said, pointing to a spur. "Get behind this ridge, follow it to that broken peak, ease along the back of that slide, and come out across from him."

"That'd be a long shot," Bryan argued.

"I don't know. Three-fifty?"

"More like four hundred. Or five," Todd countered.

"I think those two up high are bigger than Yeller anyway," Bryan said. "Let's sit tight. They should come down to feed." The wind had quieted, and the sun came out. We sat and watched. Bryan ripped open a Milky Way and a bag of M&M Peanuts. Old Yeller finally began to move when I was fantasizing about freeze-dried dinners.

"Man, look at him go," Aliya said. "It's like he's late for a date."

"He's seen those nannies down by the creek," said Bryan.

"If he keeps coming on that line he might pass underneath us, close enough for a shot," I put in.

"I still think those two way up there are bigger. Let's wait and see if they come down," Bryan argued.

They didn't, but three new billies filed out of some secret cove and picked their way down a boulder slide toward the tarn. Old Yeller intercepted them before they all disappeared in the waterfall trench. I was hoping for a fight. Rutting billies are said to circle like Greco-Roman wrestlers, throwing roundhouse punches with their stabbing horns, trying for the guts but mostly getting hair and rump. These didn't even so much as feint before the sun dropped behind the mountain and fresh clouds rolled over its top.

"I'm going down there to compare them side by side," Bryan volunteered. "I'll signal you if one's worth trying for."

An hour later a wall of flying snow obliterated my guide as he lay behind a rock, peering through his scope. Ten minutes later the rest of us were running scree slides down toward him, climbing old rockslides tied together by patches of tundra roots, then belly crawling.

"Watcha got?" I asked.

"Keep your heads down. There's one above the lake. Just came out. The other three are right under us, about 150 yards. Old Yeller fooled us. He's a dwarf, maybe two-thirds the size of these others. His horns look huge compared with his face and body, but the others are bigger."

I window-shopped through the scope. All the horns looked good, but Yeller was noticeably smaller. Todd took a turn. "The high one is slightly shorter than the best one below us, but it carries its mass farther. It will score the best." That goat had seen us and was standing, staring, trying to figure us out.

"What do you think, 9½ inches?" Bryan asked. "He won't make 50, but he'll score 48 at least."

We compared inches in urgent whispers, Bryan arguing for the two billies still high on the mountain. They were up feeding now but hadn't moved any lower. The lowest goats were foraging in happy ignorance. The billy on the rock slide was nervous. The consensus was that it would probably measure less than 10 inches, the Holy Grail of goat horns, but score at least 49 points because of its mass. I rolled away from the spotting scope and wriggled up to a tundra hummock.

"What are you doing? Are you going to shoot?" Bryan whispered.

"I'm taking the far one. Whadya figure, 350 yards?"

"About that. But I still think those two on the mountain may be bigger."

It was eight o'clock and the fourth day of our hunt. I was beyond nitpicking an inch of horn. The hunt had been good, the stalk clean. We'd studied lots of billies and had earned this shot. It was time.

The little rifle was surprisingly loud in the vast basin. The first bullet hit too far back; the second completely missed behind the animal's rump. I compensated by holding ahead of its brisket for the third shot, and that punched through both lungs, ending it. It took nearly an hour to reach the goat. A stiff wind funneling down a side chute explained the errant shots. The range had been at least 350 yards, long for a goat. In their broken habitat you can usually sneak closer, but we hadn't had time. There was barely enough light for a picture. It was fully dark by the time we got it caped and butchered, the meat distributed among four packs, mine, thankfully, the lightest.

There were no wolves howling as we hiked back to camp, but stunning peaks stood black against the moonlit sky and clouds sailed shadows over the silent tundra. Rivulets and brooks burbled underfoot. From atop the ridge the whole world curved around us, empty and new.

THE FARTHEST-AWAY RIVER

BY

PHILIP CAPUTO

Philip Caputo has often traveled to places of war: Vietnam, Afghanistan, the Middle East, Sudan. In this story it is fair to say that he has traveled, in one of the most remote corners of the continent, to a place of peace. Peace? With animals being killed? The truth is, had Caputo gone there and just sat—after first making certain that he wouldn't be crushing some subpolar insect by doing so—he would have been surrounded by an incessant taking of animal life, whether by the fish in the river, the birds in the air, the predators on the land, or that insect he spared. That is the background noise of true peace, and it is doubtful that Caputo and his friends, in this story, increased the volume of it in any appreciable way.

It was the name that beckoned—Kongakut—"The Farthest Away River" in the language of the Inupiat Eskimos in Alaska's far north. Someone told me that they call it that because it's the most distant river from Kaktovik, a native village some sixty or seventy miles west of its mouth. Whatever the reason for it, the name fits: The Kongakut is the farthest away river from anywhere in the United States. In the extreme northeastern corner of the Arctic National Wildlife Refuge, it begins on the north slope of the northern Continental Divide in the Brooks Range, flows for a little more than a hundred miles into the Beaufort Sea, and at one point comes to within a day's hike of the border with the Yukon Territory. The country it passes through is arguably the wildest in North America, an uninhabited land exempt from our Yankee-Doodle drive to tame the untamed, where nature still roars and rages and most of the rivers and mountains don't have names, native or otherwise. All that beckoned even more than the lyrical "Farthest Away River."

I'll try to keep the romanticism within bounds, the call of the wild being a summons more attractive to the man snug in his living room than to the subsistence hunter who has to wrestle nature to get through the week with a full belly; nevertheless, the Kongakut did call, because all I had been able to think about for the past year was getting back to Alaska. Once again, I was depressed by the neutering of the wilderness that remains in the Lower Forty-eight. I'd read in a recent issue of *Sierra* magazine that there is no place in the continental United States more than twenty miles from a road of some kind. The nearest one to the Kongakut is 180 miles—the Dalton Haul Road, which I'd traveled the previous summer.

There were other becauses:

I woke up on 10 June 1996 to find myself fifty-five years old—still in good shape, but those two digits looked weird whenever I had to fill out a form. They reminded me that the window of opportunity for high adventure was closing. I had an urge to go big game hunting again. Except for wild boar in Australia, I'd shot only waterfowl and upland birds since I'd quit deer hunting almost thirty years before, driven out of the woods by trigger-happy bozos, one of whom had put a round over my head in 1967; another, the following season, had fired through my tent just as I was getting out of my sleeping bag. Maybe I wanted to find out if I still could endure the dangers and hardships of going into the Big Wild after quarry larger than grouse or ducks, and if I could still shoot straight. A willingness to face danger and hardship and an ability to shoot straight are not relevant virtues in our let's-stay-home-and-surf-the-Net, safety-obsessed, consumer culture, but one advantage to getting older is the freedom to be reactionary.

Alaska means "The Great Land," and it is. The state's wolf population, estimated at between seven and ten thousand, is several times larger than that of the entire continental United States. I wanted to get to know it as well as a cheechako (tenderfoot) could. Hunting in it, hunting in the right way—that is, the hard way—seemed a path to that knowledge. The hunter achieves a depth of intimacy with his environment denied the hiker, the rafter, or the trail-biking athlete for whom wild country is an outdoor fitness center. All the good hunters I know are excellent naturalists because their success depends on acute powers of observation and hearing, and on a knowledge of game and habitat. Wilderness tourists generally see only the bold print of the natural world; the hunter reads the fine print, and if he's really skilled, that part of nature's book that is written in invisible ink. At the deepest level, he becomes an actor in the primeval drama between predator and prey.

Companions would be Dave Brown, Alan Richey, and Frank Stanskanis, all of whom work for Alyeska, the company that operates and maintains the Trans-Alaskan oil pipeline.

A two hundred-pound six-footer, Brown at forty-four has gray hair and a gray mustache and bears a slight resemblance to the actor Donald Sutherland. The son of a U.S. Army rifle champion, he's a crack shot himself and has lived in Alaska for almost thirty years. Thirteen Dall rams are mounted in his Fairbanks house. He's hunted them in every season for twenty-six years and was a hunting guide in a previous incarnation. Today he oversees the security force that patrols the pipeline.

Forty-nine-year-old Richey came to Alaska in 1976 from his native Alabama, where he began shooting and fishing at an age when city boys were trying on their first baseball mitts. He worked on a pipeline construction crew and is now an engineer with Alyeska, a job that's taken him into the Brooks Range when it's minus 60 degrees F. He's fished all over Alaska and Costa Rica and the Florida Keys. An accomplished archer as well as rifleman, his bowhunting achievements include a caribou that just missed setting a Boone and Crockett record, and a grizzly bear that he shot at a range of twenty yards.

Stanskanis, with his sandy brown hair and trim physique, looks ten years younger than his sixty-two years. He should be an inspiration to other senior citizens who think that passing sixty is a one-way ticket to an AARP life of golf courses and rocking chairs. Carrying a pack and rifle, he can outwalk men half his age over the ruggedest terrain, which isn't surprising; until a few years ago, he'd been a line-walker for the Trans-Alaskan, inspecting the four hundred of its eight hundred miles that are above ground. Through muskeg bogs and over tundra and mountain passes, he would be out for six weeks, covering twelve to twenty miles a day. He began sheep hunting with Dave about a decade ago. Sheep hunting takes you into some very hazardous, vertiginous terrain, but Frank took it up because, he says, "I figured I'd lived long enough that it wouldn't be so bad if I got killed."

We would do our own outfitting, skinning, packing, and camp chores. Whatever the difficulties of the do-it-yourself approach, it's less expensive and more gratifying than buying a hunt. Ours would be an old-fashioned hunt, with none of the doodads, such as Global Positioning Systems (maps and compasses would do for navigation, thanks) or ATVs (all travel would be by raft or on foot). Almost everything the hunter carries into the bush, from rifle to boots, is artificial, but there is a degree of artificiality that alienates him from the surroundings and makes the hunt unworthy of the dignity of the quarry.

Alan, Dave, and Frank each hoped to shoot a Dall ram, a grizzly, and a wolf.

I had tags to kill two caribou. (You won't find the euphemism "harvest" anywhere in this story. Big-game animals are not cash crops, and we hunters should avoid the politically correct obfuscations that muddle the speech in our universities and in the news media.) There were two reasons why I limited myself to caribou.

The first was practical: Alaskan game laws prohibit nonresidents from hunting brown bears or Dall sheep without a professional guide. Dave Brown, still licensed to guide, had generously offered me his services for a nominal fee. I declined because he would have been barred by law from hunting.

The second reason was mystical. I wasn't ready to shoot a grizzly. It wasn't only the long hiatus from big-game hunting that made me reluctant; it was my belief that a grizzly has a powerful spirit. I didn't feel that my own spirit was commensurate, didn't feel that I had yet earned the right to shoot so magnificent a beast. Maybe next year, maybe the year after, maybe never, but definitely not now.

The plan was for a fifteen-day hunt. We would land by bush plane near the headwaters of the Kongakut, then raft downstream, stopping every few miles to hunt side creeks and drainages. To some extent we'd be living off the land, supplementing our freeze-dried rations with whatever we shot and any fish we might catch. This wasn't to be a stunt, an attempt to play hunter-gatherer. Bush-plane fares in Alaska are expensive (ours would be more than $5,000, and that was a bargain). The more stuff you carry, the more flights are required to get you in and out. With the raft, paddles, and its accoutrements weighing almost 200 pounds, and a four-man base-camp tent adding another 50, we had to keep our food and personal gear as light as possible—an average of 65 pounds per man, including rifles and ammunition.

There are ski bums and surf bums, so I guess Stu Ballard, a bush pilot for Alaska Flyers, is an aviation bum. He has no wife, children, or fixed address, and stays with friends or pitches his sleeping bag in the hangar in between hops. A Green Beret usually covers his thinning hair, and he wears a goatee and a cracked leather jacket that might have belonged to a World War II ace.

"I've never landed there, so I'm going to make three or four passes. If I don't like what I see, I'll take you to Kaktovik, and Walt will fly you in," Ballard said to us as we stood on the airstrip at Deadhorse. Walt was Walt Audi, owner of Alaska Flyers, and "there" was a gravel bar on the Kongakut, about two miles upstream from a feeder stream with the unlovely name of Drain Creek. "Is that OK with you guys?"

Bad weather had delayed our departure by three days (it was the third coldest August on record in the Brooks Range; blizzards had dumped half a foot of snow on the mountains), but Ballard's caution was OK with us. Not that caution and flying skill were guarantees of a happy landing. A few days before, two very experienced bush pilots had died in a crash in the western Brooks Range.

Ballard's Super Cub could not carry all of us, the raft, and our gear in one flight; we would have to shuttle in, two men at a time. Frank and I went first. We took off into a crystalline blue sky, the first clear sky we'd seen in days, and flew along the northern rim of America. On one side, between the shore and ice pack where polar bears ranged, was a dark blue corridor of the Beaufort Sea. In a few weeks that lane of open water would be frozen solid, and you would be able to walk to the North Pole if you were so inclined. On the other side, the Arctic coastal plain—flat, brown, fissured by cracks in the permafrost into polygonal shapes resembling rice paddies—stretched east and west as far as we could see, and southward fifty miles to the jagged wall of the mountains. The plain is the spring calving grounds of the Porcupine caribou herd, 200,000 animals, and ground zero of the fight between, on the one side, oil companies that want to drill in the Arctic Wildlife National Refuge, and on the other, environmentalists and Gwich'in Indians whose lives and culture depend on the caribou as much as the lives and culture of the Lakota and Cheyenne had on the buffalo. (Personally, I'd like to see the Indians win this time around. Yeah, yeah, an oil field would take up only a tiny fraction of the refuge, but to my mind that's like installing roulette tables in a cathedral and then saying, Well, they only cover a few square yards of floor space.)

I looked down, hoping to see caribou. The herd's migration, an awesome, ever-moving tide of flesh and antlers, has earned the coastal plain the nickname "America's Serengeti." This migration is a sight never forgotten by the few who have seen it. But the early winter storm appeared already to have sent the caribou south. Empty of game, the plain was a depressing monotony of tundra grasses broken by small thaw lakes and the silver, serpentine braids of rivers. The Canning, named by British explorer Sir John Franklin for Prime Minister George Canning, passed beneath us, then the Hulahula, christened by Hawai'ian whalers who had hunted bowheads on Yankee ships in the nineteenth century. Then came a succession of rivers with Eskimo names that hobbled the most nimble tongue: the Okpilak and the Okerokovik, the Niguanak and Aichilik and Ekaluakat. Finally, with the British Mountains of the Yukon Territory in sight, Ballard turned south, and we winged over the Kongakut.

Within half an hour, we were skimming the shining peaks of the Romanzof Mountains. Ballard, accustomed to the low ceilings of the North Slope, was ecstatic; he hadn't flown this high in weeks. Cresting at 9,000 feet, the Romanzofs are the tallest mountains in the Brooks Range. That isn't much by the standards of the Alps or the Rockies; yet their rise from the plain is so steep and sudden that they possess a forbidding drama, their sharp peaks, razor-edged ridges, and spired battlements giving an impression of a guarded sanctuary in which you might not find a hospitable welcome.

There was snow everywhere, from the summits down to the Kongakut valley; great gray boulders and limestone crags and long black rivers of shale and scree showed through the snow. Meandering sheep trails striated slopes so steep that I could not imagine any creature surefooted enough to walk them. The river, now a bright pewter in the sun, now a deep jade, twined and braided past stands of willow and browning aspen. It might have been August on the calendar, but down there it was late November.

Ballard made a pass over the landing strip, which didn't look different from any other gravel bar to my untrained eye. We made a second pass and saw patches of maroon and blue in the snow of the valley: the tents of a hunting camp. Those hunters and their guide, along with a handful of Eskimo and Gwich'in subsistence hunters, were the only human beings in the refuge's 32,000 square miles. You have to imagine Maine with a population of about twenty.

A third pass. Ballard was peering out to check for ruts and large boulders on the strip. I began to ponder, somewhat tardily, the concern my wife, in-laws, and parents felt for me, going into so remote a place at my age. No doctors or hospital or telephone within 200 miles. In bush Alaska, you come as close as a modern American can to experiencing what our country was like in the days of Lewis and Clark. It's a wilderness that doesn't forgive mistakes or rashness, and randomly metes out bad luck even to the prudent and experienced. If a freak downdraft doesn't cause you to die in a bush-plane crash, you might stumble into a sow grizzly with cubs (a hiker from Washington, D.C., had been mauled to death in the western Brooks Range a week before). If a bear doesn't get you, your raft might overturn in a river so cold that you have about, oh, five minutes before you go into fatal hypothermia, as my son Marc almost had last year. Or you might die in a fall from a cliff (the body of a British hiker who had tumbled into a gorge this summer was found about six weeks after he disappeared). It's not surprising that bush Alaskans don't worry a lot about their cholesterol.

After a fourth pass, Ballard decided to go for it. The Super Cub touched down, bouncing crazily over the rocks. This is what Frank called "blue-collar flying." We rolled to a stop. Frank and I off-loaded our rifles, packs, and other gear. Ballard taxied to take off and got his nose wheel stuck in sand. We helped push him out—and then the plane lofted away to pick up Alan, Dave, and the raft.

All around was a world of white mountains and white tundra meadows, and, when the echoing buzz of the plane faded away, a world utterly silent except for the whisper of the cold, green, transparent river. John Voelker, the novelist and outdoor writer (*Anatomy of a Murder*, *Trout Madness*), once said that he fished for trout because he liked where trout are. I thought about that and realized that I wasn't after caribou. The hunt was important, imposing a kind of logic and discipline on what otherwise would have been aimless wandering. If I saw a suitable bull, I certainly would shoot it; but the true quarry wasn't on land. These days of budget air travel have made it easier than ever to put several thousand miles between you and home, but cell phones and CNN, among others, have made it harder than ever to flee the familiar, the pressures, and the trivial chatter of modern civilization. I had come to the Farthest Away River, not only to *be* far away, but to *feel* that I was. And I did.

The day was calm and pleasantly warm, about 50 degrees F. We idled away the next three hours. Frank fished for a while, then took a nap. I talked and drank tea around the fire with the guide, Dave Marsh, and his two clients. A wiry, bearded man of medium height, Marsh had been in the mountains for several weeks without much word from the outside world. Said he'd heard something about an airliner blowing up near New York, and did they find out what caused it? Nearby was evidence of a successful hunt—a boar grizzly's hide, fleshed and salted, a caribou rack, a Dall ram's skull and horns, and game bags, packed with meat. The blizzard had made things miserable for a while, Marsh said, and one of his packers had been charged by an angry sow with cubs. The grizzly swiped the man across his backpack, knocking him flat, but she must not have been in a murderous mood; having made her point, she ran off to rejoin her young.

Ballard landed with Alan and Dave. Marsh gave us a hand packing the raft, then photographed us as we shoved off. He was the last human being we would see until we flew out.

The river carried us down, through the mountains. We pitched our first camp on a gravel bar at the mouth of Drain Creek, which wound away to the west, galleries of yellow aspen along its banks. There were wolf tracks in the fine black sand, and in the last glimmer of the long Arctic twilight, a young bull caribou plodded along the Kongakut, only thirty yards from our tent and crackling driftwood fire. Caribou aren't known for their intelligence, but this one's obliviousness struck me as monumentally stupid, if not evidence of a death wish. Shooting it would have been no honor; it was too small, in any case. But I took its appearance as a good omen, and after a meal of freeze-dried beef and noodles, I had a jolt of Johnny Walker and crawled into my sleeping bag. The four of us lay awake for more than an hour, made mildly insomniac by the anticipation and unrealistic expectations that precede every hunt.

Waking to a frosty but cloudless morning, my Alaskan friends marveled at the weather. The North Slope of the Brooks Range wasn't supposed to be so benign in late August and early September. The excellent visibility allowed them to scan a distant mountainside for Dall sheep. With the naked eye they spotted a dozen or so, all ewes and lambs. Even with my binocular, all I could see were patches of snow and white rocks.

Alan, with whom I've fished in Mexico and the Florida Keys, told me that the art of spotting sheep was a little like the art of spotting bonefish wakes on a tidal flat.

"When you've done it a thousand times, you know what to look for," he drawled. "They're dirty white, not like snow or rocks, and you look for a little movement. Rocks don't move sidehill or uphill."

Finally, I focused on them, clinging to what looked like a sheer rock face in apparent defiance of gravity. My next problem was how to discern their age and sex. I couldn't tell which were adults, which had ram's horns and which didn't, so I had to take my companions' word that the flocks were ewes and lambs.

Hunters are allowed to shoot only mature rams—males with a three-quarter to a full curl. Dall rams rut in the late fall, but they are not nurturing fathers or loving husbands; for the rest of the year, they live apart in small bachelor groups. We went off to find them, or caribou, or bear.

Stuffing spotting scopes, game bags, survival gear, and food into our backpacks, Alan and I crossed the Kongakut in hip boots to hunt a drainage on the east side. Frank and Dave hiked up Drain Creek on the west.

That stream and its surrounding ridges (which had equally unpoetic names, like Bathtub Ridge—the surveyors of that country must have been plumbers in another life) were rich in game, particularly sheep. The reasons offer a lesson in why the hunter must be able to read nature's fine print. In the Brooks Range, as in most other wild areas, nature doesn't believe in equality, distributing plants and animals unevenly. One stretch of terrain is full of game, another is not; but because nature is also jealous of her secrets, she often makes the difference between the two landscapes too subtle for most people to notice.

From morning till early afternoon, Alan and I hunted five miles up one side of the eastern drainage, then the other side back to base camp. We saw a few old caribou tracks, a golden eagle's nest, and two or three female Dalls; Frank and Dave, striking ten miles up Drain Creek, saw two dozen sheep (though none were legal rams), a moose, ptarmigan, merganser, and teal, in addition to fresh sign of caribou and grizzly. The mouths of the two watercourses were separated by less than a mile; the banks of both were covered with willow and aspen. Both were surrounded by identical natural communities—wetland, alpine tundra, treeless mountainside. What accounted for the abundance of the one, the barrenness of the other?

Anyone but a blind man would have noticed that Drain Creek had more water in it; only slightly less obvious was the density and age of the vegetation—Frank reported seeing aspen with trunks eight inches in diameter (in the austere Arctic, trees that size are the equivalent of giant sequoia). But there were other, more hidden answers to the puzzle, inscribed in the shale on Drain Creek's bars—fossilized corals and marine organisms that

lived in the primeval sea basin from which the Romanzofs arose, sixty million years ago. That's recent by the geological calendar, so the shale is still rich in nutrients that not only help vegetation flourish in the creek valley and on the lower elevations but also provide minerals that the sheep need. Periodically, they come down from the safety of their high ranges (whose limestone formations are comparatively sterile) to lick up the phosphorus and nitrates leached out of the rocks.

The rest of the answer lay in the architecture of the land. The creek that Alan and I followed was narrow, its canyon almost sheer-sided—a still, shadowy corridor that rose steeply toward its source. The Drain Creek valley was several times as wide, and it ascended gradually. Its width made it a natural wind channel, while its gentler sides allowed more sunlight to fall on the south-facing slopes above. Dall sheep like wind channels, and also south-facing slopes. In the winter, the gales that make the Brooks Range only slightly more congenial to human life than the moon scour the snow from the high meadows, exposing tundra grasses that the sheep graze on. In the warmer months the sheep move onto the ridges with southerly slopes, because those are the first to green up in spring and because they remain the most luxuriant through the summer. All of this illustrates another lesson, an old one learned by Native Americans over millennia and by ecologists through science: If you significantly alter one thing in nature, you alter everything, because all things are connected, in time as well as in space. Interred within the very rocks are creatures that died when dinosaurs reigned; their microscopic skeletons help sustain animals living today.

Two golden eagles, wings black against the blue sky, gyred on thermals rising from a limestone pinnacle, swooped across a tundra meadow, and then soared away and vanished over a distant ridge. I sat on a gravel bar and watched the eagles, just because their grace and effortless speed made me feel good. The Kongakut surged slowly against a cliff on the far side. The river looked like liquefied jade, so pure that only the movement of the eddies told that it was water and not air. The clarity created an illusion of shallowness—shoals and bars that appeared no more than a foot or two down were in fact four or five feet below the surface. The greenish rock bottom was speckled with gray oblong spawning beds, or redds, scraped out by the tails of mating char, hundreds in this pool alone, the females long and silvery, the males with black, red-spotted flanks, bellies the color of fire.

It was our third day out, and we were a few miles down from Drain Creek, on our way to another campsite. Looking northward, we saw dark clouds filling the notch of the Kongakut valley. The mountains were through giving us a break on the weather, so we decided to move on.

Farther downriver we secured the raft and set up base camp, but we weren't going to spend the night in it. We would trek up another unnamed drainage and spike out deep in mountains where friends of Alan's had shot and seen everything there was to be shot and seen a couple of years ago: That wilderness teeming with game that has been a sportsman's fantasy for centuries, and the Indian shaman's vision for much longer than that.

There is a saying that everything in Alaska is twice as far as it appears, and twice as hard to get to. With some thirty pounds on our backs, we tramped over the jumbled rocks of dry creek bottom, through muskeg, over tussock tundra, the tussocks rolling underfoot like bowling balls. We must have crossed and recrossed the creek a hundred times, and the icy water eventually breached the triple layer of waterproofing on my boots. The moose trails that wound through the willow and alder breaks were a comparative joy to walk on; those monsters had tramped the tundra to the hardness of pavement. But there was a certain tension in the thickets, and we had rounds chambered and scope covers off in case of a point-blank grizzly charge.

Frank and Dave, those marathon hikers, had gone on ahead. Their spike was to be pitched about ten miles up, Alan's and mine half that distance, under a mountain on which one of his friends had bagged a ram with a thirty-nine-inch curl. I was happy to have Alan as a companion, because he was hobbled by bad knees and I by a bad ankle and right foot: traumatic osteoarthritis in the ankle, traumatic neuroma in the foot, and the trauma arising from two AK-47 bullets fired at me by Muslim militiamen back when I was a war correspondent in Beirut. I've often wondered if the experience of being hit by a high-powered rifle had something to do with my reluctance to shoot big game. A certain empathy.

We came across a long stretch of stream that inexplicably flowed underground. It must have dried up suddenly; dozens of juvenile char, caught unaware, lay rotting on the rocks. The tracks of a very large wolf were printed over Dave's and Frank's tracks in the snow, and every spooky Russian folktale I'd heard came back to me.

At dusk we pitched the small mountain tent near a stand of dead willow. The mountain rose to the northwest, its summit slightly bent, like a half-straightened fishhook, and crowned with limestone slabs. The peaks to the east glowed in the light of a sun we could no longer see. The days were still long, sunset arriving about 10:00 P.M., but we were losing light at the rate of eight minutes a day. For the next hour, we watched steam rise from our drenched boots and socks, arranged around the fire; we ate some more freeze-dried rations before turning in. With the bolts open, to chamber a round quickly if necessary, we slept with our rifles beside us, the muzzle of Alan's .300 pointed to the back of the tent, the muzzle of my .30-06 toward the front. In Alaska, grizzles always stalk your imagination, but never so much as at night.

Rain and sleet were crackling against the tent when we woke up. Next came a breakfast of instant oatmeal and coffee, and then a short walk in our raingear to a low bluff downstream. From that perch we watched the valley for caribou and bear and glassed the mountains for sheep. The easterly wind turned north, and banks of fog and cloud settled into the draws and canyons above. If there were any Dalls up there, we would not see them now. Not a living thing appeared in the valley, though it was crisscrossed with game trails. The Arctic is a spare environment, its climate severe, but with 200,000 caribou in the Porcupine herd, I expected to see a lot of *Rangifer tarandus*—and with an estimated 960 grizzlies in the refuge, a least one *Ursus arctos horribilis*. But even in the West early in the last century, white explorers and Indians alike often faced starvation. In his biography of Meriwether Lewis, *Undaunted Courage*, Stephen Ambrose notes that the Lewis and Clark expedition, in country abounding in elk, antelope, and buffalo, was sometimes reduced to eating dogs and horses, as were a few of the tribes they encountered. Hunger was such a constant threat to Native Americans that it haunted their souls as well as their bellies. The Ojibwa of the northern Middle West and central Canada believed in the *windigo*, an evil spirit that resorted to the practice of cannibalism. In Alaska today, the Koyukon have a similar myth— Woodsman, a human being exiled to the forest because game shortages had driven him to survive on human flesh.

The idea that the amount of game is directly proportional to the degree of wildness is partly illusion. Of course, you won't find grizzlies in Manhattan, nor bison in Iowa cornfields, but true wilderness is vast and unpredictable. I wasn't seeing any caribou because the Porcupine herd ranges over an area as large as all six New England states put together—plenty of space in which to disappear. They can be whimsical nomads, born under a wandering star, and often change their migratory routes without prior notice. True wilderness also is harsh on game populations. Sheep in the Brooks Range have lost a half to three-fourths of their population in the past several years* because severe winters (severe, that is, even by Arctic standards) have buried their alpine pastures under several feet of snow. The sheep have either starved or have been driven to concentrate in valleys in which they can find graze— and in which they are easy prey for wolves. The moose season was closed in the northern part of the refuge this year because the calf survival rate was close to zero. In the Kongakut herd alone, only three of the two dozen moose calves born last year lived through the winter. The calves couldn't forage in the deep snows, and those that didn't die of hunger were killed by grizzlies, which often stake out a calving area and devour the newborns.

After four fruitless and chilling hours atop the bluff, Alan and I decided to return to camp, put on an extra layer of clothes, and move to another spot farther up the valley. I was scouting the creek for a ford when Alan whispered:

"Get down! Stay quiet! Big bull caribou!"

---

*Editor's note: This was written in 1996.

I caught a glimpse of it through the willow and alder thicket behind us. It was meandering along the side of a ridge about 400 yards away. In the open, with no trees or shrubs to make a contrast, the bull did look big. Its velvety rack branching handsomely, its cape a grayish brown, its flanks dark brown, it moved at a stately pace, pausing to browse on tundra grass. Alan raised his binocular and said in an excited whisper:

"He's got a double shovel! There's only one in a thousand with a double shovel!"

A double shovel means two antler spades that jut from the base of the rack, parallel over the caribou's forehead.

My heartbeat immediately shot into buckfever range, and I was telling myself to calm down as we stalked through the thicket, bent low, trying hard not to crack branches underfoot. I was thinking "Trophy!" and about camp meat and that it was up to me to bag insurance in case we got weathered in—a frequent emergency in Alaska. During his guiding days, a storm had trapped Dave Brown in the mountains for seven days. His partner had broken his leg on the last day of the hunt, and their food was almost gone. If they hadn't shot a sheep the day before, they would have been half starved by the time the weather broke and the plane picked them up.

I took three or four deep breaths to steady myself as we came out of the thicket and crouched down. Between us and the bull was a wide-open muskeg bog, perhaps two hundred yards across. The caribou was standing some fifty or sixty feet above it, its side toward us.

"Better shoot now," Alan muttered.

I had a 4X fixed scope for my Weatherby, but there wasn't anything other than a flimsy willow shrub to rest the rifle on. An offhand shot of more than two hundred yards was longer than I cared to make, especially in the rain. On the other hand, I didn't dare venture farther into the open muskeg— even a dumb caribou would spook if it saw me. I'm not too bad on an offhand shot—ten years ago in Australia I'd dropped a wild boar from the standing position, with one shot and with iron sights. And on the rifle range at home, I'd put twenty killing rounds in a row through the silhouette target at one hundred yards. But that was at a cardboard deer, on a warm, sunny day.

I shouldered the rifle, slipped the sling under my arm for stability—and found myself looking into a fog. The scope had misted over in the rain. I wiped it off with a bandanna and raised the .30-06 again. The bull was on the move now, almost prancing, its head held high. I led it slightly, fired, and saw it stumble.

"Good shot!" Alan said, looking through his binocular. The caribou didn't think so—it was still moving, although a little more slowly. The rifle was sighted to hit dead-on at two hundred yards, but there must have been more bullet drop than I'd counted on. I figured I'd hit low, on the upper part of the foreleg. Still, the 180-grain bullet should have knocked it down. Maybe I'd led a little too much and only winged a leg. (I found out later that's what I'd done.) Overcompensating, I put the next shot high, and, watching the round throw up dust in the ridge, was amazed that the animal didn't sprint off—or at least try to.

Now it was atop a knoll, and I saw that it was going to turn into a thickly wooded draw. The last thing I wanted was to have wounded it and lose it in the woods. I rested on a willow branch, but it was, well, willowy, and gave way just as I centered the cross hairs on the lungs and fired again. The bull's legs crumpled. On its knees now, it raised its head and seemed to look momentarily toward the strange noise that it might or might not have associated with the terrible thing that had just happened. Then its head dropped, and it rolled over onto its side and lay still. Alan was sure that the caribou was dead, but I wasn't; the shot must have been thrown off when the willow bowed under the weight of the rifle.

The cheechako was right. After slogging across the muskeg and up the knoll, we found that the bull had hobbled into the draw, where it now knelt on all fours, blood matting its fur from a wound behind its lungs. It was looking at me from thirty yards away, and I saw in those dark eyes glowing from under the antlers all that I had felt when I'd been shot—not pain, because I can attest that you don't feel a bullet wound's pain right away, but a stunned bewilderment. I also saw that the rack was not as big as it had appeared from a distance.

But there was no choice now. I sat down and made sure that the rifle was as solid as if it were benchrested. Watching the caribou's legs give a few final kicks from the shoulder-breaking shot, I told myself, *Remember this and how it makes you feel, and maybe next time you won't come hunting until you've made* five-hundred *bull's-eyes at the range.* I'm not sentimental about the deaths of animals, and antihunting zealots who aren't strict vegetarians strike me as sanctimonious hypocrites. Our lives are sustained by the deaths of other creatures, whether they're steers or free-range chickens or wild caribou. But when you hunt for any reason other than to stave off starvation, you have a moral responsibility to kill as quickly and cleanly as possible.

"That wasn't shooting, that was butchery," I murmured as we began to skin and gut the carcass.

"Hey, we all like 'em to be pretty, one shot and down, but they can't all be pretty. You got the job done," Alan said, forgiving me.

I wanted to say that's what it had felt like—a job, and a messy one at that—but there is nothing more tiresome than the whine of self-recrimination.

Stripped of felt and bloodstained, the rack lay near the fire we'd managed to get started in the steady downpour, and chunks of caribou tenderloin were roasting on willow sticks when Frank and Dave tramped in, soaked with rain and sweat after a five-mile walk from their spike camp.

"You guys are just in time for dinner," I said.

"Yours?" asked Dave, gesturing at the rack.

I nodded.

"One shot, right?"

"Not quite."

Dave dropped his pack, squatted by the fire, and sampled the meat.

"What the hell's going on here?" he said. "The Connecticut gentleman, the East Coast dude, shoots the only game?"

"Anytime I can provide for you sourdoughs, give me a call," I answered.

He and Frank reported that they had seen a number of ewes and lambs, but not a ram, a moose with a rack of fifty-five or sixty inches, and about ten caribou filing along the far ridge, led by an enormous bull with antlers like small trees.

"That's the kind you want next. You'll have to be selective," Dave said, commenting indirectly on the size of my caribou's rack.

Through the afternoon and into the early evening, we boned the quarters and stuffed meat into game bags. I was hoping for a leisurely night, but Dave, who was more or less in charge, noted that the creek had risen several inches and that the clouds were racing overhead. We couldn't feel the wind, broken as it was by a wall of mountains to the north, but we could be sure that it was howling down the Kongakut. A blizzard was coming. We'd better hoof it back to base camp and make sure all was secure. If the big river rose our raft could be carried away, and then we'd have to walk the fifty-odd remaining miles to the pickup point. That's a five-day march in the Brooks Range.

With the meat adding twenty pounds to Frank's, Alan's, and Dave's packs (as the resident East Coast dude, or perhaps in deference to my bum ankle, I was given the lightest load), the return to base camp took more than three hours. Alan's bad knees grew wobbly under the sixty pounds on his back. I relieved him for an hour, and that was penance enough for shooting badly. And so was tramping through bear country stinking of caribou meat and blood.

It was snowing by the time we got back, a little after nightfall, our feet drenched and half frozen. The tent was still standing, but it was billowing and snapping like an unsheeted sail in the thirty-mile-an-hour wind. Too tired to build a fire, we stripped off our wet clothes and leapt shivering into our bags.

The gale blew all the following day, more snow fell, and dense gray clouds shrouded the mountains. The water in our water bottles froze solid. We built a roaring fire behind a tall willow bush and rigged tarps over the bush to break the wind further; then we hung our wet socks and trousers over the branches on the lee side to dry them by the fire. Despite the weather—the Brooks Range was through showing us its smiling side—there was a kind of cozy domesticity about camp and an atmosphere of cheerful comradeship. We reorganized gear, trimmed and roasted caribou meat, and dried our boots. One of the benefits of hunting the hard way is that it teaches you how most humanity once lived—you hunted, you ate what you killed, and you did your best to stay warm and dry.

By late afternoon we were on the river again, and we set up another camp some three or four miles downstream. Hunting long and hard the next day, with each team of two covering at least fifteen miles, we saw the usual ewes and lambs, golden eagles, and plenty of moose, caribou, and grizzly sign—but never the animals that made them. The day wasn't without its rewards, though. Once, I found a perfectly preserved mayfly in a field of *Aufeis*—overflow ice that remains frozen all year—and the ice itself was beautiful, seven or eight feet thick, with aquamarine chambers beneath it.

Later, far up a canyon as innocent of human footprints as Mars, I sat on a bed of glacial till and experienced the absolute "otherness" of the natural world, a world independent of human endeavor, careless about human fate, whether one person's or the entire race—a world complete unto itself. The silence was different from the silences of wild places in the Lower Forty-eight, where, even when there isn't a manmade sound to be heard, the atmosphere seems to carry the echoes of the logger's chainsaw or of mine machinery or of tourists' laughter and shouts. The stillness of the Brooks Range was virgin, a quiet never broken by humanity's industrial and commercial clatter. Compared with it, the noise I'd left behind—campaign speeches, sound bites, talk-radio yelps—seemed as significant as the chirping of crickets. I listened for an hour, and once I thought I heard voices, faint with distance. It must have been a trick of the wind, but I like to think the mountains were talking, though in a language I couldn't understand.

The next morning dawned foggy and cold, and there were fresh wolf tracks in the sand only yards from the tent. Half a mile away, three caribou appeared like apparitions out of the mists. Tossing willow leaves in the air to test the wind, Dave and I stalked to within 250 yards of the animals—a bull, a cow, and a calf. We crept a little closer. The bull raised its head majestically and grew wary; the cow and calf paced nervously. We'd been quiet and were well downwind, so they could not have seen or scented us. Then we realized that they'd cut the trail of the wolf. The bull had a fine cape that fell like a silver apron over its front and made a beautiful contrast with its chocolate-brown flanks and haunches. Its rack, however, was no larger than the one I already had, so I didn't shoot, but just watched the three animals walk off and was happy to do so. What a sight that silver-chested bull made, prancing with its crown of antlers beneath the mountains.

At midday, it was downstream again to a new camp, a new drainage, the river falling now, its rapids becoming more frequent and more demanding. Beaching the raft near a summit called Mount Greenough, only twelve miles from the Canadian border, we caught several char in a half-mile stretch of smooth, swift water. We seasoned the fish with salt, pepper, and lemon-pepper, then wrapped them in tinfoil with chunks of butter and baked them over the coals. Although it was sleeting and we ate hunched over the fire in foul-weather gear, picking the meat off the bones with our fingers, that meal tasted better than anything I've had in those Manhattan restaurants in which the waiters are called "servers" and the numbers on the menu look like the down payment for a used car.

The weather partly cleared later on. Alan, glassing a ridge some three miles off, announced, "I see my ram!"

I was again amazed by his ability to pick it out among the snow patches and rocks, but eventually I found it with my binocular. It was grazing on a ledge in the concave face of the ridge, 2,500 feet above.

Checking it out through the 60X spotting scope, Dave said that it had a full curl, and Alan declared that he was going after it. I couldn't see how he would manage the climb, but I decided to go along to photograph the ram and to help pack out the meat if Alan bagged it.

Off we went, following a bluff alongside the Kongakut to mask our approach. Dalls, Alan said with only slight exaggeration, had eyesight equivalent to his spotting scope. The horizontal part of the stalk, the easy part, was hard enough—for almost two miles, we picked our way over and around boulders strewn above a roaring rapids. A cross-fox—half Arctic fox, half red fox—scampered across our path.

Coming to the base of the ridge, Alan pointed toward two slabs of rock rising from near the crest like the humps of a camel. If possible, he would make his shot from there.

The ridge was covered with immense rockslides too treacherous to climb. Though many of the boulders were the size of small cars, they were precariously balanced and could give way under a man's weight. Then that man would be dead, if not immediately from the fall, eventually from exposure as he lay with his legs or back or arms broken. We scaled the tundra fells and willow thickets between the rockslides, the slope far steeper than it had looked from below—so steep that we had to turn the bills of our caps up to keep them from bumping into the mountain.

Sometimes the willow brakes were too dense to get through, forcing us onto the slides. Never in my life have I been so careful, watching and testing every step, feeling a pain in my chest like a heart attack when a boulder shifted or I heard scree sliding away from under me with a sound like breaking crystal.

The weather changed again without warning. The wind picked up—20 miles and hour, 30, 40. Great sheets of snow swooped down like curtains from the onrolling clouds to the north. It was 7:45 P.M. by the time we got above the willow line, roughly halfway to the top and a thousand feet above the Kongakut. As we sat with our fingers digging into the mountainside (because the wind threatened to blow us off), I remembered that my mother-in-law had warned me not to do anything stupid or to take unnecessary chances. This was stupid. By the time we got to where we were going, it would be too dark for a shot with rifle or camera. I told Alan that we should pack it in. He said he was going on. I considered advising him not to, but there was a bright, wild, predatory determination in his eyes, and I knew he wouldn't listen.

Some three hours later, in pitch blackness, I stumbled back into camp, very happy not to have broken a leg or bumped into a bear. Dave and Frank were snug in their sleeping bags.

"Christ, we were wondering when you guys would give it up," Frank called out.

"Make that 'guy.' Alan's still up there. He wanted to go on," I said, now embarrassed that I hadn't insisted he return with me. "Maybe I ought to go back and find him. . . ."

"The hell you will," said Dave. "Then we'll have two guys stranded up there in this weather. If he's not back by morning, we'll backtrack him and find him."

We lay awake for a long time, listening to the wind that blew so hard it made snowflakes crack like hail against the tent. We didn't say it, but each of us wondered how Alan could survive such a night up there. Then, around midnight, we saw the beam of a flashlight outside and heard him say:

"High adventure on the Kongakut!"

He'd made the climb, arriving at the two humped rocks at last light—just in time to see that the ram had moved to a pinnacle almost a mile away. He had returned by the same route as I, navigating by starlight and moonlight. While working his way back along the river bluff, he'd heard something snarl in a willow thicket above him. Was it the fox we'd seen earlier? Bear? Wolf? He couldn't identify the sound, what with the wind and the noise of the rapids. When the creature snarled again he whirled around, leveling his rifle and turning his flashlight on. But he couldn't see a thing.

"So I started talking to it," he said, "'Now listen, whatever you are, I'm trying to get back to camp and into my sleeping bag, all right? I've gotta .300 Weatherby here, but if you don't f— with me, I won't f— with you.'"

Sometimes nature had a sense of black humor. When Alan and I awoke, late the next morning, we spotted the same ram standing on the same ledge. Had we waited, we would have had a whole day to stalk it. Now, so worn out that it tired us just to gather firewood, we couldn't muster the strength.

With only three hunting days left, Dave and Frank had left camp at first light. They made their most epic trek, walking out of the Romanzofs and into the British Mountains to within a long rifle shot of Canada. Somewhere up there, at a point that Dave later described as "several miles east of Jesus," they saw ten sheep—all ewes and lambs, but with a beautiful ram nearby, its horns curling into nearly perfect circles. The two men began their stalk, scaling scree meadows past waterfalls and glaciers. When they had finally reached the top, some 4,500 feet up, they watched the ram amble over another ridge and out of sight.

They had to settle for the scenic rewards, which were not inconsiderable. Mountains climbed and fell and climbed again, tier upon tier, for a hundred miles in all directions, the ranges stitched by rivers and jeweled with glacial lakes—a world as pristine as when those crags and peaks were born in the thunder of the earth's colliding plates.

The two then climbed down into the drainage they had followed from camp. In midafternoon, rounding a bend in the creekbed, they spotted a fine grizzly of some seven feet and four hundred fifty pounds, with a honey-brown coat. Frank had never killed a bear. Taking the rifle off sling, he eased the safety. Then they saw a cub come out of an aspen stand. You do not shoot a sow with young, because you have then killed more than one bear. It was unusual to see a female with only one cub; possibly the brother or sister had been killed by a boar. Like lions, male grizzlies sometimes commit infanticide to induce females to go into heat.

It that's what had happened, this sow probably would be extremely defensive, so Dave and Frank looked for a way around her. But she scented them first, bolted up to a knoll above the aspen, and rose onto her hind legs to get a fix on them. (Grizzlies have acute senses of smell and hearing but poor eyesight; they stand upright to see better.) For a few seconds, men and bear faced each other; then the sow tossed her wide head side to side and popped her jaws. Dave and Frank could hear her teeth clacking, even from over a hundred yards away. It's one of the most dreadful sounds in nature. It means that you're going to be charged, an experience that can be approximated if you stand on a football field while two enraged NFL linebackers, each with a fistful of jackknives and roofing nails for eyeteeth, come at you at full speed.

Dave pointed to a spot some thirty or forty yards away and said: "She gets to there, I'm afraid that cub will have to fend for itself."

With a *whoof*, the sow dropped to all fours, bursting through the underbrush at racehorse speed, ears flattened, saliva flying from her jaws, her teeth still popping, her claws clattering on the rocks of the creekbed. As the two men raised their rifles, the sow suddenly turned, just short of Dave's imaginary line in the sand, and lunged off toward her cub. It was a false charge, a bluff. One could say that Frank and Dave sighed with relief, but it was more than a sigh. The bear's agility stunned them.

"She didn't slow down before she turned, like a man would," Frank said later. "I never saw anything reverse field like that."

Now only two full hunting days remained. My three companions were getting anxious; they'd been skunked so far. There was much strategizing around the fire that night, discussions about the dearth of sheep in the Brooks Range and how much blame to assign to bad weather, how much to wolves. Nothing could be done about the weather, but if a wolf pack appeared, my companions intended to do some serious culling. I said I wouldn't join in because, coming from the Lower Forty-eight where wolves had been trapped, poisoned, and shot to the edge of extinction, I viewed the wolf as an almost mythic animal. They had a more pragmatic outlook about that much-maligned creature. They weren't obsessed with wolves, like, say, farmers and ranchers, and they appreciated having them around; on the other hand, they didn't look at wolves or anything else in the natural world through Disneyworld glasses. Living in a land in which the wild dominates, they saw the wild for what it is—a place of astonishing beauty and freedom, but also of an indifference that amounts to an unbearable ruthlessness.

Some years ago, when he was a guide, Dave was glassing for sheep when he saw a pair of wolves attack a bull moose many times heavier then their combined weight. For almost an hour, they worked the moose like skilled banderilleros preparing a bull for the matador's kill.

"The first wolf would charge the moose from the front, and the moose would go at him, hooking its antlers," Dave said. "But the wolf would dodge away in time. Meantime, the second one would back off, then charge the moose from behind. The moose would turn to face that one, but then the other would charge from the back, and it would have to spin around again. Finally, the moose was exhausted. Its head was hanging down, its legs were spread wide. One of the wolves paced back and forth in front of the moose, making quick charges, and then ran away. The moose was distracted by it. The other one circled around behind and waited. Then something told that wolf it was time to go in for the kill. Don't know what, but something did, and it charged, so fast I almost couldn't see it, right between the moose's hind legs and bit into its belly and ripped it open.

"The moose's guts spilled out like groceries out of a bag. Both wolves tore at the intestines, snapping them up while the moose stumbled and weaved.

"The moose was being eaten alive, but it was still on its feet," Dave went on. "Then one of them jumped onto its hindquarters and tore out a big chunk of meat. The other one jumped on from the other side and ate some of that leg, and the damned moose was still on its feet, its insides trailing on the ground, the two wolves hanging on and tearing at its hindquarters."

At last the huge beast fell, though Dave could see by the motions of its head that it was still alive as the wolves devoured it, sometimes from the inside out, sometimes from the outside in.

"There's nothing up here that dies easy," said Alan, supplying the moral to the story.

We paddled ten or twelve miles the next morning, after a frigid night. The sky was clear and the wind down, but the river got serious, falling more sharply toward the coastal plain, flinging itself around cliffs in frothing bends, and tumbling down rocky staircases with a steady roar. There were Class III rapids in places, with standing waves a yard high and enormous boulders with back eddies and whirlpools spinning behind them. Experienced whitewater rafters would have found this four-mile stretch a piece of cake, but for us, it was exhilarating and occasionally a little scary. Complicated eddies combined with our, let's say, modest rafting skills to sling us into rocks or careen us against cliff sides; once, in a booming rapid, we wound up high-centered atop a boulder roughly the size of a pickup truck. We shifted our weight and rocked the raft, ever so careful not to capsize in that beautiful, clear, absolutely deadly water, and then piked with our paddles and at last succeeded in refloating ourselves.

The Kongakut swept us around a conical mountain and into a wide, wooded valley below Whale Mountain, so called, I assume, because it is shaped like a whale—or because its massive breadth makes it a whale of a mountain. To the east, a broad side drainage split through the Romanzofs for miles, showing us the snow-crested, serrated wall that marks the Yukon border.

Dave and Frank hunted this drainage in the morning, while Alan and I worked the meadows on the west side of Whale Mountain. We came across fresh bear sign—tracks and holes dug by a grizzly hunting for ground squirrels. Sometimes called "parky squirrels" because Eskimos made parkas from their fur, they are a mainstay of the interior grizzly's diet (moose and caribou are rare treats, the ursine equivalent of a night out at a five-star restaurant). Otherwise they subsist on berries and the roots and leaves of boykinia, or bear flower, which is why their meat (unlike that of the fish-eating bears of coastal Alaska) is excellent, tasting a little like sweet pork.

We trailed the bear all morning without success. It must have doubled back on us, because our partners, we found out later, spooked a grizzly only a fifteen-minute walk from camp. They didn't get a shot at it, but three miles farther up the drainage they encountered another bear, feeding on a caribou. Here was Frank's chance. He raised his .300, firing high on the first shot. A second dropped the bear; it leapt up and started running, and the third shot killed it. At almost the same moment, a wolf burst out of the trees and raced up a ridge, out of effective range. The wolf let out a howl, and another answered, and then a third. The caribou must have been killed by a wolf pack, which the bear had driven off. While the two men skinned and dressed out the grizzly (it taped at 6 feet, 8 inches, and weighed about 400 pounds), the wolves circled the ridges above, calling to one another. What were they saying?

Miles away, Alan and I were perched on a spur of Whale Mountain, looking for a sheep. I was feeling a little woozy, from fatigue and a touch of vertigo, for we occupied a narrow shelf, above a long, almost vertical shale slide. After a couple of hours of glassing we saw only a shaggy muskox, climbed down, and hunted our way back to camp, arriving there about an hour before dusk. Having eaten nothing but a few granola bars and boxes of raisins all day (we'd run out of oatmeal the day before), our first act was to fire up the camp stove and boil water for a luscious meal of freeze-dried chicken gumbo. I hitched my belt another notch. I was shedding a pound a day by consuming

2,500 calories while burning three times that much. It made for an efficient weight loss program, though I doubted I could market it to the general public.

After dinner, Alan went toward the river to draw more water for coffee. He was back fifteen seconds later, with that focused, predatory brightness in his eye.

"I see him!" he said in a tense undertone, jacking a round into his Weatherby. "See my bear and he's coming this way."

I pulled my binocular from my jacket pocket. The bear was a little more than a quarter of a mile downstream, ambling along the side of the mountain on the opposite side of the river—a big, classic grizzly with dark brown fur silvered at the hump, a long nose, and short, powerful legs. Each bristling hair seemed alive as it walked, its nose down a little, its small black eyes in a head, as wide as an average man's chest, looking straight ahead, its gait exuding sovereignty.

Between us and the river was a broad gravel bar with no cover except for one big boulder the color of weathered copper. We low-crawled to it, Alan resting his rifle on a clump of brush alongside. The bear was downwind of the caribou meat we'd cached well away from camp on the near side of the river. We figured that it would be drawn to the scent and come down to the bank on the far side, giving Alan an easy shot of less than a hundred yards. Instead, it climbed up to some scree, as easily as I might climb a short flight of stairs. The light was fading, and the bear did not make a distinct target against the black shale. It was almost directly across from us now, about 225 yards distant and 100 feet above the river. It hadn't scented us any more than it had the cache; it displayed that total absence of wariness that marks the predator at the top of the food chain.

Alan didn't want to risk a long shot in the dim light. In a crouch, he stalked quickly to where the raft was moored and used the raft for a benchrest. I followed him with my camera and binocular.

My light meter told me that I would need a flash, but I didn't dare use one before Alan fired.

"Put the glasses on him and mark my shot," he whispered, tracking the bear as it sidled down onto the tundra just below the shale.

Lying flat, I felt my heart thumping against the gravel. The bear was just a little to our upstream side by this time, its whole broad, brown side facing us, and its pace quickening a little. In a couple of seconds it would be in a willow thicket and out of sight, and in my mind I was shouting, "Shoot! For Christ's sake, shoot!" when the .300 cracked. All four of the grizzly's legs left the ground, and it cartwheeled in midair. The next thing I saw were its haunches as it ran into the willows. Alan looked at me.

"You hit him solid, but he took off. He's in the brush," I said.

If going in there after a wounded bear with night quickly coming on was unthinkable, not going was unconscionable. We walked upstream, glassing the mountainside, and saw its head showing from behind a rock. Just then a big gray wolf, materializing out of nowhere, came loping down the mountain. It seemed to be making a beeline for the bear, then squatted to pee. Alan's snap shot hit close enough to convince the she-wolf to leave. She ran back up and vanished.

We then launched the raft, paddled across the river, tied up, and climbed well above where the grizzly had fallen. If it was still alive, it would either flee or charge. If it fled, it would be downhill; if it charged, the steep slope would slow it enough to give us time for a killing shot.

Rifles in our shoulders, safeties off, we crept toward the willows, thick and shadowy. In another five or ten minutes we would need flashlights. Well, I thought, with some resignation, if the son-of-a-b— comes and kills us, I sure wouldn't blame it.

"There he is!" Alan said, pointing downhill.

The grizzly lay on its side, its back toward us, and though it was motionless, those rippling hairs suggested life. We went down cautiously, stopped, went down a little farther, stopped again. When we were perhaps ten yards away, I centered the cross hairs of my scope on the grizzly's upper back while Alan circled around behind it and poked it with the muzzle of his rifle—once, twice, a third time. The bear never moved.

The bullet—a 180-grain Federal with the appropriate brand name of Bear Claw—had gone through the lungs and out the other side; the short run it had made had been more reflex than anything else.

We dragged the bear from behind the rock and onto a flat spot to begin skinning, and I was awed by how heavy it was, and by the black claws as long as my fingers and the fangs and jaws that could have broken my neck as easily as I could crush a bug. The emotions I'd felt up until then, a fusion of exhilaration and fear, swiftly changed to relief and . . . well, I don't know what to call it. Pity seems too cheap, and so does guilt. A kind of reverence, I guess, an awareness that the death of that great animal had been no small event. At such moments, the hunter understands in his bones and guts why Native Americans apologized to the spirit of an animal they'd killed.

Night fell before we could start skinning. It would have to wait until morning. We laid our packs and stinking undershirts on the carcass, figuring that our stench would keep scavengers away. It would have kept almost anything away, except a skunk.

That night we built a big fire against the cold and roasted caribou and pieces of succulent bear tenderloin from Frank's kill. That seemed fitting: After they have killed a grizzly, Koyukon hunters eat the bear's best parts to placate its spirit. Later on we each poured our customary nightcaps. As we drank, a partial moon rose, and the snowy mountains stood out in stark relief in its light; they looked in fact as pale and unearthly as the lunar mountains themselves. Dave pricked his ears for a moment and gestured for us to be quiet. Far off a wolf was howling, possibly the female Alan and I had seen. The northern lights came out. We'd seen them almost every night, but they put on their most dazzling display that night, appearing first as ever-shifting, pale green curtains, then as rising columns that whirled singly, like ghostly tornadoes, or twined around each other, forming gigantic double helixes. A moment later, in silent explosions of pink and rose, the lights shot horizontally across the skies, dancing rings over the rims of the mountains with movements so vigorous and rhythmic that I swore they would make music next. Two bears killed on the same day, game meat roasting on a campfire, whiskey drunk from a tin cup with good friends, wolves and the moon on wild mountains, and the aurora going crazy overhead—that was one night for the record books.

Alan's bear taped out at 6 feet, 10 inches. It probably had weighed 425 pounds. While skinning it the next morning, the biggest bull moose either of us had ever seen lumbered to within a long stone's throw before it whiffed the stench of bear and man and trotted off. Its rack would have gone over five feet.

The wind turned northerly in the early afternoon. Ahead of us lay a twenty-five-mile float to the pickup point at Caribou Pass. The bush plane was coming for us the next day, weather permitting. But now snow-laden clouds tumbled in, and fog lay in the valleys. I was sure that we would be weathered in for at least two days. We were nearly out of freeze-dried rations, and I was glad for the game bags of bear and caribou stowed in the bow of the raft.

We paddled with the wind in our faces. Some gusts were strong enough almost to stall the raft despite our efforts and the four-knot current. It got colder and colder. Wearing wool long underwear and lined fleece trousers, a thick wool shirt, lined wool sweater, and a pile jacket, I shivered nonetheless. And so did the others. "I have envied the early explorers not for their discoveries but for their sufferings," says a character in André Malraux's *Man's Fate*. Not me. No more penances.

After covering some six miles, we had to beach the raft and build a fire behind a clump of alders. Those flimsy bushes made an enormous difference, cutting wind and windchill in half. But the vegetation downriver began to grow sparser, the mountains lower and more rounded; we were getting closer to the coastal plain. The barren landscape took on an alien, menacing quality. It looked Paleolithic.

Twelve miles. Another stop. Another fire.

"Only eight miles to go," said Dave cheerfully. "Maybe this will let up soon."

When we got back on the river, with no feeling in our fingertips and little in our feet, the snow started to fall harder. Actually, it wasn't falling—it was whipping along almost parallel to the water.

"Yes, this *is* better," said Frank dryly. "Really splendid conditions."

More than cold troubled us.

"Man, we don't find that thing, we're screwed," said Alan, voicing our concern. He meant the landing strip at the pass.

Ballard, our pilot, had told us that we couldn't miss it, and I don't suppose we could have on a clear day. But in a blizzard, with clouds and fog obscuring landmarks and darkness only a few hours away, all we would have to do was take the wrong braid in the river and we'd shoot right past.

Considering that possibility, what happened next was just this side of totally insane. Hawk-eyed Alan spotted a grizzly trotting down to the river. Dave, the only one not to have shot anything, went after it, with Frank backing him up. From the riverbank, Alan and I watched the whole show. We saw the two men skirting an alder-choked ravine, and we saw the bear (which Dave and Frank could not see), about twenty yards away on the other side. The hunters thrashed through the underbrush, but the bear heard them. It reared on its hind legs, then dropped and bolted off, making for the hills at top speed. We watched Dave raise his rifle and heard the shot. Considering the range, the weather, and the fast-moving target, the miss wasn't surprising. The bear ran on, vanished for a moment in a gully, then reappeared, lunging up a hill in the snow, dark brown against white.

"You know, I'm glad I missed. If I'd killed it, we'd be here all night dressing it out," Dave said when he got back with Frank.

Maybe there was another reason to be glad. The great bear, galloping across the snow-covered tundra, made a sight that might have been seen by the first nomad hunters who crossed the Bering Strait into North America thousands of years ago.

At twilight, we caught the briefest glimpse of a blue fuel barrel peeking through some underbrush. Above it, a shred of pink surveyor's tape fluttered from a tall willow branch—the bush pilot's windsock. That tattered little ribbon was what we weren't supposed to be able to miss. It was miraculous we hadn't.

It was midnight by the time we had the tent pitched, the raft deflated, and our gear ready for loading. We enjoyed our (possibly) last campfire, more caribou and bear meat for dinner, and then the last of our whiskey. Never had a warm sleeping bag felt so good.

The storm began to break up the next morning, 8 September, and the clearing weather brought one of the most memorable events I think I'll ever see. The cold winds had convinced the snow geese and speckle-bellied geese, fattened on the cotton grass of the coastal plain, that it was time to leave the Arctic. All morning and into the afternoon, the birds staged for their 3,800-mile journey to California's San Joaquin Valley and the bosques of New Mexico. On the ground, the snow geese were grouped so thickly that they resembled drifts. In the sky, with high, shrill cries, skein after skein after skein flew by, hour after hour without end. I learned later that many of the refuge's game biologists have never seen the migration at its beginning; we four felt graced and privileged.

In a chapter in his book on the wars in North America, military historian John Keegan mentions that some anthropologists have noted that the life of the nomadic hunter, for all its privations and hardships, is the happiest. Watching the geese, I fully understood what the anthropologists meant—not with my mind but with my heart and in my belly, which may be the premier seat of understanding. The night before, I had been ready for a warm bed and the pleasures of the hearth, so it now surprised me to feel a hope that we would get weathered in for a few days. The far-off buzz of the approaching bush plane, which we heard around midafternoon, was not entirely welcome.

We were going to be shuttled out again, and in my enthusiasm, I volunteered to be the last one to leave.

Dave said: "You've seen how fast the weather changes up here. He could bring us back and then get socked in before he can pick you up. You could be out here for days, on your own. It's your call, Phil."

I pondered for a few seconds and answered.

"Nope. This is no place for an amateur."

From Ballard's plane, I looked down 5,000 feet to the Farthest Away River, twisting out of the Brooks Range and onto the coastal plain that reached to the Arctic Ocean, where ice floes sailed on the currents. Out of the corner of my eye, I saw what looked to be a bright, low-flying cloud; turning, I saw that it was a wedge of snow geese, necks like white arrows, pointing southward.

TOP OF THE WORLD

BY

AARON FRASER PASS

Some sing of arms and the man, but Aaron Fraser Pass has written a paean to old legs, and old aches and pains in general. Knowing what you can still do—and harder, knowing what you cannot—is knowledge not easily won, or admitted to. There are hunters in their seventies and eighties who can still reach the summit of a steep mountain in one go—but only a very exceptional few. There is a time when all rams, sheep and man alike, have to quit the climb, and the manner in which that is accepted is yet another definition of courage.

> [We] came out on top of the world, in a land of Arctic sheep pastures . . . clad in a thick, damp carpet of mosses, lichens, grasses cut by deep canyons, black with shale, formidable with cliffs, . . . and behind them rose a mighty series of crags black as ink.

Jack O'Connor, arguably the dean of American gunwriters and patron saint of North American sheep hunters, wrote this accurate and evocative description of mountain sheep habitat in his article "A Day in Ram Heaven" in a 1947 issue of *Outdoor Life*. (In actuality, the late "Sir Jack" probably missed sainthood by a considerable margin but was truly a notable sheep hunter.)

In the ensuing half-century plus, little has changed about mountain sheep or the majestic country they inhabit. Indeed, relatively little has changed in regard to the "on-the-ground" tactics of sheep hunting. However, the totality of sheep hunting has changed profoundly since O'Connor glassed the windswept basins and benches of the sheep pastures.

O'Connor once opined that only the rich and the poor could afford to hunt sheep. His premise was that the rich need have no regard for time, and the poor, whose time was worth little or nothing, needn't be overly concerned with it either. In O'Connor's day a sheep hunt was a rather open-ended affair, and hunting time was expandable. The implication was (and it was substantiated by O'Connor's stories) that a sheep hunt was a pleasant and leisurely horseback amble through the high country that meandered along until success struck. While O'Connor correctly identified *time* as sheep hunting's critical element, the paradigm and the context has since shifted. Today, the *scarcity of time* is sheep hunting's significant limiting factor, and the costs have risen.

In the big picture, sheep hunting involves both getting to sheep country and then penetrating that country to where the sheep are. These are somewhat separate endeavors. In O'Connor's day "getting there" involved steamboat, train, and later passenger aircraft. The actual hunting involved substantial horseback and packtrain travel. Hunts of two to three weeks' duration were common. Today, jet and bush planes have accelerated the velocity of access to and from sheep country, and the actual hunting involves mostly Shank's Mare. The modern sheep hunter goes in fast and light, and the stay is short.

During a tightly scheduled capsule of time, a certain proportion of skill, endurance, and luck must conspire to reward the hunter with his trophy. The usual hunt duration is five to six days, at a time of year when changeable weather conditions can easily blank out half or more of the actual hunting. "Do-overs" and rain checks seldom happen. The modern sheep hunt is a constantly closing window of opportunity.

Along with rising hunting costs, the trophy value of mountain sheep has risen as well. Largely because of the writings of O'Connor, Jim Rearden, and some other "top-end" outdoor scribes, the mystique and prestige of hunting mountain sheep has climbed as high as their lofty habitat. Sheep are seen as a "major-superlative" North American big-game trophy, rivaled only by the great bears in bragging rights. This worth is also based on the inherent beauty of the sheep (and that of their habitat), the difficulty and the expense of their hunting (both considerable), and their relative scarcity and remoteness from dreary day-to-day commonality. In short, mountain sheep hunting is imbued with a heavy dose of romance.

Men of a certain age should be wary of romance in any form. Nevertheless, when I was offered a Dall sheep hunt in Alaska's Brooks Range, my common sense capitulated faster than a French girl's virtue on VE DAY. I'm a sucker for anything Arctic, and sheep hunts don't look you up every day. I accepted with a mixture of alacrity and trepidation.

The invitation, based on a late cancellation, gave me less than six weeks to prepare. Added to that, an old knee injury made me less than nimble in the first place. So I proceeded on the solid illogic that I was in such rotten shape to begin with that no amount of preparation would equip this old man for a young man's sport. I resolved to give it my best shot, no matter how feeble that effort might be. That last qualification was as close to prophecy as I've ever come.

I already had most of the necessary northern gear, the result of previous Arctic hunts. As to rifles, I bowed at the O'Connor shrine and took a Winchester Model 70 Featherweight in .270 Winchester. I had aftermarket engineered (lightweight synthetic stock and small 1.5-6X Burris scope) this gun into a true mountain rifle. Loaded and slung it weighs 8 pounds and shoots 150-grain Nosler Partitions into 1¼ inches. I never argue with a rifle over which load it prefers.

Setting off well equipped, if in less than the greatest physical shape, I encountered some of the modern traveler's typical frustrations. This included a missing airplane in Seattle. (The airline had literally misplaced a plane and wasn't telling where it was or when it would show up.) A quick transition to a second airline got me, but not my luggage (including long underwear, sleeping bag, and rifle), to Dead Horse Airport in Prudhoe Bay, Alaska. Following a tense and uncomfortable night, the errant luggage arrived, and the next day I was trucked eighty miles down the Trans-Alaska pipeline haul road to the Happy Valley bush plane base on the Sag (short for Sagavanirktok) River. There, a Piper Super Cub spun up for my flight into sheep country in the heart of the Brooks Range.

Coming into sheep camp after three legs of jet lag, a less than restful night, and a bouncy ride in a wind-buffeted bush plane, we touched down to a truly jolting landing among the humps of tussock grass on an impossibly short stretch of "level" tundra. It is a cliche to say that a bush plane landing is a barely controlled crash, but cliches become cliches for a reason.

My elation at surviving the landing was dampened by the sight of the departing sheep hunter. As sheep guide and writer Rearden once observed, "Each season, only about 40 percent of Alaska's sheep hunters bag a ram." I knew I was looking at one of the other 60. He wore a "1,000-yard stare," a flannel shirt, long-john bottoms, and blood-soaked socks. Boots poorly fitted or simply not well broken in had spawned a simple blister—a common business cost among sheep hunters—which had then turned major and ended his hunt. He had nothing to say, but his every nuance screamed defeat and exhaustion—extreme exhaustion. The previous night, on his last evening, he couldn't make the climb to a nice ram. Six days of hunting. Ran out of time, ran out of steam—no sheep.

Nor was the view from sheep camp a huge comfort. Upriver the vista included O'Connor's "damp carpet of mosses, lichens, grasses" but cut quickly to "deep canyons, black with shale, formidable with cliffs" with the requisite "mighty series of crags black as ink" looming above it all. Dominating the whole valley was a large, isolated mountain rising from the tundra. It looked like Dracula's castle on steroids. Natural rock formations suggested spires and parapets, and its top third was shrouded in fog. It was a visual, visceral gut check that gave form and substance to the nagging suspicion that, this time, I might have bitten off more than I could chew.

A heart-to-heart with the guide seemed wise. I laid out what I was and what I wasn't. (The latter list was longer.) I said I probably had only two or three good climbs in me and didn't want to waste them. The guide said he could probably work with that. These guys can accomplish a lot if you are straight with them.

Ultimately, mountain sheep hunting means climbing and glassing—they don't call them mountain sheep because they live at the bottom of the mountains. This is sheep hunting in its classic

form, and that part hasn't changed. It's mostly an uphill business, or so it seems. You climb, sometimes on stable patches of soil and grass but often on the eternally shifting and sliding scree slopes of loose stone. Sometimes, something close to rock climbing is required to negotiate a cliff's ledge that is the only path to success.

Not every sheep seen is a sheep stalked or shot. The severity of the terrain or a lack of cover often overrides apparent opportunity. "Can't get there from here," is not an uncommon situation when hunting sheep in the high country.

The rugged nature of sheep country is Darwinism unleashed. It flings its first challenge at the weakest link of either the hunter or his equipment and progresses from there. As noted, something as simple as blistered feet has ended hunts and dashed hunters' hopes. More obvious dangers include climbing steep terrain, wading swift glacial streams, and short-strip landings and takeoffs in bush planes. All these contribute to the overall pucker factor of the endeavor. Also, in much of sheep country "Old Ephraim," the grizzly, still lurks. However, in the high country, other threats are more subtle but no less severe. Getting "caught out" in a sudden weather change or in a whiteout of either snow or dense fog is, for the unprepared, dangerous and perhaps deadly.

To recapitulate, modern sheep hunting involves considerable expense, a degree of risk, and no assurance of success. In short, it is much like real life.

Cutting from the generalities of sheep hunting to the specifics of my own quest for a fleece, in this case white rather than golden and with a full curl attached, the first day was basically a shakedown cruise. In the morning we took an easy hike downriver to check on the ram the previous hunter couldn't reach. That ram wasn't at home. The afternoon upped the ante with a more serious climb up a small glacial valley behind camp.

Lo and behold, we found a sheep. A smallish ram was bedded down on a rocky point. It had about a $7/8^{ths}$ tight curl that the guide estimated at 30 to 31, "*maybe 32, maybe . . . ,*" inches. Nevertheless, it showed the eight annular rings that made it technically legal game. The stalk, as indicated by the guide, was of moderate difficulty, but the shot would be long, very long—about four hundred yards or more. The guide left the decision to me.

I pondered the situation. The ram was no giant, but, considering my limitations, it met reasonable trophy standards. First day? Five days to go. Good chance to do better but no guarantee. The climb tough but doable. The shot? Ah, the shot. Much longer than I was comfortable with across the windy ridges. Reluctantly, I passed on the ram. That decision would come back to haunt me.

The first day had used up most of the sheep hunting near the main camp, and apparently my fitness had been assessed as only fair at best. The decision was made to climb higher and establish a spike camp up in the really high pastures. This traded a tough initial climb for easier daily access to prime sheep country.

It was a great idea in theory, but sheep hunting reality intervened. A fog bank rolled in the first night and settled. Hunting white sheep in a white cloud is a low-odds proposition. Even relocating the spike camp in the fog, if you leave it to hunt, is a poor wager. After being trapped for two days in a dripping tent by a driving mist, we trudged back down to base camp. Bad weather can cut severely into sheep hunting time, and that fog bank had erased any comfortable margin of time for my hunt. Suddenly we were in the late innings with nothing on the scoreboard, no runners on base, and the equivalent of two outs. My window of opportunity was closing.

The next morning a yearling and a nonlegal three-quarter-curl ram wandered right by camp. We trekked back up the valley of the small ram of the first day. It would look pretty good about now. We hunted that whole valley hard and finally spotted two rams, one probably legal. However, they were bedded very high on the mountain, above an immense scree slope. From our position, and with my climbing ability, they might as well have been on Mars.

The morning of the sixth day, my last hunting day, broke bright and sunny—in considerable contrast to my mood. My window of opportunity had all but slammed, and that verdict seemed sealed when a long trek upriver revealed no rams. After lunch we commenced to break camp, and I resigned myself to joining the majority of (unsuccessful) sheep hunters.

However, the mountain gods do occasionally favor the halt and the lame. The guide had left his spotting scope set up and kept looking at the ridge across the river from camp. Late in the day he announced that he could see a bunch of sheep, and that one of them was a ram. "If he's the one we chased up there last week, he's a good one," the guide said. "The stalk is long but not terribly steep. Think you have it in you?"

Possibly only Abraham has ever been more grateful for the sudden appearance of a ram. I resolved to put all I had left into this effort.

We crossed the river and used the rocky canyon of a small tributary stream as stalking cover well up the side of the major ridgeline. When we finally topped out on a rocky bench, the sheep that should have been there weren't.

"Either they've stopped or turned downhill," the guide said. "If they had gone back uphill, we could see them."

This was doubtless his way of encouraging his gimpy client that we were still in the game. Obviously, I didn't have a hell of a lot of uphill left in me. However, there still was a considerable expanse of loose scree to traverse across the bench, and that's tough walking on a bad knee. Luckily, I found a sheep trail that provided decent footing most of the way.

I was only a few yards from a stand of dwarf birch and stable footing when six sheep erupted from a hidden fold in the hillside. They headed up and away, climbing a nearly vertical cliff face. I could see the ram's broad rump bouncing among the running ewes as it climbed, but it offered no good shot. What was worse, I was prone on the sliding scree and could not hold a steady sight picture.

Suddenly, in what can only be called an "it's better to be lucky than good" turn of events, the loose stones under me crunched to a halt and the big ram stopped and turned broadside. My elbows were dug into the gravel and my cross hairs were benchrest firm on the ram's neck when I squeezed the trigger—and the ram came tumbling down.

What came next was one of those intensely personal moments of self-confrontation that arise unbidden from truly significant events. After six days of mostly fatigue and frustration, sudden, unequivocal, and unexpected success was, to say the least, overwhelming. Raging cross-currents of relief, exultation, and triumph crashed like waves against the breakwaters of somber reflection, thankfulness, and a good dose of humility. The final analysis was: "I don't deserve this, but I'll take it." Experienced hunters will understand. I'm sure even Jack O'Connor would have.

Postscript: The ram's horns measured 37 inches, which I am told is quite decent for the Brooks Range. I would be lying if I said that wasn't important. However, it would be equally untruthful to say that a steel tape can measure hunting mountain sheep on top of the world.

THE BEST COUNTRY

BY
CRAIG BODDINGTON

If anyone would be qualified to pass judgment on what is "the best country," then the nod would probably have to go to Craig Boddington. In a vigorous lifetime of hunting he has seen more of it than any two or three others combined. As you will note from the story below, he has turned not just his riflescope but also his eye—and heart—onto that country. He lets us know that where we hunt is never merely a physical landscape; it is also a terrain of memories.

You know how memories somehow become enlarged? Your grandparents' home was vast and rambling, and their yard that you played in as a child was an endless open field. But when you visit the neighborhood as an adult, you find just a normal suburban house on a normal suburban lot. For more than thirty years the Cassiar Mountains of northern British Columbia have loomed large in my memory. Not in size, because I remember them as gentle mountains, but in pristine beauty that, during those same thirty years, I have compared all other game country against.

I remember hillsides of virgin timber rising to muskeg-carpeted ridges, with emerald green basins below the rocky tops. In late August the largest moose were still high, finishing their antler growth among the stunted pines near timberline. The mountain caribou were high, too, feeding along the open ridges. Higher still were Stone sheep, white rumps and salt-and-pepper bodies seen as tiny specks in the spotting scope.

Over the years I have often wondered if the country of hunter-explorer Andrew Stone's sheep was really so beautiful, or if it was a trick of a special memory. It was not my first big-game hunt, nor my first out-of-state hunt. I grew up in Kansas in a time when we had fabulous bird hunting, but there had been no deer season for forty years. Kansans were bird hunters, and those who wished to hunt big game traveled to other states—mostly west to the Rockies. By August of 1973, when I was twenty, I'd hunted pronghorn, mule deer, black bear, and elk—and I'd hunted them in Colorado, Wyoming, and Montana. So, for a Kansas boy of my generation, I was a seasoned big-game hunter (or at least I thought I was). But that trip to northern British Columbia was a very special trip, and it was a trip of many firsts.

It was the first out-of-country hunt for both my Dad and me, a college-graduation present. It was our first hunt for northern game and, with active duty in the Marines to follow for me, it could have been our last hunt together for a while. So it stands to reason that I remember it as a special hunt in a special place. The lakes were crystal clear and full of trout, and I remember expending no effort getting up the mountains. After a few days of fishing and moose hunting, I spiked out with a broken-nose, barrel-chest Indian guide, returning a few days later with a nice mountain caribou and a beautiful ram on the packhorse.

It was country that I always wanted to return to, but I never did. In 1973, Dad and I went on a moose, caribou, and goat hunt for $1,250. Student of Jack O'Connor that I was, I also bought a sheep tag for, as I recall, $25. That was a time when Canada was still full of U.S. draft dodgers. Our outfitter, crusty old Frank Cooke, liked my short haircut and offered me a Stone sheep for a few bucks more. Times changed. Resident pressure increased, nonresident tags went on an ever-shrinking quota, and prices skyrocketed. Like so many things, I could have returned to Stone sheep country if I'd wanted to badly enough, but other countries beckoned.

I spent much time in Africa and a lot of other places, and over time I did a lot of sheep hunting in other ranges with wonderful names: Wrangell, Brooks, MacKenzie, Bonnet Plume, Rockies, Pamir, Kophet Dagh, Ennedi, del Seri, and more. The sheep were always beautiful and the mountains always magnificent, but I never again saw sheep mountains with the gentle beauty of the Cassiars. I did make one other attempt for a Stone sheep, far to the west in the Skeena Mountains. Like all mountains the Skeenas were gorgeous—but the Skeenas were beautiful only from a distance. Up close the slopes were steep and treacherous and choked with near-impenetrable devil's club. On the last day we finally spotted a band of rams, but they were two tough days away. With the spotting scope at 60X, I could see their white rumps and dark bodies and perhaps just the hint of a curling horn. That was as close as I got.

So it was thirty-one years later, in August 2004, before I could compare memory with reality. My old friend Dwight Van Brunt and I took a charter plane from Whitehorse in the Yukon, landing on a strip cleared by hand in a narrow valley. Outfitter Randy Babala and his crew were there to meet us with saddle horses and packhorses for our gear and the supplies that came in with us. Babala had his spotting scope set up, and on a gentle ridge above the airstrip he showed us two bedded rams, both youngsters. I had come home.

Technically, I was not in the Cassiars of northern British Columbia. Specifically, I was fifty-odd miles farther north, in the triangle of dark sheep country that extends up into south-central Yukon. These were the Pelly Mountains, but they were sisters to the ones I remembered. Timbered valleys rose to open ridges, with emerald basins heading the valleys. The tops were rocky and the approaches steep, but neither high nor treacherous as sheep country goes.

The short airstrip was carved into a major drainage, ending on a bluff so that a skilled pilot, probably overloaded, could fly off the end of the strip and drop down several dozen feet to gain airspeed before starting to climb. We checked our rifles there at the strip. The echoing explosions disturbed the sheep, and Babala clucked as two unseen rams, one clearly legal, joined another pair and made their way up the ridge and over the top. Then we loaded the packhorses and followed a good trail up a side canyon to its divide. There, between two tall ridges, we found a meadow of good grass with a small cluster of tents and cabins at the upper end. Wood smoke rose from the cook shack; camp cook Lenore Vinson had coffee on. We were home, and the mountains awaited us.

It is probable that the Cassiars of my youth were a bit steeper than I remember. At twenty, fresh out of Officer Candidate School, I was in the best shape of my life. We rode, on that hunt, into a high basin and spotted two rams in the heather maybe six hundred yards above us. One was a youngster, the other clearly full curl. We slipped off the horses and into the brush, my Indian friend saying simply, "Sheep can't count."

We counted on the horses, though, to hold the attention of the sheep while we made our way up a steep chute, coming out a bit above the two rams. I do not remember being tired from the climb, and in those days I probably wasn't. I do not remember being out of breath when I sat down with a tight sling to shoot, and I probably wasn't. I do remember quite clearly missing with the first, easy shot, then rolling it with a much more difficult running one, but I don't recall blaming my miss on what must have been a very tough climb.

Now past fifty, I was clearly aware that those slopes, so gentle from a distance, were plenty steep. Come to think of it, even the valleys were plenty steep. I was grateful for good horses—at least some of the time. Randy Babala had the best mountain horses I have ever been around. Calm, perfectly trained to ground-rein, and in exceptional condition from the lush grass, they were wonderful—and Babala intended to keep them that way. We led them uphill and we led them downhill. Sometimes we led them on the flats. There was a point when I asked my horse why I'd brought him along, but in a few days I understood the method behind the seeming madness.

Babala, a horse outfitter for forty years, saved his stock for when they were needed the most. At the end of a really long day, when we'd climbed hard and failed to see the kind of ram we were looking for, I noticed that we rode the horses much more—including up and down places that, in the mornings, when we were fresh, we'd lead them through. In sum it made sense, and I was glad I wasn't doing this all on foot.

In any mountain hunt you wind up alternately cursing and blessing your horses. Eventually you must tie them up and proceed upward on foot. You never know where the day might lead you, but you know you must come back to the horses—even if they're

in the wrong direction from camp. Most of the time we were glad to see them, especially after we figured out we'd ride a lot more on the way back to camp than we did on the way out.

On the day Dwight got his ram, late in the hunt, we wished for horses. That day we'd gone out on foot, expecting to glass from the backside of the high ridge north of camp. We found his ram, a real beauty, but it took us far up a big mountain two ridges away, and then to the backside of that big mountain. Dwight shot it just before sunset far down that mountain. We packed it out in the long Arctic twilight, negotiating a tough boulder field in half-light and making the last ridge above camp at midnight, just at full dark. Horses left somewhere along the way would have been a blessing that day!

However many horses there were, there was no shortage of sheep. During the twelve days of our hunt we saw legal rams each and every day, an uncommon occurrence for Stone sheep hunting in modern times. Many rams, in bands from three to twenty, were glassed from Lenore Vinson's handmade lawn chairs in camp, either on the big ridge to the south or at impossible distances up a long valley at the end of that ridge. If they were on the ridge the distance was little more than a mile, and we could judge them easily with good optics. If they were on the big pyramid-shaped mountain at the far end of that valley they were too far to be sure, so it would take a long day and a tough climb for a closer look. None of these panned out; we weren't looking for barely legal full-curl rams, but older rams with deep curls and flared tips.

It was perhaps the sixth day when we all rode out together: Randy, Dwight, guide Mark Greenlee, wrangler Craig Jarvis, and me. We took the horse trail from the divide down the drainage, away from the airstrip, intending to look at some new country several big ridges away. Hardly a half-hour from camp we glanced up and saw two rams on a little bench perhaps sixty yards above us—almost exactly as I'd seen my Stone ram thirty-one years before. The mix was much the same, a young ram, not quite legal, and an older ram that looked very, very good.

As we watched they fed up over the ridge, and we planned our approach. I fully expected Randy to say, "Sheep can't count" as we began a frontal assault. Instead, we rode partway around the mountain and tied our horses, then ascended an incredibly steep, grassy slide that should bring us to the top well above the sheep. This time it hurt, and I felt every inch of the climb. It was not a matter of simply scrambling up the slope, as I probably had done so many years before. This time it was more like taking twenty steps, stopping to blow, then taking twenty more. Randy Babala, several years older than I but in his own mountains, led the way with no apparent effort. At least I never had to ask him to stop, although I desperately wanted to.

I figured it would end about as it had so long ago. We would top out a bit above the rams and they would be there. So we stopped just before the crest for one last blow. Then I chambered a round and we crept forward. At this point the past and the present diverged. We were looking down at a perfect basin, just a few hundred yards above where our sheep had topped out. It was perfect . . . except the sheep weren't there. The basin was completely empty—and then we saw the rump of a ram disappearing around the ridge on the far side, much farther away now.

We skirted the basin and then moved slowly along the ridge. This would be my shot, if there was a shot. We'd gotten a good look at the larger ram; it looked just fine to me, at least a curl and a quarter and into the high 30s. So Randy and I moved forward while the rest of the crew dropped back.

It was late morning now and the rams should have been lying down in that first basin. That they were still moving this late was a bad sign; most likely they were on some sort of a sheep mission, crossing from one drainage to another. I didn't really expect that we'd catch them, but we did. They were feeding in a much smaller basin well around the ridge, just below the rocks. It was simple. Randy and I crawled forward, seeing only the tops of their backs for a long time. Then we reached the lip of the basin and I set up prone.

Now I could clearly see the smaller ram, much lighter in color, but the larger ram was in a depression, only its backline showing. The wind was good, the distance barely one hundred yards. We had it, provided I didn't let panic set in. I concentrated on breathing and staying relaxed, and eventually the ram moved out of the gully, feeding straight away. More waiting while we took a last look at the horns. The shape was perfect, the mass good, the age right. It was a far better ram than the one I'd taken so long ago, and it was plenty good enough for me. The minutes passed like hours, and then it turned to the left, quartering just slightly away. Steady in the sling, I slipped the safety and squeezed the trigger of the little short-magnum .270. It took a few steps, then was down and still.

The pictures and the chores of dividing up the load for the long pack back to the horses could wait. For a little while I just sat with the ram, admiring its horns and its wonderful gray coat, drinking in the green basin around me, the talus slopes above, and the dark timber of the valley far below. I wished my Dad was there with me, enjoying the best country we'd ever seen, as beautiful as I remembered it.

SHEEP

BY
SAMUEL WESTERN

Vertigo is the last thing you would want on a sheep hunt, yet there is something fundamentally vertiginous in the hunting of sheep. It isn't a physical state as much as an emotional, perhaps spiritual, one. Hanging on the side of a sheep mountain can pitch the mind into a whirl of conflicting thoughts: go up, go down, stay here forever, never again, I must reach that ram. Sam Western understands that, and all the other peculiar torments, confusions, and joys contained in this story's title, a single word that speaks volumes.

Each morning of the bighorn hunt, I ritually went through my pack, hoisting, with the exactitude of Shylock, each item, pondering its necessity. The pack itself was a cavernous affair that, empty, exceeded eight pounds. If I shot a ram, I'd be grateful—sort of—for its capacity to hold meat. Our camp sat at 9,600 feet above sea level. We ascended each day to greater heights, sometimes atop peaks over 11,000 feet, walking four to five miles up and down precipitous, ankle-snapping slopes of scree and loose volcanic terrain. I was eager to lighten my load.

Could I cut it down to one water bottle? Oh sure. Write your own morgue report, why don't you? Temperatures during week two of the hunt set new records. At this elevation, the sun's intensity burned the top of my head through a camo doo-rag. Remind me not to have a buzz before sheep hunting.

So that meant the raingear could go. Nope. These mountains brew their own weather with astonishing speed, dictating a constant stripping or pulling on of gear. It's as if someone had a remote to a celestial medium and, bored with the current feature, pushed a button every twenty minutes. Snow. *Click.* Blistering heat. *Click.* Wind. *Click.* In such patterns, a sheep hunter changes outfits more often than a fashion model. The heavy coat and long underwear must also stay.

Binoculars? Might as well rip out your eyes. First-aid kit? The sun really has parboiled your brain.

What went was food. The heat, dehydration, and fatigue chased away hunger, even though I was burning somewhere between 5,000 and 7,000 calories per day. Two thin strips of peppered jerky and a handful of gorp was enough.

Herman Melville said that true places are never put down on any map. But this place was as true and authentic as any place I've been, and cartographers have charted this terrain. Yet under threats from sheep hunting addicts who have threatened bodily harm if I reveal the exact location, I'm limited to reporting that I hunted in Wyoming's North Absaroka Wilderness, about a mile, as the peregrine falcon flies, from Yellowstone National Park. It's among the most isolated area in the Lower Forty-eight states.

The pull of sheep hunting is nothing short of a *force majeure*. As a child, I read *Lives of the Hunted* by the Canadian naturalist Ernest Seton-Thompson. In one story, "Craig the Kootenay Ram," a sheep so fixates a trapper that the stalk leads to the hunter's demise. He gets his quarry, all right, but the hunt induces a black cosmic shift into the life of an otherwise happy-go-lucky fur gatherer.

This obsession left a deep, if a little scary, imprint upon my young mind. However, the older I got and the more I hunted, the better I understood the trapper's fixation. And it had everything to do with finding the edge of that blackness that doomed the trapper. I didn't want to fall in; I just wanted to touch it (or be touched by it) and recognize its power.

I know a man who has guided more than thirty hunters to successful sheep hunts. He's never taken so much as a penny. Why? "It's one of the few primordial activities left on earth," he says. "You just can't predict what will happen. Some [obstacle] always arises, something that's really difficult. With the weather and the terrain, you wonder if you're going to make it. That feeling of death is right there in your mind. You reach total despair that you're not going to get that sheep, but somehow you find it in yourself to go on. And the world opens up. It's like participating in a hard battle and actually winning. You can't really do that in many places in the world."

The terrain is half the struggle. Too rugged for an outfitter's horses and mules, these cirques and coulees provide refuge for some of Wyoming's stateliest bighorns. These guys did not acquire horn mass by being dumb; discovering their whereabouts requires time. Hunting them for a week or more mandates a stripped down camp that you can bull up the mountains on your back. It's minimalist hunting in a land of maximum demands.

We—my partner Jim O'Neill and I—went through the gear-culling process three times, attempting to jettison anything of serious mass. "I haven't actually drilled holes in my toothbrush," said Jim, "but I've thought about it."

A rough sorting-out occurred the evening we first met at a U.S. Forest campground and compared supplies. Two stoves? Out of the question. Then, the next morning, after a breakfast of hardboiled eggs, sweet rose-colored chunks of dried papaya, and cup after cup of stout camp coffee, we undertook a serious elimination. Extra footgear, eating implements (a single spoon will do), and any clothing not meeting a strict utilitarian code all went. Since the weather's been so obligingly clement, we take a tarp, not a tent, and save ourselves three or four pounds.

And before we actually hoist our packs upon our backs, a third selection occurs. We substitute instant coffee for fresh, a major concession: don't want the weight of an extra pot. I hem and haw but finally I elect to take the pepper spray. For years Yellowstone Park released their problem or rogue grizzlies in this drainage. But people who have been in this country plenty say that bears, while most decidedly present, have never been much of a problem—especially not this year, when drought has chased everything out of the high country.

That absence includes, we soon discovered, sheep. After packing in five miles (including a vessel-busting climb up an avalanche chute) and setting up camp under a hardy cluster of subalpine fir, we begin glassing. For five days we combed, first casually then inch by inch, deep shadowy draws and boulder-strewn hillsides only to spot the occasional sickle-horn or barely legal ram. One such young specimen actually popped out about forty yards from where we sat, looked us over, then strolled leisurely on its way, not the least bit disturbed. "He's probably never seen a human," said Jim, "at least not one this close."

Furthermore, the morning before opening day, a rifle shot boomed from the very basin that we'd hoped to hunt the next day—not an auspicious sign. Older rams are not so forgiving as the young sickle-horn who coasted past us. Rifle shots combined with the sight of humans send them hoofing it to the protection of Yellowstone.

So at the end of the first week we gave it a rest. The weather had been unaccommodating for the last three days: rain, snow, 50-mph winds. We decided to see if this change from summer heat would coax the sheep out of hiding. We broke camp and planned to return in a week.

From the comfort of my home, I delighted in noting that more rain and snow pelted the Absarokas. Still, I worried about squandering my precious ram-hunting days. It's usually a once-in-a-lifetime affair, this sheep hunting. It's akin to winning the lottery. In the year 2000, for example, 7,013 resident and nonresident hunters applied for Wyoming's 260 sheep tags. Although I endured eight consecutive "did not draw" messages for my license, some hunters wait as long as thirty-four years. When you finally pull one, most friends cuss in jealous disgust, accuse you of being whelped rather than born, then vigorously pump your hand in congratulations.

Such a license also translates to an unparalleled opportunity to buy stuff. ("C'mon, honey. This is a once in a lifetime hunt.") Sheep tag in hand, I spent more money on hunting/outdoor accoutrements than I'd spent collectively in the previous seven years: new pack, Nikon rangefinder, a set of gossamer Gore-Tex raingear, a passel of Capilene, high-altitude stove, and box after box of premium ammo that I've been wanting to run through my .30-06.

Six days later Jim and I returned to the Absarokas to find a decidedly autumn light reflected off the limestone outcrops. Indian summer winds knocked the mottled yellow leaves from

aspen trees, bouncing them off Jim's tent like fat raindrops. Last week's 2:00 A.M. snowstorm reminded us that tarps and snow do not mix, especially when accompanied by high-elevation winds. Jim remedied that by purchasing a white, ripstop nylon, single-poled tent shaped like a teepee. It came with a small (about 8x12-inch) stainless steel collapsible stove. Tent and stove together weighed a total of 14 pounds.

But that meant, of course, that we had to forgo other items to make room for our new quarters. With great reluctance, Jim left behind key sheep-hunting tools: a spotting scope and tripod. As a substitute, he brought a doubler for his Swarovski binocular (it screws into one eyepiece), which does indeed double the magnification power of the glass. It weighs a slim 6.2 ounces.

Coyotes obliged as our alarm clock when we awoke the next morning to pack in, this time prepared for cold weather. But Mother Nature, the cunning vixen, instead delivered heat of blast furnace intensity. It was almost as if we were stalking desert sheep. The rams continued to remain elusive.

Between hunts, I'd called various sheep experts to ask their opinion on where to find rams. "The heat's driving them into the timber," was the consensus. But the timberline in the Absarokas runs from its base, about 7,000 feet, up to green pockets that manage to survive at 10,000 feet. Sheep ordinarily don't like hanging out in the trees. Unobstructed vision and steep rock faces are their defensive weapons.

I forgot sunscreen and was saved by a tube of mountain-expedition-strength balm that Jim had brought. Hour after hour we walked, then glassed, walked, then glassed. Heat waves danced in front of our binoculars. We were repeatedly fooled by rocks with sheeplike characteristics. We glassed the real estate so many times that it became almost as familiar as our living room. Any movement got our attention. We spotted elk, bear, marmots, and falcons, but few sheep. We would return to camp cooked by the sun, windblown, grit covered, and parched. My poor rifle, a faithful Ruger Number One, looked as if it had been the scratching post for a pride of lions. If ever there's a case for a synthetic stock, it's sheep hunting. Our little stream near the camp shrank daily; the alternative source for water was a l-o-n-g way down the hill.

In the day's last light, we would squint over maps, looking for new territory. The contour increments might just as well have been measured in microns. The operative word was "ugly," as in: "Man, check out the terrain of this little canyon to the southwest. That looks ugly. Seriously ugly. Just the place for older rams. Want to go look?"

The nights remained unseasonably warm. At camp, we padded about in bare feet. The pine needles felt deliciously cool under our swollen soles. A garish butter-yellow harvest moon made the barren peaks glow with neon intensity. I could tell roughly the time by the position of moonlight on the inner tent wall. We had a number of almost spookily quiet nights. And there is no silence quite so profound as the high-altitude silence when the wind shuts down. No bird songs. No water gurgling. No sighing pines. Just the resonance of breathing, your own heart struggling with the thin air, and the rustle of sleeping bags.

Yet the heat and moonlight occasionally addled the wildlife. One night around 10:30, a pair of blue or ruffed grouse roosted in the trees above the tent and commenced to coo, cluck, murmur, and generally carry on before finally thundering off.

Mornings arrived balmy, the cloudless sky the color of burnished aluminum. One afternoon we spotted two sickle-horns and a ram that was definitely legal. We hung around until dusk and "put them to bed," as the saying goes, then returned the next morning for a possible stalk. Sometime in the night, though, the big guy had chosen to move to a saddle with an expansive view of the drainage—including our approach. We were pinned. Finally the trio wandered off up an 11,200-foot peak.

A day later, we decided to head in the general direction in which the rams had disappeared. It was a steep go, probably low Class V in rock-climbing terminology, and we were mindful that the sun and high altitude had sapped our energy. Going uphill, I estimated only eighteen inches between footsteps. If we did shoot a ram in this unexplored drainage, it meant finding an alternative route out and probably an overnight bivouac.

Sure enough, once atop this peak (from where I could see both the Tetons and the Bighorn Mountains), Jim spotted three rams, perhaps the same sheep we had seen the day before. They were 450 yards directly below us, licking a snowpatch, grazing, and resting in the shade. One ram seemed to have a respectable set of horns.

Then followed a twenty-minute assessment of a possible target. While not after a Boone and Crockett, I wanted to take an older ram, one that had had its chance to contribute to the gene pool. Jim, who's shot Stone, Dall, and argali sheep, concluded that while the ram had the big body of an older animal, it was probably quite young. He studied it through the doubler, then summed it up: "Around five years old, I'd say. He's broomed off on one side to just barely legal [in this unit, Wyoming law requires a three-quarter curl on at least one horn] and about an inch past legal on the other. Pretty symmetrical set of horns."

Although the season runs to 1 November, I realistically had only three additional days to hunt. Would I get another chance? Unlikely, I finally determined. Jim, who had waited over ten years for his tag, very graciously gave me first dibs on the sheep. "You want to commit to this ram?" he asked.

"Yes."

"Good. Let's go get him," said Jim.

This mountain afforded no leisurely routes, up or down. But a quick study of the map revealed a possibly navigable avalanche chute about two hundred yards to the south. A small ridge separated us from the sheep, providing good cover. We found the chute and gingerly descended, Jim in the lead. It was highly unstable terrain, a mixed medium of scree, dirt, rocks, and boulders. Five minutes into the descent, Jim kicked out a Maytag-size geological specimen (that almost took him with it), which bounced in gravity-defying leaps until it shattered three-quarters of the way down the chute with a terrific crash.

After such a racket, my ram, I concluded, had to be approaching the Yellowstone border. But then again, the sound of falling rock is an everyday event to sheep. When I first looked over the edge of the ridge, I thought that my first assumption had been correct. No sheep. Oh well, the stalk had carried nice potential, I mused. Then, peering over the very edge, I saw the sheep bedded tight against the mountainside. We dropped our packs and prepared for a shot.

We moved three times. Finally, atop a mighty unaccommodating pile of andesite, I got comfortable enough, barely, to make a shot. Grit clung to my hands, and I had to keep wiping them off to get a proper grip on the rifle. The shot was at an acute angle, not too far from straight down. The sheep got up, stretched, then rebedded. Jim kept track of my target and kept reminding me that time was on my side because the animals had no idea of our presence.

It was a 162-yard shot. Ignoring any theory of aiming low when shooting downhill, I put the cross hairs just above the ram's shoulder joint (it was bedded down) and sent a 165-grain boattail screaming out of the taped-up barrel of my .30-06. The ram's head flopped, then it rolled out of the bed onto its back, kicked a few times, and was still.

"That's one dead f---ing ram," said Jim. Suddenly, I was very thirsty.

The other two rams just stood there, wondering what had happened. By the time we scrambled off the ridge (it took us almost fifteen minutes to reach the ram), they had bedded down beside their fallen alpha male. In a testament to the remoteness of this area, the sheep still refused to see humans as a possible danger. We almost had to chase them off with rocks. Reluctantly, they ambled down the drainage. We saw them the next day with another band.

Then the work began. We indulged in the obligatory photo session, then boned our boy out. I wanted a European mount, so we could do without the caping. Because of weight restrictions, we could not take the hide, a decision that later gave the taxidermist a near coronary.

We packed up the meat and skull, then aimed our tired bodies toward a possible bivouac site. Like an oasis rising from the sands, an ideal spot appeared within a mile. Next to a stream of bone-chilling temperature was a level spot on the lee side of a cluster of bristlecone pine and scrubby firs. Nestling giant boulders, the evergreens provided excellent protection against the weather. Various moose and elk beds gave testimony to the spot as a safe harbor. On muskegy ground Jim constructed a fire ring using large, flat stones. After the blaze got going, he arranged the sheep ribs against these rocks. The welcome sound of sizzling sheep meat rose in the still, warm air. The ribs were delicious. With the moon above us offering benediction, we ate ribs, then hurled the gnawed bones down the hill.

With eighty pounds of sheep meat lying about in Ziploc bags, a ram's head set up on a rock like a propitiation to the gods, and two bodies covered in sheep blood and coated with ram fat, the campsite was a pre-denning grizzly's wet dream. The vision of a griz's wide dished face poking around a boulder prevented much shut-eye.

At dawn I packed up the sheep and, map in hand, headed out to a trail, hoping that the cartographer knew his stuff. Jim set off back toward camp. The trip out set new pain records. My burden weighed, I'm guessing, in excess of one hundred pounds; I was making birthing noises within hours. But I didn't want to tarry. My black pack acted as a heat magnet, and I wanted to get the meat on ice as soon as possible. Five miles later, when I stumbled into a small mining district, a mine owner—up on a Saturday to work his claim—took pity on me and shuttled me the last couple of miles down to my vehicle. I found my way to Cody and to a motel room, where after scrubbing the grit and blood off my skin, I collapsed into bed.

The next day I hiked back into the mountains to help Jim break camp. Sleep deprived and his body screaming for carbohydrates, it had taken him nearly eight hours to get back to the tent. Catnaps had been obligatory along the way.

The ram's specifications were almost exactly as Jim had thought. It was about four and a half years old, too young really and certainly no candidate for any record book other than my own, as the finest hunt I'd ever undertaken, really the only record that matters. And Melville, in turns out, was at least partially correct. I discovered that the basin where I shot that ram is barely on the map. And it has no name.

DINING WITH BEARS

BY

JAMESON PARKER

It seems probable that in both confronting bears and trying to ply one's trade as an actor, a touch of fatalism is in order. Auditioning for a part couldn't be much less unsettling than facing a bear that might be bent on eating you. Fatalism does seem to underlie all the encounters with bears that Jameson Parker writes about here. Then there is irony over that, topped by humor. It almost seems as if Jameson is out to prove those famous last words attributed to more than one actor: "Dying is easy. Comedy is hard."

My troubles with bears have usually revolved around food. Theirs, not mine. Or at least a difference of opinion as to what belonged to whom. When I was sixteen, two friends and I were on a camping trip in the Shenandoah National Park in Virginia when we were attacked by a black bear with a tin can stuck on its tongue.

In many of the Eastern parks, including the Shenandoah, bears have perfected the smash-and-grab technique of the urban mugger. In fact, the smash-and-grab has been brought to such a high level of perfection in some places that force is not necessary. The bear simply walks into the campground, flexes its muscles, and the campers leave without bothering to pack up their food. That was the technique our bear had perfected.

On this bear's tongue was a can of blackberry syrup that some unhappy camper had opened with a church key; consequently, all the metal points, jutting down, had dug deeply in. Park authorities had shot the bear three times with tranquilizer darts to no effect—not as uncommon as you might imagine. Finally, realizing that death by starvation is both unkind and dangerous to campers, they hired a professional hunter to put the poor beast out of its misery and their hair. The PH knocked it down from three hundred yards with a .300 magnum, but the bear vanished into the woods before he could finish the job.

The morning of the day that we found it, the bear had decided, for reasons of its own, to walk into a farmhouse kitchen down in the valley. The farmer's wife, unaccustomed to having bears at the breakfast table, emptied a .38 revolver into it, and the bear went back into the woods and up the mountain with a total of seven slugs in it and presumably feeling rather testy.

Enter Jameson and his friends Rowland and Dieter.

It was the dogs that got our attention. We were deep in the woods, and we heard baying a few hundred yards below the trail. So we dropped our packs and went down to investigate. At the base of an old red oak were three hounds. Standing on a limb, about thirty feet up, was a large bear with a tin can on his tongue.

We were teenagers eager for adventure, and a bear with a tin can on its tongue was adventure of the highest order. We all three crowded in close to the trunk, peering up at it, discussing possibilities and options. It never occurred to us that if the thing decided to come down out of that tree we might see it a whole lot closer than any of us wanted.

Clearly, a bear with a can on its tongue was a Bear In Trouble. Clearly, we had to do something about it. As the runner in the group, I was elected to run back up the mountain to Skyline Drive— better than seven miles, I later found out—and notify the authorities.

As I started for the trail I glanced at Rowland and Dieter, still standing at the base of the tree, looking up into the branches. Thinking back, it amazes me that we could have been so incredibly stupid.

When I reached the ranger station with word of the bear, I was loaded into a Willys Jeep. As we lurched and bumped our way back, the very excited ranger told me about our bear, about its history as a mugger, and about how it had already been shot. The magnitude of what we had done, standing around the trunk of the tree with a starving, wounded bear only thirty feet over our heads, left me breathless. I had a sudden, sickening image of

Rowland and Dieter, thin red smears over the landscape. I felt as if I had prickly heat, I was so anxious.

The sun was setting by the time we pulled up next to our packs. I bailed out and ran down to the tree. Far from being red smears, Rowland and Dieter had sat down under the tree with their backs against the trunk. At some point during the afternoon the bear started to come down the trunk, and not even the dogs had heard it. About eight feet up it had stopped and peed, mostly on Dieter. Dieter was a German boy, visiting for the summer, and perhaps Germans are less tolerant of such things than we Americans. With high courage and low I.Q., he jumped up, grabbed a stick, and hit the bear on the ass. Miraculously, the bear climbed back up the tree.

The ranger listened to all this open-mouthed, all the while jockeying to keep himself upwind and as far away from Dieter as possible. We all did. Even the dogs didn't seem to want to get too near.

Then the ranger went to work. He found a place, about forty feet from the tree, where he had a clear shot. He told us to stand behind him. He leaned up against the trunk of a sapling, steadied himself, and took careful aim.

Nothing happened.

We kept waiting, looking at the bear, silhouetted against the setting sun. No shot. Finally, I looked at the ranger and in a little moment of clairvoyance, I realized that he was scared—more than scared, terrified. He was armed with a 12-gauge pump action shotgun loaded with slugs—he had told me so himself—but he was too scared to shoot.

The bear started looking around, and not in any casual way, either. This was a bear that was making plans. We could all see that. Dieter stepped up next to me—I nearly gagged—and said softly, "*Er müsst schiessen!*"

But the ranger didn't.

And then the bear took the initiative.

The speed with which that bear came down the trunk of the tree was truly unbelievable, faster than if it had jumped off the limb. It hit the ground and came right for us. The ranger fired, too late, the slug churning up dust three feet to the right of the bear, and started to run. He may have been running when he fired, for all I know. There wasn't much to do but follow his example.

It was the hounds that saved us. They lit into the bear with reckless courage, and for a moment there was a maelstrom of snarling fur. Then the bear went up another tree, the dogs leaping vainly after it.

That ranger was quick. He had gotten farther away than any of us. And he wasn't coming back.

"I'm going to get the hunter to do this. You guys stay here and keep an eye on that bear. Don't let him get away."

He turned and was gone.

Don't let him get away? Three boys with one hunting knife between them and night coming on? How did he expect us to stop that bear from getting away? Reason with it?

But we were teenagers, and this was *fun*. This was *adventure*.

It was dark before the ranger came back. He had another ranger with him and a tall, lean, hard-looking man with a rifle who, unlike the rangers, inspired me with confidence. We went down the hill by flashlight to the tree where the dogs still lounged around the base. We shone our flashlights up into the branches.

There was no bear.

Then followed all the confusion you might expect—yes, this is the tree; no, of course we didn't see it go; no, we don't know where it is; look at the dogs, they're still here—with the rangers attacking us as if we were somehow in collusion with a bear with a tin can on its tongue. It was the professional hunter who took charge, directing us to shine our flashlights up into other trees. For several minutes we all milled around in different directions, shining our lights up into the leaves with no success.

I got a rock in my shoe, and I was leaning against a tall young tree, digging around in my boot with my finger, when I realized that I could feel the trunk moving beneath my hand, just as it might in a strong wind. Only there was no wind.

We all shone our lights upward, but the foliage was too thick to see. Both rangers started pooh-poohing me, but the hunter put his hand on the trunk just as I had.

"He's up there."

He had us all back up. He told us to keep our lights on the trunk of the tree, no matter what. One of the rangers was to shoot his shotgun, loaded now with buckshot, into the branches. When the bear came down the trunk, we were to keep it in our flashlight beams until the hunter fired. He would try to kill it at the base of the trunk.

It all worked just as the hunter said it would. Almost.

The ranger fired once. Nothing. The second time the bear came down just as fast as it had earlier, but we managed to keep it in our lights. At the base of the tree it paused infinitesimally, and the hunter fired. The bullet whipped the poor beast around the trunk, and then here it came.

I was standing next to the hunter, and the bear was heading straight for us, faster than seemed possible. It had been a long, exciting day, and I had had just about all the fun I wanted. I decided I didn't wish to be part of the proceedings anymore and turned to leave.

Never run in the woods at night while looking over your shoulder. I hadn't gone three steps when I slammed into a tree so hard that it knocked me backward, toward the bear.

I had the wit to cover the back of my neck with my hands as I fell, and I curled up into the fetal position while I promised the Almighty all kinds of things I could never possibly deliver. I had my eyes clamped shut, but that bear came so close I could smell it.

Again it was the dogs that saved me, lighting into the bear almost on top of me. The dogs and the bear fought so close to me that dirt was kicked into my hair and down the back of my shirt. Then, somehow—I had dropped my flashlight, and nobody else had lingered to watch—bear and dogs rolled down the hill in a massive, snarling ball of variegated fur. They rolled together down into a clump of mountain laurel, where the bear took up its final stand.

The professional hunter prudently decided that, as long as the bear was on the ground, going after it in the dark was not the thing to do. We retreated a little ways and sat down to wait.

All night the bear and dogs went at it in the laurel. We would hear savage, primeval snarling and grunting from the bushes and occasionally a sickening *thuck* followed by a squeal of pain, and a dog would come arcing out of the bushes, land with a thud and another squeal, jump up, shake itself, and rush right back into the fray. Other times there would be long, apparently mutually agreed upon round breaks, when all the contestants would sit watchfully, panting heavily and rapidly, until some unheard ringside bell would sound and they would resume hostilities.

The end came at dawn, very anticlimactically, with a single shot. So much for putting a bear out of its misery.

Fifteen years later, I was doing some preseason scouting for an elk hunt in southwestern Colorado. It was a glorious, God-given day, and I was walking by myself along a logging road in the mountains. I was a grown man used to being by myself in the woods, and I had a .44 Magnum on my hip, for no better reason than that it made me feel macho. But suddenly, for no discernible reason, I had a major panic attack. I was terrified, my heart was racing, I was having trouble getting enough air into my lungs, I was sweating, I had to make a conscious effort to override my instinct to run. I was so scared—and so scared that I was this scared—that I actually started talking to myself, out loud.

"OK, Jameson, get a grip, calm down. Let's think about this. What's going on here? What's happening? What do you see? What do you hear? What do you sm . . ."

And I realized that I was smelling something I had smelled once before, long ago, while I lay curled in a ball in the Virginia woods.

Either a bear had just crossed the logging road, or there was a bear somewhere very close by—but I smelled it, and my body reacted before my brain knew what it was reacting to. I pulled out my .44 Magnum and cautiously went back the way I had come.

Since then I have hunted bears in different places and in different ways with a spectacular lack of success. Not just a lack of success, but with the kind of close-up, intimate contact—occurring just *after* the nick of time—that made me think that God or fate or the Infinite was having a good deal of fun at my expense.

I sat in a stand over bait in Canada and never saw anything bigger than a Labrador retriever.

But just a few months later I was filming a movie out in the sticks in British Columbia. I had a little time off and went for a walk along an abandoned railroad track. The blackberry brambles along the track were all heavy with berries and I was happily eating my way through when a bear stood up in a very unexpected manner about thirty feet away. It may have been a black bear, or it may have been a grizzly—it was about fifteen or sixteen feet tall, maybe more—but I didn't linger to examine it closely. I know all the good advice about standing your ground and speaking forcefully in a low voice, but it slipped my mind at the moment.

I live up in the mountains of central California where there are enough bears to constitute a significant minority voting block. In fact there are so many bears that when I got permission from a local rancher to hunt deer on his property, it was on the condition that I kill a bear first. I never saw anything but tracks and scat.

Yet that same year, not long after hunting season closed, my dogs woke me one night, roaring threats and imprecations at something in the backyard. There were two smallish things running around through the apple trees inside the fence. It was a dark night, and I had left my glasses in the living room, and my brain was still a little fuzzy with sleep, so for some reason I came to the conclusion that they were elk calves. For some equally obscure reason I opened the sliding glass door, stepped out onto the deck, and started down the stairs in my pajamas. When I was about halfway down there was an unmistakable *woof* from the dark, and I realized, with terrible clarity, that the two smallish things were young bears, which meant that there was a mama bear somewhere close by. Probably a very protective mama who might object to a middle-aged man in mauve striped pajamas getting overly familiar with her cubs. Bed seemed like a very desirable place to be just then, and I returned there.

I went all the way back East to spend a week running after hounds in New Hampshire. The only thing we treed was a fisher.

Yet the week after I got home from that trip, I was leaving my house one day just after lunch, and as I put my hand on the door to the garage one of the dogs insisted on being petted. I bent down to give her a smooch, and as I straightened up, I looked out the window in time to see a prehistorically large bear amble out of my garage. If I had walked in, it might have been embarrassing for both of us. It went up the walk and onto my front porch. It then proceeded to examine the house closely, as if it were a prospective buyer, before walking the entire length of the porch and off into the yard on the far side. I remembered to stand my ground this time, being safely inside. I even had the presence of mind to call to my wife, in what I still maintain was a perfectly normal voice, to bring the camera. She claims she thought Minnie Mouse was calling her.

There have been other contacts with bears, invariably out of season or in places where I didn't have a bear tag. When finally everything—bear, hunter, season, tag, rifle—came together, it was unexpected and dramatically quick.

There were three of us—Bee, Dave, and I—joining forces to help Dave's young son get a deer on his first-ever hunt. Dave had already taken his deer, so he was unarmed. I was still hoping to find a monster buck (by California standards). I had glassed just before the season opened, so I was carrying a rifle. That turned out to be a very good thing.

We ended up separating into two groups, not by choice, but rather by topographical accident. The southern Sierras are remarkably steep, and the boy, Jonathan, had worked his way down to the bottom of a very deep canyon with Bee, while Dave and I were up top. In an act of Christian mercy, we decided to get the truck and drive down to pick them up. We hiked up to the two-track and came around a curve. There was the truck, and there was the bear.

It was the size of a walk-in safe, and the way it turned to look at us made me confident that it had no intention of running—from us or from anyone. It was the same look I used to see on my opponents, during my short-lived career as the worst amateur boxer in recorded history, just before I got knocked out. It was a look that said—in addition to something about my mother that I wouldn't tolerate from a man—"I don't like your face. I don't like the way you smell. I don't like the way you dress. I don't like your haircut. I don't like a single damn thing about you, and I especially don't like your being in my neighborhood. P–s off."

In the secret life of Jameson Parker I have often fantasized about precisely this sort of do-or-die situation, how with icy nerves and blinding speed I would mount my rifle, standing my ground in front of the charging (pick one) Cape buffalo, lion, bear, rhino, or leopard before dispatching it cleanly with a single, perfectly placed shot.

Instead, I stood there with my mouth open, my rifle hanging limply and uselessly in my hand.

Dave yelled, as much out of surprise as anything else, "Hey! Get out of here!"

That bear never moved a muscle, but it did something I didn't know bears do. It actually showed its teeth and growled, a monstrous black mastiff from hell.

That stirred me to jack a round into the chamber.

"Go on! Get out of here!" Dave stepped away from me and moved around in a semicircle, keeping his truck between himself and the bear. He reached in the open window and honked the horn, yelling again, "Beat it!"

The bear kept its teeth bared and made that same quiet growl.

Dave reached farther in and turned on the engine and honked the horn once more.

Another quiet growl. It still didn't move, but this time something changed that I can neither describe nor quantify. I knew we were about to see some action.

Simultaneously, Dave said to me, "Do you have your tag on you?"

At last I came out of my stupor and raised the rifle.

The only part of my little fantasy that actually played out was the placement of the shot. It was perfect, right through the heart. Not that it did the slightest bit of good. Bears can be legally dead and remain blissfully unaware of that fact for surprisingly long periods of time. Fortunately, this bear went in the direction it was facing, which was off into a ravine, and with the safety of some forty or fifty yards between us I put two more insurance rounds into it.

When we clambered down to get a rope on it we found the dead horse it had been feeding on. Of course, if I hadn't had a rifle, it might have dined on us.

DINING WITH BEARS

Statistically, your chances of running afoul of a bear are considerably less than your chances of being struck by lightning, but if it happens it will be because there are either cubs or food nearby. If it's the bear's food, it can keep it—especially if it's a dead horse. If it's mine, I intend to share.

WILLIWAW

BY

TERRY WIELAND

The wind is no more than the wind, until it gathers into a squall—or a williwaw—and charges in to sweep down whatever is in front of it. Something similar holds for brown bears: You may cross paths a thousand times with them, without a glance between you; then there comes the 1001st time. Only one of you will be left standing afterward— and sometimes in the end, because of the way a brown bear's nervous system can absorb the shock, and postpone the consequences of a killing bullet, neither of you may be. As Terry Wieland shows, this is something he knows in both a literary and literal sense.

The good ship *Lornie B.* was riding at anchor in the lee of the storm, and riding is truly the word. Every minute or so a swell would round the long point from Prince William Sound and bear down on her, heaving the bow into the air. She would rear up, totter, and then plunge and buck as the wave swept away under the stern to savage the flock of lobster pots in the bay and finally crash onto the wet black shore. Through the porthole, beyond the point, bigger swells rolled down the sound and out to sea. The killer whales, usually dancing on the surface, were far below in the calm, dark depths.

Inside, the cabin of the *Lornie B.* smelled of damp wool. The rain drummed on the deck in a steady beat, but, after fourteen straight days, we no longer heard it. The rain was just there. It would, it seemed, always be there.

Periodically I would smear my sleeve across the porthole and peer out through the raindrops at the gray sea rolling, then settle back with my mackinaw pulled tight and pick up a book once again. After three days holed up against the storm, conversation had dwindled to nothing. All aboard the *Lornie B.* were withdrawn into their own thoughts—Dale with the barometer and the ship's radio; Linda bustling in the galley, cleaning the stove yet again; the rest of us with books or maps or just staring off.

The ship's library was limited. I had brought some Jack London—appropriate for cruising off the Alaskan coast, nosing into the fjords among the seals and whales—and Frank Hibben's account of hunting the great bears a half-century earlier. *Buck* and *White Fang* and *Wolf Larsen* occupied my time, in the bunk beside the fogged-over porthole. Only the periodic cups of coffee were in any way warm, but even they were wet. Alaska in October. What joy is mine. And cracked a book once again . . .

. . . Allen Hasselborg was a young man of 22, but already tall and assured, when he boarded a ship in Seattle in 1898 and disembarked a week later in Ketchikan. His Viking forebears in Minnesota had bequeathed him a wandering bent, and he drifted west as a mule skinner, and later a buffalo hunter, chasing what remained of the bison herds. He came to Alaska, not to pan for gold, but to hunt the great coastal bears for their pelts.

Hasselborg's hunting ground was the islands: Admiralty, Chichagof, Baranof. He shot the bears and sold their skins for $15 apiece in Ketchikan, a small enough reward for the hardships and the danger involved. Aside from the bears themselves, there was the cold grey sea and the Alaska storms, but Hasselborg was at home here. When Frank Hibben sailed up the coast in the 1930s to hunt Alaska brown bears, he found Hasselborg quietly ensconced in a lonely cabin on Mole Harbor, on Admiralty Island, where he homesteaded in 1900. A difficult man as only hermits can be difficult, tall, gaunt, and bearded, never seen without a pack on his back and a rifle in his hand, Hasselborg looked to Hibben "like a prophet in hip waders." But Hasselborg took a liking to the young college professor and big-game hunter, and guided him to a big brown bear on Admiralty, climbing into the interior through the dripping foliage, camping in the rain.

"I haven't killed a bear in twenty years," he told Hibben. There was a reason for that.

The rain was still rolling by in clouds, hammering the sea into submission, but the weather reports were becoming friendlier. Rain was not the problem—hell, one year it rained here for sixty-three days straight. It was that wind! But small-craft warnings were now tempered with promises of lower seas to come.

Dale stood up suddenly.

"If we're gonno do 'er, let's do 'er."

We weighed anchor and hauled the bow around until it was facing due south—due south and Montague Island, the long, spiny mountain range that protects Prince William Sound from the worst of the North Pacific. Montague Island, home of the deadly *williwaw*, and (sometimes) deadlier Montague Island bears.

Montague was discovered by Captain James Cook in 1778. Later, Captain George Vancouver took shelter in the lee of Montague Island and discovered—accidentally and to his dismay—the phenomenon known as the williwaw. His ships, riding at anchor in Port Chalmers, a bay on the inland shore, and protected, he thought, from the North Pacific, were struck by a horrific wind that came barreling down the mountain, sweeping all before it, snapping masts, ripping ships from their anchor chains, and driving the craft onto the rocks.

The williwaw is sudden and deadly—a unique phenomenon wherein the wind off the Pacific builds up against the mountains that run the length of Montague, finally spilling over the top and roaring down the lee slope like an avalanche.

Four hours after leaving the shelter of Naked Island, four hours of dodging drifting logs in three-foot swells, the *Lornie B.* limped into Port Chalmers and dropped anchor. It was raining. It was always raining.

Charles Sheldon was the first on record to hunt Alaska brown bears on Montague Island. He landed here in 1905 and took several specimens he believed exhibited unique characteristics—thick, chocolate-brown fur, and noses that were distinctly turned up. Sheldon took five bears, and later wrote about his experiences in The Wilderness of the North Pacific Coast Islands.

Three years later, the Alexander Expedition arrived to study all the flora and fauna of Montague Island. The leader was Annie M. Alexander. She and her hunter took several more bears, and she called the Montague Island subspecies Ursus arctos sheldoni *after the man who had taken the first recorded specimens.*

Alexander's contract hunter viewed all this with some bemusement. His name was Allen Hasselborg.

At one time, when the biological "splitters" were in their heyday, there were some seventy-six subspecies of grizzly bear and eleven different Alaska brown bears; then the splitters gave way to the "lumpers," and the arcane and often trivial distinctions were swept away. Today, science recognizes only two types of grizzlies and browns: the Kodiak bear, and all the rest. That they are no longer distinctly *Ursus arctos sheldoni* probably matters not to the brown bears of Montague Island, since their remote little tribe has already been watered down through intermarriage with bears that swam over from Hinchinbrook Island, or troublemaking bruins captured on the mainland and sent there to get them safely away from civilization.

The days when Alaska brown bears were casually killed for invading someone's backyard are long since gone, and today even self-defense is rigidly defined. For example, the limit on black-tailed deer along the coast is five per hunter. On Kodiak, and elsewhere, bears have learned that the sound of a rifle shot can mean a free lunch, and they will come running to drive a hunter off his deer and take it for themselves. Killing a bear in defense of your deer is no longer acceptable. You have a limit of five and there are lots of deer, say the game wardens; go shoot yourself another, and let the bear dine in peace.

Of course, self-defense works two ways, and the bears have no doubts whatever about their rights in that regard.

Allen Hasselborg was a man in his prime when he sailed into Chichagof Island's Basket Bay one day in 1918. He had built the small boat himself, with a tiny cabin and a cookstove. It was massive and solid—a one-man boat for heavy seas— and Hasselborg was powerful enough to handle it on his own. He anchored offshore where it would still be afloat when the

233

tide went out, with a draw-line to a tree in the event he returned at high tide. It is a system still used by bear guides along the Alaska coast. With his boat secure, Hasselborg turned inland through the tall, wet grass, skirting a large beaver swamp. He was following a trail when he came upon the fresh track of the largest bear he had ever seen. The footprint was more than eighteen inches long and he could only imagine the size of the beast.

As he approached a dam, he spotted what appeared to be a small bear dozing in the grass, but then it moved and revealed itself to be, not a small bear, but the hump of a truly immense bear, snuffling and feeding, and occasionally raising its head to look around.

Mesmerized by its size, Allen Hasselborg began a lengthy stalk, moving silently in his hip boots through the shallow water of the beaver swamp. As he closed in, his rifle across his chest, his toe jarred an alder branch wedged in the mud. It kicked loose in a shower of water. The bear's head came up. Seeing Hasselborg only fifteen yards away, the bear charged. The rifle came up and fired and the bear went down, blowing blood, and slumped in a motionless heap. Hasselborg sloshed to dry land and leaned his rifle against a bush. Excited by the thought of a huge pelt that would bring twice the normal price in Ketchikan, he forgot all the rules of bear hunting he had learned in his twenty years on the Alaska coast, and turned, knife in hand, to start skinning.

Hasselborg found himself confronted by a wet, black wall. The bear was towering over him—a bear twice the height of Hasselborg, who was himself well over six feet. The bear's head was as big as a washtub, and his immense jaws gaped open in a nightmare of frothy blood and yellow-white teeth. His front paws, with their six-inch claws, hung before Hasselborg's astonished eyes.

Looking doom in the face, the hunter turned and dived into the muck, burrowing down, protecting his head with his arms, and preparing for the mauling he knew was to come. The bear's first pass with his claws tore away Hasselborg's shirt and belt, and he felt the bear's head come down close to his shoulder. Its breath was hot with rotting salmon as the jaws spread and the teeth sank into Hasselborg's shoulder. He later recalled the strange sensation of the teeth scraping along bone and the sound—the distinct ripping sound—of his shoulder being torn away before he lost all consciousness.

There are many myths about the great bears of the north, not least of which is the myth of size. It is generally conceded that a Kodiak bear can run 1,500 pounds, or three-quarters of a ton, and a big one—a truly huge one today—squares 11 feet. The "square" is calculated by adding the nose-to-tail measurement and the paw-tip to paw-tip measurement, and then dividing by two. When we hunted Alaska in October 1988, Dale told me that the average Alaska brown bear taken then squared 7½ feet.

Scientists today insist that grizzlies and Alaska brown bears may have some genetic differences from region to region, but they are essentially the same bear. Any variation in size is attributable to differences in diet, with a bear that eats fat salmon all year on the coast inevitably growing to be considerably more hefty than one that ekes out a living on berries and marmots on the high mountain slopes and hibernates half the year.

The difference between a 600-pound grizzly and a 1,500-pound Alaska brown is huge on a weigh scale, but it's not so significant when one is intent on eating you. The jaws look immense regardless.

All the coastal bears love to eat salmon, but that is not their sole diet. The salmon are available only when they are swimming up the rivers to spawn, and there are far more bears than there are river drainages. Bears are territorial; the bigger bears get the prime salmon grounds and the better diet, which makes them bigger and more able to protect their territory. The rich get richer, while the poor become hungrier, testier, and more ready to attack and eat anything they can get, responding to the prospect of an easy meal with quick and deadly determination.

Hasselborg regained consciousness some hours later. He never knew how many hours. One shoulder was useless. Blood lay around him in huge clots, like chunks of raw liver. Of the huge bear, there was no sign. The rifle was broken, crushed in the huge jaws. Hasselborg slowly gained his feet and began to stagger the two miles back to his boat. Several times during the journey, he passed out. Each time, he would come to and struggle on, and eventually he reached the shore on his knees and one good arm. There, he confronted another problem: The tide was in; the water was chest-deep at the boat; he was unable to climb over the gunwale. He slept on the beach that night and into the next day.

Finally, he was able to pull the boat into water shallow enough that he could clamber in, where he passed out once again from the effort. Now, he found himself a prisoner of his own anchor chain. It was almost forty-eight hours since the bear attack. His cheeks were sunken and he was becoming weaker by the hour. With only one good arm, he could not budge the anchor. Wrapped in a blanket like iron with clotted blood, shivering in the incessant rain, Hasselborg tried to heat some soup but could not master the cookstove. He slept once more, knowing that when he awoke he would have to break free of the anchor or die where he was.

In desperation, he looked over the boat he had built himself, a man facing death and surveying his possessions one last time. His eye fell on his ax, still razor-sharp as he meticulously kept it. Taking the ax in his one good hand, bracing himself for the pain, summoning all his remaining strength, he raised the ax over the anchor chain where it dug into the gunwale, and directed one despairing blow.

The next day, a small boat drifted into a bay by the Indian village of Hoonah. Slumped unconscious in the stern was Allen Hasselborg, still wrapped in the soggy, bloody blanket.

From that day, Allen Hasselborg was never without a pack on his back—something for the bear to rip for. As he said, "One bite is enough." And a rifle in his hand—never, ever, out of reach.

And, for reasons he never explained to anyone, he never again hunted Alaska brown bears.

Dale and I eased ashore on Montague Island with backpacks and rifles. We pulled the inflatable boat up onto the rocks, secured it, and headed inland.

We had lost the toss. There were two bear hunters on the *Lornie B.*, but only one river drainage with a late-season run of silver salmon, and room on it for only one hunter and his guide. That left Dale and me to improvise.

"Best way I know to find bears is to go hunt something else," Dale said. "Let's climb the mountain and camp. We'll hunt deer and see what turns up. With bears, you just never know."

Deer calling, as it is done in Alaska, is an arcane art unknown elsewhere in North America. It is not like rattling, which depends on the urgencies of the rut and the desire to fight. Calling with the coastal Alaskan's homemade deer call works at all times of the year, on deer of both sexes and all ages.

Dale cut a green branch from a tree, then split a six-inch chunk lengthwise and hollowed out a shallow gap in the middle. He stretched a piece of electrical tape across the gap, sandwiched it between the two pieces, and taped them firmly together at the ends. The tape down the center acted as a reed; he put the call to his mouth like a harmonica and blew across it. The sound was somewhere between a snort and a wheeze; Dale blew it thoughtfully a half-dozen times, then dismantled the call, stretched the reed more tightly, reassembled it, and blew again. Satisfied this time, he tucked the call into his pocket and we continued on.

"You need to make a new one each time," he told me. "The tape dries out. Then the tone is wrong."

"What do the deer think it is?"

"I don't know," said Dale, shrugging. "A wounded fawn, maybe. I've had does come in so hard, they run right over me. But it calls bucks, too. All I know is, it works."

Montague Island is long and narrow, with one long mountain down the center like a spine. The coastal meadow is a couple of miles wide, running from the shore to the base of the mountain, waving with yellow-brown wet grass and dotted with clumps of trees and alders. The landscape is gently menacing in its wet silence.

The mountain slope comes upon you suddenly. One minute you are on level ground, the next, you are climbing up the slippery grass and trying not to touch the devil's club that invites your grasp and waits to bite. At the base of the mountain, there were two deer trails intersecting where a creek bubbled down, and a clump of brush.

"Let's see if we can't get one here," Dale murmured, settling down in the cover. I sat beside him. We were facing the trails and the mountain slope. My .300 Weatherby was in my hands, Dale's .338 across his knees. He raised the deer call and blew a long, low moan. Then another. And a third, deliberately weaker. Then we waited. Dale looked to the right while I kept an eye to the left. Neither of us looked behind. He raised the call again.

No sooner had the sound died away than a movement above and in front of us caught my eye, and I saw a huge black-brown ball barreling down the slope at a dead run. It was coming straight down toward the trails, the creek, and the thicket where we sat. I nudged Dale, who turned his head and snapped, "Take him!"

The rifle came up, caught a patch of black in the scope, and I pulled the trigger. The shock of the blast caused Dale to jerk his trigger and shoot wide. The bear spun, stung by my bullet, which had hit its collarbone and disintegrated. My second shot grazed it as it whirled, but Dale's second went in behind the ribs and ranged up into its chest. Shocked, the bear stopped, broadside now, and its huge jaw dropped open to roar as only an enraged brown bear can roar.

My cross hairs settled on its neck, and I pulled the trigger. The bear hit the ground with never a sound. It lay seventeen yards from where we sat. In the space of thirty seconds we had become the richest men on earth. The bear had come like a williwaw, and we were still alive.

In November of 1988, just one month after we left Montague, a party of hunters from Juneau crossed the channel to Baranof Island to hunt deer. They split up, with one of their number going off by himself. He sat down on a log and pulled out his deer call.

Some hours later, when he had not returned, his companions began a search. They found the log where he had been sitting, and the unmistakable signs of the Alaska brown bear that, attracted by the call, had come up behind him, killed the hunter, devoured part of his body, and carried off the rest. Too frightened to search further, they returned to town and raised the alarm.

The next day, a search party returned from Juneau determined to hunt the bear down and recover the hunter's remains. Three of the men lost their nerve and remained behind, while a game warden and another man followed the bear's trail. The bear, however, was not about to give up. He stalked the three men as they sat, attacked them, and was towering over one of them when the warden, attracted by shouts and gunfire, hurried back and shot the bear.

Allen Hasselborg dwelt alone on Admiralty Island until the summer of 1955 when, at the age of seventy-nine, destitute and too weak to live by himself any longer, he was taken in by the Pioneers' Home in Sitka. The strain of living with other people— and without his beloved bears—for the first time in a half-century must have been too much. He died, six months later, on 19 February 1956.

Frank C. Hibben had by that time published his book *Hunting American Bears*. It was dedicated *"To Allen Hasselborg, of Admiralty Island, the one human who has come the closest to knowing all there is to know about bears. . . ."* Why did Allen Hasselborg never hunt bears again after his dreadful encounter? It was not fear of the bears, for he chose to live among them as close as a man could. We will never know, now, for he never explained it to anyone.

As the *Lornie B.* plowed her way back across Prince William Sound toward the Valdez Arm—home, safety, and a dry bed that did not toss in the night—I climbed up to the foredeck and looked to the southeast. A fine mist hung over the sound, not quite rain, not quite fog, and not going anywhere. At times I could just make out Hinchinbrook Island, or thought I could. Admiralty and Chichagof were many miles south of that again. Killer whales danced in the waves, which were friendly and slapping the sides of the *Lornie B.*, instead of trying to swamp her or dash her to bits. Montague Island receded until I could make out only the snow-covered, very highest peaks. Finally, even those dissolved into the clouds and were gone.

As I stood up top, with the mist in my face and beading on my wool mackinaw, I wondered about Allen Hasselborg and Frank Hibben, about Annie Alexander and Charles Sheldon. Even about

Cook and Vancouver. About the unexpected. About williwaws and the great bears and tall ships driven onto the rocks. Jack London. Buck and White Fang and Wolf Larsen. Wolf Larsen would have liked it here. Now, doesn't that say it all?

THE BIGGEST DEER IN THE WORLD

BY

MARK T. SULLIVAN

It seems a curious ability to take the hunting knowledge acquired in the whitetail woods of Vermont and Montana and transfer it to the rain forest of southeastern Alaska, but that is what Mark Sullivan did. It is similar to what he has done with all that he has learned over the years in the outdoors, carrying it over into a substantial body of adventurous novels. The salient fact he brought with him into this piece is that for all its size, the moose remains a deer, pure but maybe not so simple.

The Bering glacier loomed six miles in front of us, an earth-churning ice machine that supercooled the coming rain. Fifty-knot gusts lashed the cloud of sleet at us, over the last blue ice at the moraine, across a river silver with silt and salmon, across tens of thousands of acres of mud flats, flooded meadows, and tag alder jungles separating the glacier from the Gulf of Alaska, twelve miles to our south.

"Hold on tight, this squall's gonna hit us right in the chops," growled Marcus East, a lanky, dour man with a copper beard and an absolutely uncanny ability to spot game in cold rain forests.

East and I were sixty feet up in a soaking-wet, moss-coated spruce tree that towered over a two-mile by five-hundred-yard oblong maze within the greater swamp. It was sheer madness: We had no safety belts and no time to climb down before the microburst struck. Following East's lead, I hooked my arms around branches and braced my legs on two stout limbs.

The wind reached us first, whipping the alders far below us into a raging olive sea. Seconds later the frozen rain pinged off the Gore-Tex and commercial fishing gear we wore head to toe. The tree began to lurch, buck, and sway, and I wondered what in God's name my wife would say if she could see me now.

Frickin idiot came to mind. So did, *You could have taken me to Tahiti with the money, but no, you had to go to Alaska and sit in a tree!*

Common sense dictated that East and I turn our backs to the gale, hug the tree, and pray for divine intervention. Instead, we jammed our spines against the spruce trunk, dipped the hoods of our rain jackets into the wind, and squinted against the driving sleet, trying our damndest to focus on one particular swell in the churning alder chaos, eighty yards out and sixty feet below. We were chattering. Our hands were numb. But there was no way we were taking our attention off that spot— one of the biggest deer in the world was lurking right there in that little patch of swamp.

Every once in a while we'd catch flashes of it: its blackened hump scarred from fighting, the pendulous bell dangling below its chin, one monstrous left antler with an obscenely wide paddle and at least seventeen points, five of which jutted off the brows, one of which hung like a club near the eye.

A drop-tined Alaska-Yukon bull moose. Bring on the hurricane. There was no way this frickin idiot was leaving the tree, even when the big gusts struck and I feared being blown out. Hanging on for dear life, I kept myself sane by reminding myself of the photograph of my great uncle that had gotten me into this predicament.

When I was eight, my mother got a Christmas card from her uncle that included a black-and-white snapshot of him and an Indian guide crouched beside a giant moose in a foggy swamp. Both men looked exhausted but happy. Indeed, I've never seen a picture that evoked a sense of adventure more than that one. I was born into a whitetail-deer-hunting family in Vermont, but right then I knew someday I'd go to Alaska as my great uncle had and hunt the biggest deer in the world.

For the next thirty-five years, I read up on Alaska-Yukon moose, their territory, and the men who specialize in hunting them. For a long time I figured I'd never be able to raise the money to go, but then a miracle happened and one of my books was purchased for film. My wife wanted to celebrate by going to Tahiti. I wanted moose. By then I'd already chosen where I'd go if I ever had the chance: the swamps around the Bering and Tsiu Rivers east of Cordova, Alaska. The region accounts for roughly twenty of the top one hundred Alaska-Yukon bull moose scored in the Safari Club system (total inches of antler with no deductions), including the number one moose of all time.

In 1999, on the Okalee Spit west of the Tsiu River, within what is known as the Bering Unit, Michigan hunter Debra Card shot the largest racked moose ever measured. She killed the bull on opening morning that year. The rack was 75 inches wide, had 56 points, and measured an astounding 731⅛ inches.* Marcus East, the lunatic in the tree with me, had been Card's guide.

Few men know the behemoths of the Tsiu country as well as Marcus East and his boss, Sam Fejes, an Alaskan master guide and outfitter who has been flying and hunting the region since his early teens. His uncle flew the mail route across the vast sodden wilderness between the Chugach Mountain Range and the Gulf of Alaska and would drop his nephew off to hunt there for days at a time. Soon Fejes's knowledge of the Tsiu became legendary among serious hunters. So there was no question about whom I'd hire to organize the hunt after I'd sold the movie and pulled a limited-entry tag for bull moose in the Bering Unit.

Fejes picked me up in Cordova in late September of 2001. I'd had a tense week after September 11, wondering if I'd be able to fly at all. But things had worked out, and we flew east in his De Havilland Beaver, one of the classic Alaska bush pilot aircraft, toward his base camp near the Tsiu. We soared across mud flats and river courses, over bays choked with floating ice, over flooded thickets thousands of yards wide. To the north, glaciers swept down from 13,000-foot mountains. To the south, surf pounded a gray-sand coastline that was deserted for forty miles.

"It's rugged country," Fejes said, in one of the biggest understatements I ever heard. "But it takes rugged country to hold an animal as big as the one you're after."

*According to the Safari Club International scoring system.

Upon arrival at base camp, he cautioned me not to expect to see many bulls during my hunt. Despite the area's reputation as a hot spot for gigantic moose, the Alaskan government does not categorize the Bering Unit as a trophy hunt. Instead, the state allows twenty-five residents and five nonresidents a "subsistence" or meat hunt in the area. To get their moose meat, the locals use Everglades-style airboats to go deep into the Bering Unit. Fejes vehemently opposes the use of the boats, calling it unfair chase, but he has not been able to convince the government to ban the practice. Airboat hunters killed twenty moose in the nine days before I arrived. The big bulls, Fejes said, were hiding deep in the alder thickets with their cows, behaving like pressured whitetail deer.

"It'll be tough," he warned me. "But if you're willing to hunt hard, the rewards here can be huge."

That afternoon after a hot meal, I hopped into a Super Cub with Marcus East, and we went flying. Within an hour, we'd spotted a very big bull in the northern reaches of the Bering Unit. It was not particularly wide by Tsiu standards—in the mid-60s—but it was massive, with many points and a drop tine off the left paddle. I wanted to hunt it.

Before dusk, Fejes flew East and me to a sandbar in the Bering River, several thousand yards from where we had seen the bull. We waded to shore in hip boots, our gear held high overhead. Then we climbed the bank, crossed a brown bear trail, and used machetes to hack our way into the thick, dank alder jungle that lined the river. By sundown we had set up a spike camp with tent, fly, and tarp.

"Where's your lover?" East asked me at one point.

"Huh?"

"Your lover," he repeated, thrusting his chin toward his .375 H&H. "This place is crawling with bears. Keep your lover with you at all times."

My .300 Winchester did not leave my side the rest of the trip. Shortly after dark, it began to drizzle. Within an hour the drizzle had turned into a downpour that lasted all night, and by dawn it was a deluge. Around 9:00 the next morning, the storm had abated by several degrees, and we donned fleece, wool, Gore-Tex, hip

boots and commercial fishing bibs, coats, and gloves. We began to slither, slop, and chop our way northeast through the dripping alders toward the big bull's last known position.

An hour later we reached the edge of a flooded, foggy meadow several miles long and as wide again. Across the vast expanse we could make out the shadows of other alder jungles.

East pointed to a nearby spruce and whispered, "We're on as flat a piece of ground as you're ever likely to see. The only way to spot moose in this country is by climbing."

And so it went throughout the day. We'd climb a tree in our rubber gloves, take a long look around with our binoculars, then forge out into the flooded reeds, heads bent against the driving rain, peeking into the fingers of the vast meadow. Where the cursed airboats had crossed, our legs sank to mid-thigh in the stirred-up muck. We walked for miles in the stuff. At dark, we returned to the spike camp exhausted and drenched. We had not seen or heard a single moose.

It rained hard again that night but slowed before dawn, and we set out. East was interested in a line of spruce trees that towered over an alder tangle four thousand yards to the northeast, and we headed toward it. Some hours later, we found ourselves in a glen where the ground and the trunks of the gnarled spruces were covered in spongy black-green moss that put me in mind of a Hobbit hole. Winding through the moss were trails beaten deep and muddy by hoofs as big as a Clydesdale's. The alders that lined the glen had been stripped and frayed by giant antlers. A musky perfume hung in the air near huge ovals that looked like whitetail scrapes, only magnified. East got on his knees, sniffed, and grinned.

"Moose," he said.

We left our guns and packs at the bottom of the biggest tree and climbed it. The breeze was strong but the rain had stopped, and we had a clear view of a second flooded plain that ran out toward the glacier. East spotted our bull almost immediately—it was traipsing after a cow in the alders, 150 yards from the spruce.

We climbed down and eased into a finger meadow that ran from the spruce glen to the alder thicket. East used a moose shoulder bone to rake tree branches and grunt-called to the bull.

But the breeze had become a steady wind, and our calls were drowned out within fifty yards.

We crawled back up the big spruce and relocated the bull just as the microburst of gale-driven sleet hit. For more than an hour I rode the tree, petrified, trying to keep track of the bull's location and not think of Tahiti. We lost it for more than fifteen minutes, only to have it appear in an opening right out in front of us at less than sixty yards. Then, just as suddenly as it had come, the wind died and the glacier emerged from the gray clouds again. East motioned that we should get back down the tree. We got to the bottom, weak-kneed from the experience, and eased forward to where we could look back out at the narrow maze of alders where the bull hid.

East grunted and used the shoulder bone again. We heard a tremendous crash and then nothing. East scrambled back up the tree and then came down fast.

"That bull's a lover, not a fighter," he said. "He's moved off about a hundred yards. Maybe if we can get your gun up the tree, you can shoot him from up there, whitetail style."

It took us ten minutes to get my .300 safely into position and reloaded. East balanced on a limb behind me and braced me by holding my jacket while I rested the rifle over a branch. All I could see was the bull's neck and drop-tined rack. Under ordinary circumstances, I would have attempted the shot. But the wind had stirred again, and I could not keep the sights steady. The bull disappeared.

We didn't see the bull the next day or the morning after that. By then it had been pouring on and off for nearly four days. Our equipment was so wet that it was unusable, a situation that made the difficulties and dangers of coastal Alaskan moose hunting profoundly clear. If the temperatures dropped, we'd be facing hypothermia.

At noon on the fourth day, Fejes flew us back to base camp. We took a hot shower and dried our equipment in a shed designed for that task. By late afternoon, Fejes was urging us to finish our hot meal and grab our gear; he'd been flying all afternoon and had seen the drop-tined monster again, lying out in the flooded meadow northwest of the big spruce.

We flew back to the Bering River for the fourth night of the hunt and re-erected our camp in the alders. Long before dawn we started to feel our way north through the jungle, gripping our lovers, intent on being at the big spruce at first light while avoiding the brown bears feeding on silver salmon in the river. In the pitch black, we jumped a moose that grunted and lumbered around us in a large half-circle. We heard its hoofs splash and then fade, until all was silent.

The entire fifth day we sat in our perch, sixty feet up in the big spruce. We listened to the chortle of ravens and watched bald eagles soar. We saw a young bull trot the entire length of the flooded meadow in minutes. But we never saw the drop-tined bull.

Right around dusk, shortly after we'd stumbled back into camp, we heard splashing in the river. We sneaked to the bank and through our binoculars saw a brown bear wading along the opposite shore, fishing for salmon.

"Bear!" East yelled. "You stay over there now. This is our side."

We slept with our lovers right along side our sleeping bags all night.

On the sixth morning, we once again made the long trek through the muck and reeds to the spruce, climbed up and sat there for seven long hours. The only moose we saw was a yearling cow chewing on alder shoots.

"What do you think?" I asked East as we shouldered our packs for the long slog back to the tent. "Should we ask Sam to move camp?"

"He's gonna fly over and talk to us by radio before dark," East said. "Let's see what he says."

For the next hour we pushed our way through the thickets and waded across the weed-choked bogs, hoping against hope to see the drop-tined bull. In the six days afield, I'd noticed again and again how Alaskan-Yukon moose seemed just like the whitetails I'd grown up hunting, in the way they would rub trees, make scrapes, and move hot cows into thick cover. They were just deer. The biggest in the world, but deer nonetheless.

But by the time we were almost across the last flooded meadow and to the dense alders that lined the Bering River, I figured that we were never going to see the drop-tined monster again. It must have moved off, I told myself, trolling the vast swamp in search of other cows.

The rain stopped. The clouds broke, and the snow-clad peaks of the Chugach appeared all around us. I halted my march to take it all in and smiled. I told myself that even if I didn't get a bull, I had enjoyed the kind of adventure I'd imagined as a little kid looking at a snapshot of his great uncle—and that was what counted.

By the time I began slogging again, East was sixty yards ahead of me, almost to the tree line. I stumbled up out of the water grass onto a firm, mossy spot between another spruce glen and a thicket of alders twenty feet high.

That's when I heard the crash, off to my right. I stopped, got up my gun, and for some reason did not think "Bear!" Instead, I listened intently, heard a second crash, and then the unmistakable grunt of a rutting bull moose.

"He's coming out of there," I called to East.

My next thought was, *It's just a big, big deer.* And if I'd learned anything over the years hunting timber bucks back East and in Montana, where I now live, it was that when big deer are jumped in dense cover, they often run at an angle to danger, watching their backtrail. So I started running at an angle, too, sprinting through the muck back toward the flooded meadow I'd just left, chambering a round in the Winchester as I went.

I reached the edge of the meadow, thumbed off the safety, and got the gun up just as a cow moose broke free of the alder tangle at 70 yards. Then a bull crashed out at 125 yards. This was the first time I'd seen an Alaska-Yukon bull from ground level and in the open, and it was so titanic that it took my breath away. I thought, *That's just not possible!*

It slowed to a trot and swung its head toward the cow, revealing the drop tine. The cross hairs of my scope found the bull's front shoulder. I led it and fired, hitting it in the heart. The moose lurched to a halt, wobbled, and I fired again. It took one more step, then collapsed on the only reasonably dry ground in a solid square mile.

I stood there, absolutely stunned at my reversal of fortune. Suddenly East grabbed me around the shoulders, and we started yelling and giving each other high-fives. When I could think straight, we walked toward the fallen monster. I knelt beside it in complete awe and held its great rack in my hands.

I know it sounds corny, but my heart swelled and my eyes misted over, because it was only at that moment that I fully understood the exhaustion, reverence, and elation my great uncle must have felt so long ago at the end of his adventure hunting the biggest deer in the world.

FOLIAGE AND FIRST BLOOD

BY

SAMUEL WESTERN

Sam Western, in his second appearance in this anthology, could very well be toying with the reader with this title, which might be taken as a metaphor for a son. Certainly there is a son, and a father in the piece, and what is not a little remarkable is Sam's avoiding the temptation to romanticize either, or the relationship they share. Except that "romanticize" is the wrong word, with "sentimentalize" coming closer. It is almost impossible to continue hunting in this time without some sense of the romantic, even, or especially, if that hunting is primarily for meat, and involves a son.

The scrawled blue ink scribble on my son's hand reads: *get homework.* For the first time in his life, I've removed my son from books and classrooms so that we could hunt together. He was two years old when I first entered the draw for a moose tag in Wyoming's Bighorn Mountains. Now he is fourteen, and I've finally got that permit. To share the experience with him seemed only natural. Pulling him from school, however, required him to complete all school work in advance of playing hooky—hence the crude epidermal notebook.

By ten o'clock, opening morning tedium sets in. He's been gently protesting the hunt since I roused him at 5:15. "God doesn't even get up this early," he said, slurping his hot chocolate.

Walking toward our hunting area in the dark, his size thirteen feet *whap* the hard ground like Sasquatch. He scuffs the dirt. His legs are longer than mine, and he puts them to use, moving out quickly. The concept of walking slowly, listening, and glassing a meadow as dawn turns up the solar rheostat is alien to him. He is fourteen and has got to move.

Ice creeps around the edges of a stream we cross. He pauses to bust it. As shadows turn to light, I put the binocular on willows around a bog. He balances on the peaks between frozen ruts.

What is he thinking about, I wonder. Girls and Pepsi and salt-and-vinegar potato chips. Or maybe he's thinking about how in camp last night his dad gave him a beer to drink around the fire and how, since dad forgot an ax and we couldn't split kindling, the paint thinner inadvertently left in the back of the Land Cruiser made an excellent fire starter.

I am not optimistic about the morning's chances. Although scouting the previous week revealed a grand set of tracks, three bow hunters for elk we chanced to meet the previous night said they had seen no moose in this drainage. Still, I wanted to show my son the importance of following up on scouting.

Besides, I don't really mind a barren drainage this morning. In twenty-plus years of living in Wyoming, I can't recall a fall of such color. We haven't had one of those September storms that strip a crown clean in a matter of minutes. The aspen leaves have a reddish tint, swirling in veins among the yellow, shaming any maple. The beauty invokes reverie.

"Dad."

"Umm?"

"What are you doing?"

"Looking at the trees."

"Again?"

Four hours of hunting bring great vistas and a lesson in tree morphology. We marvel at how the branches of blown down, but not dead, Douglas fir have taken over the growth duties from the main trunk. We delight in finding two patches of ground raked clean by bears searching for roots.

But no moose or moose sign. My son displays signs of advanced boredom and asks if he can push over a rotting tree.

"No. Moose could hear that two miles away."

"Pal-e-e-e-ze? We're never going to get anything this morning."

I look at him: 6 foot, 2 inches, and almost 200 pounds, a mass of copper hair upon his head but the red cheeks of a cherub. I tell him he has chink peaks. He pauses for a moment, gets the spoonerism, then gives me a grin of braces and a guffaw. I realize for the umpteenth time how much I love this kid and love this age of discovery.

I give up and resign myself that hunting is over for the morning. Besides, the bow hunters last evening told of seeing a bull in a drainage not twenty minutes away that was B&C material. "I'd say at least fifty-six inches," said one hunter of his rack. I'm prepared to pull up the tent and go look for him.

I relent on the fir. "Sure. Go ahead."

After considerable effort, he succeeds and the snag crashes into a bed of cones. He jumps up and down. "This is cool!"

He pushes over another one. Then just for good measure he chucks rocks at a massive old-growth spruce and revels in the hollow *thwack*.

We come across new elk sign, tracks made in haste—and no wonder, with all the racket we are making.

Not half a mile from camp, I catch a movement in a meadow up ahead and to my astonishment see a bull moose trotting up the hill. It disappears into the timber.

I cuss and tell my son to shush.

A cow hastily follows the bull but stops halfway up the hill and turns to inspect the noisemakers. For five minutes, she stares at us. I'm partly behind a tree, so I can signal my son to be still. Soon enough the bull comes back into the meadow, more interested in the cow than in us.

It's only a modest-size bull, I'm guessing about three or four years old.

This is what goes through my head:

What about that fifty-six-incher? It took you a dozen years to get this tag. Chances of your getting another, especially another tag in which both you and your son can hunt together, is close to nil. You have a whole month to fill this one.

No, you don't. In ten days you've got to go guide for two weeks. You won't get to see your son but for a few days. You took him out of school for a day. You won't do that again. Furthermore, moose hunting wisdom says to get your animal in the first couple of days of the season. "I don't know what happens to them," said one of the bow hunters we spoke to the night before, who'd shot two moose with a bow. "They just disappear."

Man, that moose sure would be good eating.

Affirmative.

He's close to a road. You could probably drive the Land Cruiser to him.

Wimp.

Don't be wimping me, jack. This guy weighs eight hundred pounds.

Yet this line makes the most logic: *The most important aspect of this hunt is not an entry in the B&C book. It is to make a kill with your son.*

The cow finally gets nervous and runs away. The bull follows, but I grunt. It stops like a dog that has come to the end of its leash.

The bull humps up from the impact of the bullet; then its front knees buckle. But it collects itself and then stands still. I had missed the heart, damn it, but gotten the lungs. I wait for it to fall, but instead it turns to face me to see if, before it collapses, it can figure out what caused that awful sound. If alone, I would have just waited for it to buckle. It would be dead before the magpies—a rifle shot their dinner bell—flicker into the pines. But my son's presence urges me to reduce any suffering. So I shoot it again, front on. The moose wheels and buckles. All four legs go this time. Wasting a bullet, I shoot it a third time on the ground. It rolls down the hill.

I'm grateful for a cool morning, lots of light, and an open meadow providing an uncramped space for the task ahead. My son sizes up the job, frowns in disapproval, and immediately suggests we get the Land Cruiser to maneuver the critter into gutting position. I counter that sweat equity, if properly employed, would do the job. It does.

When I slit open the belly my son, who is holding the legs, turns away.

"That is disgusting, Dad. A knife cutting moose hair and hide is not one of my favorite sounds."

He is not at all enthusiastic about the gutting job. The prospect of getting blood on his pants hardly seems manly. So I have him just hold the legs and head, so I can reach all the way inside the cavity. Within minutes, my T-shirt is more red than white.

Grunting and tugging for four or five yards at a time, we pull the gutted carcass to the shade of a fir. Then comes the critical reconnoitering to see if we can indeed get the Land Cruiser in without tearing up the country too badly. It's mostly dry, open meadow, but I hate crossing creeks in anything motorized unless absolutely necessary.

For a quarter-ton of meat and bone, I'm willing to be contrary. In four low, we drive to the carcass. I take off the head, remove the legs below the knee, and cut the body in half. My son fiddles with my rifle and examines a spent cartridge. "It's amazing how something so small can bring down something so big."

Necessity dictates, however, that he abandon ballistic speculation and disdain of blood to help me lift each half into the Land Cruiser. It requires several tries. The carcass takes up so much room that I must strap most of our camping gear to the roof rack.

On the way home, the Land Cruiser, older than my son, protests the load. He loves this vehicle and spent bored moments of his youth marring its interior. Now he wants the title. He looks out the window, happy and singing along with Blues Traveler. He's still probably thinking about girls and potato chips, but he's also got moose meat on the brain. At least his parents have done one thing right. My kids prefer wild game to almost any other meat.

He wants jerky and he will get some, even though I hate to jerk something so good as moose. But I want him to play rummy, drink Pepsi, and eat jerky, remembering the October day when that moose fell in a meadow of golden grass, and recall that he was part of it—even if it was just holding the legs.

THE RAIN CROW

BY

NICK POPOVICH

The first, too-quick thought is of Hemingway's "Fathers and Sons," until you hear the strains of Faulkner, and more. Nick Popovich would probably point to less modern influences, such as Chekhov or Dostoyevsky. But the story, the third and final work of fiction in this anthology, is undilutedly the author's. Who is that author? That is not easy to say—or rather, it is easier to declare that his story is a refutation of all those little men in their windowless cubicles on one or the other of the "coasts" who edit the outdoor magazines today and who believe that there is no longer any use for writing about hunting that is both complex and lyrical.

Wildflowers grew next to what would become the fairway, where he had just scraped away the sod, exposing naked dirt. The flowers were alive upon the gentle tension of their stems, and on the fresh black silt where the flowers grew there lay a snake.

He knew it was a moccasin by its body: heavy about the center, tapering to either end, its skin a plaited web of coal and cinnamon. What he didn't know was where each end lay and which one held the head. He leaned out farther, hands on knees. He had no stick, no gun. His face was only a foot above the flowers when he saw that it wasn't just the snake's body that had been camouflaged by earth. As he stared at the matted whiteness of its open mouth, he saw that the living flowers had also camouflaged its head.

He stepped back as the snake lay frozen into a shepherd's crook, its head raised on a hook-backed neck. He watched its head and neck subside, like shadow lowering into shadow, cursive as a living rune, and then it slid away into a fallen oak rotting into what once had been its own shadow.

On his way home he thought not just about the moccasin he had seen that afternoon but also about how he had once been so close to others that he had stepped into their den.

But that was in another time, he told himself. *Another place.*

He had been thirty then. Now he was thirty-four. The incident had sunken deep into a part of him he rarely visited, the part that once had lived far north and seemed to wander still among the rocks that floored the shallow valley where he and his father had once gone hunting.

Now he lived in the South. There were no valleys: only clay and swamp and a lack of seasons—moons that shone down on the sea and cast no shadows save the ones of ocean grass and reeds and what few trees had found earth enough to root against the hurricanes. But seeing the snake uncoiled something in him that had lain asleep, and after that he looked for it and soon understood its home to be the rotting oak.

After he moved on to other sections of the island he went back to the flowers, even after they had withered, and looked for the snake. Soon it seemed to wait for him; he would see it lying loosely looped within the shadows the living trees cast on the rotting log.

At times he left his bulldozer next to the woods and went to find the snake. When it was not lying in the rotting log, he would wait for it, often seeing it glide through the weeds, a fresh-killed bird clamped in its jaws, or swimming in a pond beyond the strip of earth he had cleared, and he would think, *It's heading for the other one.*

Across another woods where he had seen the tracks of deer and boar was a large pond like a dark lagoon and, on its far side, woods where no one had set foot for years. He would try to think of words for how the moccasin moved, flapping in liquid undulations both in water and on earth. *Like there's no difference because it's going home, back where it left the egg.* Then he thought of those through whose den he had walked at home and, leaving work, drove into the twilit atmosphere of ancient oaks that filled the island, then back into light across the causeway to the mainland, thinking as he crossed the tidal flats, *Don't stop when you're across. Just get there and drive on.* But when he reached the mainland he stopped and rolled down his window and listened for the dove that often sounded—plaintive, grave, as if its sound were not mere sound but sight from a blinded beak, and just as often it didn't sound at all.

September brought a flatter warmth, the sun low-angled now, its light diffuse, the trees backlit, the moss hanging from the oaks like ghosts of foliage with their own long history.

He saw the snake more often now. Its skin had split, and yet it moved beneath his gaze as if it were his eyes and not itself that gave it impetus to move with solemn urgency.

October, soon, he thought, watching the moccasin flap lazily across the pond. *That's what we're waiting for. We need the leaves to hide among.* He smiled, then tried to steel himself against remembering but, failing, thought about his son. *I'll have to bring him here. He'll have to see it swim across the water to the woods where it was born.*

They would hunt from a stand. The island had been purchased by a syndicate of rich men who had earned their money properly. There would be houses and a golf course soon, both far beyond his means to own or use, but now there were just woods of ancient oak and fertile dirt where rice had once grown. He had not asked to hunt but had been invited after he made a gunstock for one of the men.

"If I could bring my son," he said, conditioning himself to lose the invitation because he thought, *If they say No it wouldn't bother me; I'd rather take him hunting home someday.*

But Dr. Scott answered, "Yes, of course. You take the stand on Number Five."

It was what would become the fairway where he'd seen the moccasin.

He left work Thursday evening thinking of the morning's hunt. He crossed the causeway slowly, plank by plank beneath the tires flapping lazily. The tidal basin lay serene. The tide was not yet in. The reeds stood browning in the autumn peace, but it was not this that slowed him as he drove but a reluctance to be home too soon. He reached the mainland where he stopped and listened,

but the melancholy voice he waited for didn't come. He sat awhile, thinking that the voice would be a mellow herald to the hunt, but he heard only the boastful birds, a bright cacophony of knowing that the man was leaving and the woods would soon be theirs.

It's there somewhere, he thought. *It never changed. They come beyond the passing of themselves. The voice is there, waiting for them to wake into its sound.*

To occupy his time he drove west into woods on roads of red clay flanked by stunted pine, so unlike the oaks that darkened the island where he worked. He looked for motion—deer or rabbit, boar or squirrel—to occupy his mind until he could get home and go into the room where he worked each evening shaping wood, where his thoughts abeyed in secrecy. When the sky purpled into twilight, he left dirt roads for paved ones and turned south.

The house was small and raised off the earth on timber feet. It sat in a clearing stretching from the road an acre deep and three abreast. In the house it was dark save for a light above the kitchen sink. The bedroom where he shaped the gunstocks was unlit and silent. Inside, gunstocks in varied stages of completion leaned upright against the wall like cradle ribs. Closing the door, he lit the workbench lamp and, sitting on the stool, picked up a piece of walnut, thin and wallet-sized, on which his son had practiced checkering. *Better than me at twelve,* he thought.

He had been eighteen when he made his first. He had begun it in a travel trailer pulled behind a pickup truck on his way west two years after he'd left his father's house. He had not started it before, because he'd had to work for simple sustenance with pick and shovel. And although this met the need of simply living it did not meet the hunger, which was not in his body but in his hands, and they would not be satisfied until they held tools to occupy his mind. This need had been there for years, beginning when, as a child, he had gone to the basement where he stood upon the stairs and watched his father's shadow on the wall.

The room where his father worked was small. Above the workbench was a light, its single bulb shaded by a cone of bright aluminum. Facing the workbench was a stool, and clamped onto the workbench was a cradle where rifle stocks were held on centers by two coarsely threaded screws. The basement was of concrete block, sometimes damp from seepage.

He would leave his bed at night, descend the narrow stairs, and watch his father's shadow cast from the workshop doorway onto the whitewashed coal-bin wall, the shadow bent above the cradled wood and magnified into a perfect effigy of someone small, so that the gross enlargement, instead of blurring the original, produced a giant replica of fierce immutability.

His father was a small, hard man; bony of cheek; flat-mouthed, like someone who had pressed his lips against a steering wheel and driven at high speed into a concrete wall. His eyes were those of a man rising after being knocked down in a brawl. He seemed to have no muscles, simply strings of meat bound close about the bones. His chest was like a coonhound's—flat and hard. He walked bent-kneed, as though, even without his peach-branch dowsing rod, he searched constantly and intently for things beneath the earth. His ears were overlarge, his huge hands thick and strong with upthrust knuckles, shaped to hold the tools of sculptors seeking to release the grace from blanks of wood.

Of evenings he, the son, would lie in bed and listen for his father's gentle rasping, as of mice feet on a barn floor. Then he would sneak down into the basement, watch his father's shadow until he had breathed it deeply into his own child-lungs, and then he would take it back into his bed and thereby let it sleep.

He watched for years, aware not from spoken words but from his father's fierce silence that the workshop was beyond his rights of entering. And then, when he was nine, he went into the workshop, where he stood in awe, his chin barely above the workbench, looking at his father's tools. A stock was in the cradle, scribed with master lines and shallow checkering, the wood bearing the red-brown cast he would later come to recognize as walnut. He caressed the wood gently, sensing tautened velvet curved by rasps to fit the hand or cheek, feeling where it had been sanded, scraped with broken glass, and then rubbed until it became not simple wood but a substance that reflected the coarseness of his fingertips. He knew not to touch it further but could not help himself. Taking a piece of sandpaper, he rubbed the checkering and then waited all the next day for his father to find out, thinking, perhaps, but not knowing: *He'll have to teach me now. He'll have to show me how to use the tools.*

He waited all day with the fierce anticipation of a child on Christmas Eve, but nothing happened until that night in bed when he strained to hear the gentle sounds of chisels scraping wood but heard instead footsteps mounting stairs and saw his father come into his room, switching on the lamp.

"It's ruined," his father said, holding the stock. His voice was quiet, watchful, as though spoken through his ice-blue eyes.

He could not speak. He lay in bed, his body coiled back into itself, his neck and shoulders pressed against the wall, and he watched his father lay the stock upon the bed and hold a pen and paper to him.

"Write your name," his father said.

Reaching out, his hand shook while his father's hand held steady.

"Write it," his father said.

He wrote: "James William Lee."

"Now give it here," his father said. He did, and watched his father make an *X* and hand the paper back.

"That's how I sign my name," his father said. "That's all the writing I can do. You know what people call me when my back is turned?"

"Yes," he answered, coiled backward closer to the wall.

"Yes," his father said. "Hillbilly Jim. Not to my face but to my back, or when they want a dowser for their wells or a rifle stock." He smiled thinly, like watered venom. "Or when they want to fight." His gaze was calm, not grave but deadly, patient; his eyes did not look outward but seemed focused on an inner thought, like someone waiting to be kicked or stepped upon before he struck.

"You'll be a better man than me or else you'll leave this house. You understand?"

Nodding, he watched his father step into the doorway where he struck the light and then stood silhouetted, small and thin and deadly with the calmness of a sleeping snake. Then he turned and said, "Don't ever go into my room again."

He spent three years watching, lonely, as his father came from dowsing wells or doing odd jobs in town nine miles away, but always late in the evening going to the basement where he shaped the rifle stocks, sitting hunched above the cradle while the son, awake in bed, listened to the rasping of wood, the sound not rough but gentle like the scrape of careful teeth across a bright new apple skin

And later, sitting in his own house with his wife and son asleep, he felt he had grown beyond the cage of his own ribs into a giant child encompassed by the proximity of gunstocks standing like the pickets of a cradle as he gave himself not just to memory but to truth, because, looking at the piece of walnut his son had checkered, he could feel not just his son asleep but feel his wife as well: They were both an equal part of him. *Because his mother is still here,* he thought. *That's why his hands are sensitive.*

His own mother had been a thin, worn woman with the temper of a sapling standing lonely on a barren hillside in the wind. She had few needs beyond the one to serve his father and himself. She moved about the house like someone lost to all except the walls within which she cooked and breathed and slept. Until he was nine, he was ignorant of how his mother lived despite years of watching her rocking silently on the back porch. But when he turned twelve and learned that his father wouldn't take him hunting deer, he began to feel the mother-part inside him come alive.

At nine he didn't think of this. It took three years, each year running into the next so that Time became a single length of patience laced with fear through which he spent his nights straining to hear the sounds of metal gently eating wood and his days in the woods, his BB gun displacing what to other children might have been a blanket or a doll, some token of security that, even if he had possessed them, still would not have satisfied his need to use his father's tools. But then at nine he didn't think, *It's like a hunger in my hands. It's like my hands are empty bellies crying out for food.* Unaware that hope was mere postponement of a predetermined act, he simply thought, *He'll take me to the mountains. What I did to the wood was not that bad.*

But three years later, when October came, his father had not taken him to sight the rifles, and on Thanksgiving afternoon he watched his father eat in silence then go to the basement and return bearing the red plaid hunting suit and battered leather boots and, hanging from the hanger neck, the leather belt whose buckle bore the words *Gott Mitt Uns* pressed into relief. The buckle was as much a ritual as the hunt, discovered by his father in a mountain valley where prisoners of war had been interned. He was seven when his father explained how he had come upon it, using not the peach-branch dowsing rod but two thin rods of steel.

"They're welding rods," said his father, handing him the L-shaped rods. "I cleaned the coatings off."

His father crossed the living room and sat down on the couch. Holding the short legs of the L in each fist, he faced his father nervously.

"Now walk to me," his father said. "Go slow. Pretend your mind is in your hands. Let everything come through the rods into your hands."

He stepped forward cautiously, his arms outstretched like someone walking on a wire high above the earth.

"That's right," his father said. "Don't think, just feel." And he crossed the floor halfway and felt the rods swing lazily across each other, halting in an *X* as though each fist was a hinge.

"That's the plumbing in the floor," his father said. "That's how I found the buckle in the mountains. It was in a valley full of rocks and snakes."

"Snakes?" he said.

"I went in winter," his father said, "when they were all asleep."

The valley was a washed-out hollow running downward from a mountain known as Pigeon Loft, and he would go there twice, once with his father when he turned thirty-two, and once to cast a symbol to the rocks.

So, learning he would not be going hunting, he sought his mother for comfort, for pity, for some need that lived unspoken not just in himself but in their family. Until that spring he had not made himself available to her save as a puppy might scratch at a door to ask for food. So when spring arrived he went to the back porch where, for years beginning prior to his birth, she sat late mornings or late evenings in a rocking chair shaped not from walnut (though his father's shed was full) but from willow brought from Tennessee.

She rocked in silence, straight-backed and -necked, her face not blank so much as stalwart and severe: true to the hill people that were her kind, listening for the dove to coo. He watched from the kitchen door, standing with his face pressed to the screen like an orphan gazing through a veil into a church. He didn't know and would not know for years that what the sound of the dove portended to his mother was the echo of another life, and that she had tolerated her life since he had known her through the memory of having been a girl in Tennessee. He many times heard the sound, like gentle breath passed through a throat of softened wood, but had not liked it: It sounded hollow, weak, split like a sound once shrill now rounded by its exit from a softened beak. And yet he knew the softness of the cooing brought her peace.

Later, matured and working in the West, he would think the sound of mourning was the only future she possessed. Until the day his father left without him for the mountains he hadn't thought these things, but now, years later and a thousand miles away, he thought about them, remembering the way his father left the house then turned and said, "Don't go into that room."

So he lived through winter lonely until spring, when he approached her silently. It seemed she expected him because, rocking gently in the chair, she didn't look at him but simply said, "Pap doesn't mean to hurt. When we were younger he was different."

"How?" he said.

"Pap was seventeen," she said, "and I was fifteen when we met." She smiled. "Our grandpas' farms were next to one another, and on winter evenings I'd see Pap crossing the empty cornfield, and in summer when the corn was high I'd watch above the corn to see his hat."

"His hat?" he said. He looked down at her hands clasped loosely in her lap. Her hands were narrow-palmed, long-fingered, sensitive, the knuckles chafed. Opening her hands, she held out a crude brown ring to him. "Pap made me this when we were young," she said. It was a peach pit, hollowed out to fit her finger.

Rocking steadily, she told how she would look above the tall, ripe corn and see the yellow straw hat with the bright red band jaunting above the stalks; how neither of their families knew that both their farms had long been deeded to the family of a Yankee colonel from the Civil War until the day a sheriff's car came into the yard bearing a writ that gave both families ninety days to leave the land where eight generations of their blood had worked the earth.

"They gave us each a strip of land high up against the mountainside," she said. "The land was poor. The corn grew thin. Pap started dowsing wells the way his grandpa did. We married when I was seventeen and came to Pennsylvania. You came when I was nineteen." Nodding at the house, she said, "Right in the bedroom where you sleep."

So he knew that she was thirty-two, and that she looked twice as old.

"Sometimes I sit here like I used to sit at home when Pap came courtin' me," she said. "I used to listen to the rain crow then the way I listen to it now. Pap and me used to sit for hours on the porch waiting for it to tell us things would be all right. The rain crow gave me peace. After we moved up to the mountain, every time I heard the rain crow I would promise to forgive the men who took our land because the rain crow's voice was different from the other birds. Its voice reminded me of water, evening in the valley where we used to live, the dusk and sleeping earth."

She looked at him. "You don't quit loving something when it's gone. The part of you that made you love it still exists. No matter what you do, the part you love stays with you even when the thing you loved is gone."

"You loved Pap once?"

"I still love Pap," she said. "My spirit never left those hills. That's where I've always lived, and I'll go back someday."

She smiled, her thin body shaped by the shapeless dress washed of color. Consumed by missing home, her body seemed divorced from her face as it spoke of having lived too long without the long green ridges bluish in the spring. "In fall, the leaves were like a rainbow dug up from the earth," she said.

She passed away in autumn, leaving in her sleep as though his seeking her had granted her wish to leave him not just something of his ancestry but an understanding of his father's grief.

Because that's what it was, he thought, a thousand miles away and sitting in his room where he fashioned gunstocks as his father once did. *Because he never fit into the world where others lived.*

After his mother left the rain crow ceased to sing, as though upon his mother's passing not just sound but warmth left on silent wings. The rocking chair sat empty through the winter; then, in spring, he came home from school and thought to sit in it and saw his father there ahead of him, staring into the woods and leaning forward like a man about to leap into the trees.

He stepped backward silently, thinking to leave before he was seen, but his father said, "The Yankee bastards took the land. They owned it without knowing it and took it without telling us until the day we had to leave."

He didn't answer but watched his father staring into the woods. Then his father turned and said, "Don't ever be like me. You be like me, you'll never have a moment's peace." They lived in silence after that, two effigies of one another moving through the house as partners in a single grief.

When he was seventeen he graduated from high school second in his class. There was no party, no special gift. He came home in the too-small dark blue suit and ate the supper his father had cooked. When they were done, his father looked at him and said, "There's money for your college."

"I don't know," he said.

"Don't know?"

"Not yet," he replied.

His father looked down at his plate. When he looked back up, his eyes looked the way they had the night he came into the bedroom with the rifle stock.

"Tell me tomorrow if you want to go to school or not," his father said, then went to the basement and his wood.

He would remember this as he headed west: the morning bright with June's new light, standing on the porch after his father said at breakfast, "Say it now. College or not?" and his answering,

"I want to wait a while," and then his father saying, "All right, wait outside." He went outside and waited, then his father came out to the front porch with a suitcase in his hand.

"Good-bye," his father said, setting down the suitcase and holding out his hand. "This'll get you someplace on a bus."

Looking into his own hand he saw a hundred dollar bill; then, looking up, his father walking into the house and closing the door.

It took two years to satisfy the hunger he had carried all his life. It was the hunger in his hands and would be fed by wood, but for the first two years he dug ditches, working carefully so that his work equaled the potential offered by the task. Then he learned to operate machinery, backhoes at first then earth scrapers, progressing westward as the great machines themselves grew larger so that in two more years he was in Montana, working on a dam, where he met a man who said, "You don't just scrape the dirt, you sculpt it. What else do you do?"

"I work with wood," he replied, and he soon found himself traveling south. He had a better truck and trailer now, and in the trailer was a cradle he had made for holding gunstocks.

He married in the spring when he was twenty-two. He had been in South Carolina for a year and met her at an art show where he went to look at carver's tools. She was an artist. "Oils," she said, when he asked her what she used. She stood waiting for him to speak and watching him try to understand one of her paintings, a high and narrow one depicting streaks of clouds and dark blue night with stars and, in an upper corner, something like a ball of dirty light.

"It's the universe," he finally said, and she smiled. "But what's the little ball up in the corner that looks like it doesn't belong?"

"The tragic flaw," she replied. "Nothing can be without one."

"What else do you like?" he said.

"People who smell like woods," she answered, and he had to ask, afraid lest he be wrong but realizing later he was sure how she would respond.

"You're not from Tennessee?"

"Yes," she smiled.

He went home when Mel Wetzel's letter came: "Your father broke his hip. He's better but he talks of going home."

It was November and he went by bus, taking his rifle and some clothes. Stepping from the bus, he walked through the yard around the house to the rocking chair on the back porch, empty now as was the plot that once had been his mother's garden. He stood next to the empty furrows, closed his eyes, and listened to the woods. When the cooing didn't come he thought, *I know you're gone, but still I tried.*

Inside the house he found his father healed of bone but not of age. He stooped more now. His motion, still of someone stalking things beneath the earth, was not as sure. Shaking his father's hand in silence, he returned the hundred-dollar bill.

"I didn't want it back," his father said.

"I know," he said.

"It's time we went to Pigeon Loft," his father said.

It was three hundred miles, the latter fourth of which ran through a forest of high pine. It was dark when they exited the car before a small black shanty set back from a gravel road shining pale gray. His heart beat faster now. At first he heard a sound distant and terse, as of a tiny drumbeat coming from beyond the ridges standing dark and sharp against the sky. But as he listened further and began to move, he felt his heartbeat quicken to the motion of his limbs and realized it was his heart and not a drum whose sound pulsed behind his eyes. The thin aroma of the pines came to him on twisting winds. The moon was full. He didn't know his father had been watching him look up until he heard him say, "The moons are different here. But wait until tomorrow when we go to Pigeon Loft."

They went into the shanty, where his father lit the wood already in the heavy metal stove. They slept that night each upon a thin, hard mattress, and in the predawn light they left for Pigeon Loft, a mountain whose eastern flank fell long and deep between two ridges into a long and narrow valley strewn with pale, flat rocks.

They reached the bottom near sunrise. About them it was dark save for a thin and weightless light that drifted down and gathered in the branches of the pine. The valley sides were steep, covered with shale, and as they paused he saw upon the earth faint boxlike scars where the prisoners of war barracks had stood.

"That's where I found the buckle," his father said, pointing with his rifle north.

"The buckle wasn't rusted?"

"No," his father said. "Someone had wrapped it in oiled rags and stuffed it in an ammunition can." He smiled. "Let's go a little farther where it levels off."

They saw no game. They sat a long time silent, each to his own thoughts, watching birds and porcupine. The sun rose high above them, and his father brought out cheese and bread and coffee in a vacuum bottle and they ate.

As afternoon cast shadows on the slopes, a far-off rifle shot sprang through the silence, spreading into the valley then back to its source.

"Three hundred yards," he said. He watched his father nod and all was silent, then they heard the sound of rock falling from the valley side across the way.

"Running," his father said. "A young buck, sure. An old one would have picked his way."

They sat until the sun spread along the mountaintop, and then his father rose. "We'd best be going now," he said. "We'll come back after dark."

"Hunting at night?" he said.

"You have to see something," his father said.

On their way out they were halfway up the mountainside when suddenly a buck burst from the trees behind and to their left. It broke across the valley bottom to the northern slope. He was behind his father, so he raised his rifle, turning as he shouldered it in one long motion and thumbed off the safety. The buck was old, gray as a ghost, as though what light remained had transformed into hair and hide. He followed it with the sights then swung ahead as it reached the slope and started up in one long bound. Then it seemed to hang there, running without motion as the shale slid backward in a small cascade.

Lowering the rifle, he watched the buck dig through the shale to earth, gain a purchase, then lunge forward—head down, its shoulder blades thrust up—then lunge again and disappear among the trees.

"That was the older one," the father smiled. "He let the young one go and stayed to lure the hunter's shot."

They waited at the cabin for the moon to rise. It was full, richly yellow, buoyant low above the trees. As they drove the moon appeared to wait for them to leave the car and start again into the valley, carrying no rifles now, picking their way among the rocks. They reached the bottom and his father turned.

"Look up," he said.

The moon had changed. Once yellow, it now shone like something new, as though it had just risen and then halted, tentative.

"The moons are different here," his father said, his face mild, pale-fleshed, and awed. "It's like it never shined on earth before, like when you look at it, it stops and waits for you to look away before it moves." He felt it too: a sense of endless presence, something never having-been and never to-return, the narrow valley mutely silver and the angles of the broad flat rocks defined according to their shadows.

They left with dawn and reached home late that afternoon. They sat out on the back porch where the rocking chair had become his father's place to contemplate the woods. They rarely spoke, but it was different now.

He left the next day. Standing with his father in the yard, he waited for the bus, holding his rifle case and suitcase and facing his father for what he didn't know was a final time.

"I have something for you," his father said, handing him the belt buckle. "It's yours. I found out what the words meant after Ma passed on."

"I found out, too," he said, taking the buckle and surprised by how light it was.

"Let's see," his father said, holding out his hand for the rifle case.

He watched his father slide the rifle out. Raising it to the light, his father sighted lengthwise along the wood; then, after he had turned it side to side, he handed it back.

"It's good," his father said, "real good."

"I learned it watching you," he said.

"I didn't let you in the room."

"I heard the way the chisels moved," he smiled, then saw his father work the sunken mouth.

"Do you know why I didn't take you to the mountains that first year?"

"No," he said.

"Because it was the only place I loved more than our home in Tennessee, the only place where I could love myself. That place has different moons from anyplace I've ever seen. It seemed I was looking up from somewhere other than earth. I was afraid you might grow up to love it like I did and then turn out to be like me."

"I do," he said. "I am."

"You'll see," his father said. "Someday you'll have a family, too."

"I'm having one right now," he said. "My wife is pregnant with our son."

"A son?"

"Don't ask me how I know."

The bus halted in a drawn-out hiss. He looked into his father's eyes. They held him fixed and silent, then they blinked.

"You'd better go now, Jimmy."

"Yes," he said.

They watched each other deeply now. Then, turning suddenly, he started for the bus and heard his father call.

"Jimmy."

"Yes," he said, facing him.

"I'm proud of you."

"The wood was good," he said. "The checkering was easy."

"Not the stock."

He waited, solemnly.

"I'm proud you didn't shoot that buck while it was scrambling up those rocks."

He went back in the spring, leaving his wife and newborn son at home. The day after the funeral he gave Mel Wetzel the house keys and said, "Rent it out. I'll rent a truck and take the walnut back down south."

He left the next day, not for home but for the mountains. It was different now. Spring swelled the hills, and mountain laurel blossomed; the earth spread beneath the flow of water from the hills, and in places on the roads water overflowed, eroding tiny rivers into the dirt.

Dusk found him at his father's cabin. Drinking coffee, he waited for the sounds of evening birds to cease, and when their sounds yielded to that of insects breathing rhythmically he drove to Pigeon Loft, left the truck, and looked up at the moon. It was not full this time but new, a sliver showing like a coin-edge through a velvet slit. The valley far below lay darker than before, but he still saw the shapes of rocks and trees as shadows of a different depth. He watched awhile then went back to his truck and slept, and in the morning he went into the valley with his rifle and the ammunition can.

He thought about this while he and his son drove to the island—first about the moccasin, hoping it would be lying in the rotting oak, and then about how he had gone into the valley with the metal box, the sun above the trees too low to warm the rocks, and made his way to where his father found the buckle. Crossing the valley, he hadn't thought of snakes. He made the far side where he saw the fieldstone remnants of an old foundation. He took the buckle from his pocket, wrapped it in the oiled rags he had brought, stuffed this into the ammunition can, and flung it into the brush.

So much for you, he thought. Then, walking back across the rocks, he saw the earth appear to coil in a mass of thin deceptive lines. He heard the sound of cellophane flapped by a constant breath and saw the rattlesnakes, their bodies coiling even as they struck, their open mouths short of his ankles as he waved the rifle muzzle at them and walked on, feeling more than once the gentle tick of fangs against the rifle barrel like the distant snapping of a fingernail. On the other side, he looked back where the snakes lay among the rocks as though sprung from the earth itself.

And thinking of it now, he smiled. "The snake might be there at the log," he said.

"It was a moccasin?" the son said.

"Yes," the father said.

They crossed the causeway to the island onto fresh-paved roads. There was a guardhouse now, as yet unoccupied since all the lots hadn't yet been sold.

"It looks like a place for a watchman," the son said.

"A guard," the father said.

"They have guards here?"

"It's private," said the father.

"Like a prison?"

"It's for people who own houses here," the father answered. "We're just guests."

The roads wound through the darkened trees. Dawn had broken, but there was no sun. The fragrance of the earth and grass was heavy on the dew and birds chirped randomly, but mostly it was silent, brooding, as though the woods had closed their eyes and ears against the grim potential of the hunt, and now he thought of when he and his father had gone to the valley. He felt a sense of melancholy, soft and sweet, and thought about the cooing of the dove.

They reached what would soon become a fairway. The grass had caught, and now the narrow swath between the woods was green beyond the native grass surrounding it. They left the truck.

"This way," the father said, leading the son across the fairway to the woods. The fallen oak was there, its bark dripping the wetness of the night. Leaning, the father peered and motioned to the son.

"It's here," he said.

The son approached, hunched cautiously.

"Don't move," the father said. "He knows we're here."

The snake was coiled loosely, like a thin, brown, rubber tube. The father gently stamped his foot upon the earth, and then the snake moved sluggishly. Raising its head, it looked at them. Its eyes were lidless, filmed with age. It sensed them blindly with its tongue, then stretched itself out from the log into the weeds, approaching them.

"Step back," the father said. "He's going to the pond."

They watched it crawl as if into a motion waiting in the air. Reaching the pond, it slid over the edge and disappeared.

"It's going to another pond," the father said. "One where nobody ever goes."

The son looked at the log. "That's where it lives?"

"Yes," said the father.

"Maybe it's where it changes, too."

"Changes?" the father said.

"My teacher's grandma said that after a snake crawls from its skin so many times it leaves the earth and turns into a bird."

The father smiled.

"Come on," he said. "The sun is coming up."

They climbed the stairs onto the stand. The stand was new, set just inside the woods, unpainted to blend in.

"Remember," said the father. "You're up high. You have to aim low when you shoot."

They waited silently. The woods attained a separation from the night, and soon the birds began to voice their bright reception, spaced then gathering then mounting to a shrill cacophony.

Then silence. Sudden, like a curtain had come down. The father raised his finger, touched his lips, then pointed to the woods line to their left.

There were two bucks, no more than eighty yards away. The young one stepped out first, light brown like sand, its antlers dark and glinting at the edges like the glint of sunlight on a web of rain. It stepped full out into the fairway, where it stopped to sense the air. The father touched the son's arm. *"Wait,"* he fashioned silently.

The young buck stepped out farther then stood still. Upon its halt the older one appeared, light gray, its chest arched like a lyre upward to its neck, its nape arched like the lyre's other half. Its antlers were light gray. *Like birch,* the father thought, then both deer moved into the center of the fairway, where they stopped, the young one closer to them and the older one slightly beyond.

The son raised the rifle. He leaned against the stand's low railing, aiming while the father thought, *Don't wait too long,* then heard the shot and saw the rifle-muzzle rise, then saw the gray deer lifted from the earth. It landed on its side and did not move. The young one looked at it, unfearful, calm, and then, remembering its instincts, sprang across the fairway suddenly into the brush.

The gray deer waited until they had nearly reached it then sprang up. It sailed above them as they crouched involuntarily, and then it bounded left then right then crashed into the brush and lunged between the trees. When it disappeared, they heard another shot.

They followed where the sound of the shot had come from and found a man standing above the dead gray buck. Its tongue was out. It lay as it had run: its forelegs back, its hind legs forward, as the man looked down.

"You knocked it out," the man said, pointing his rifle muzzle at the groove across the gray buck's back. The groove was clean, a perfect caliber. The meat showed clean on either side, despite there being no blood.

"He clipped its spine," the father said. Then, to the son, "Shake hands with Dr. Scott."

The doctor shook the son's hand warmly. "We'll share the meat," he said.

The father smiled. The doctor's clothes were not those one expected from a hunter who had gone into the brush in search of meat. The clothes looked new, too clean, as if they had been taken from storage after laundering.

"We're fine," the father said. "There's other deer. We thank you, anyhow."

They hunted until sunset, casually, as if to let the moment they had shared cohere into their blood-memories. They left as evening deepened softly through the trees. The woods were still. There was about them, as they drove, a sense of rest, a sense of earth lapsing into an endless sigh upon the slaying of the deer.

They left the woods. Ahead of them the empty causeway stretched, its planks and timbers reddened by the setting sun.

"He saved the younger one," the son said quietly.

"Who did?" the father said.

"The older deer."

The father smiled. Crossing the causeway he saw that the tidal flats had filled, and now the water lay peaceful and still, its surface mirroring unbrokenly the waning sky and clouds about the random beds of weeds.

"I didn't want it to be done," the son went on.

"Done?" said the father.

"I mean I didn't want the day to end."

As they left the causeway to the road, the father frowned. Leaving the road, he stopped the truck and rolled his window farther down.

"Listen," he told the son.

There was no sound. Turning his head, he listened, thinking, *It must have been my imagination.*

"What?" the son said.

"Wait."

It came this time. As though the first had been a signal opening his mind, a melancholy voice of dusk, yielded not forth but in retreat.

"What is it?" said the son.

"A mourning dove."

"Morning?" the son replied. "Like when the sun comes up?"

"Mourning like sad," the father said.

It called again: tender and shy, piped forth like sound come from a fluted throat.

The father steered onto the road. The road was narrow and eroded, and he drove with care. The dove sounded a final time, its soft cry pulling at his blood, drawing its salt into his eyes so that the road grew blurred.

"It isn't sad," the son said.

"No?" the father said. Blinking, he saw the road grow clear.

"No," said the son. "It's telling secrets to the trees."

The father saw it now, as though behind his normal sight another eye had opened softly in his mind: the swamp and pool; the water's surface flat like mercury; the water edged by cypress roots twined in the roots of gum; the young buck watching as the moccasin flapped silently across the water without waking it; the buck's neck down-stretched and its foreleg raised; the snake and buck and dove endowed with presence, place, respectful of each other's kind, each shaped upon a history of blood that rendered them at once both different and alike beneath the silent watching of the moon and stars.

"Back home some people call them rain crows," the father said.

"Rain crows?" said the son.

"Yes."

They drove. The sky was dark save for the sunset's spread, brazen and low, far to the west. They reached a stoplight at a crossroads, where they stopped.

"What was it like?" the son said.

"Where?" the father said.

"When you were small."

The father watched the red light silently.

"My father hunted at a special place," he finally said. "I went there with him once."

"Where was it?" said the son.

"A mountain valley," said the father. Silent, then, "The moons were different there. I'll take you sometime."

"Did it have snakes?" the son said, sliding toward his father on the seat.

The light turned green. They turned onto a broader road toward the distant blur of lights casting a pale illumination to the bellies of the clouds.

"Yes," said the father, "but we'll go in winter when they're all asleep."

The son slid closer to the father. Groping, the father took the son's hand, squeezed it gently, felt the broad, flat palm and long thick fingers and the upthrust knuckles so unlike his own.

"The last time I was there," the father said, "I lost something." He squeezed his son's hand firmly now. "When we go back, we'll look for it."

AMONG THE WALRUS

BY

THOMAS MCINTYRE

"It was hunted." And where the walrus are hunted is almost the farthest place you can go to find the big game of North America. It is also where the last of the hunting peoples live. Outboards may have replaced paddles, and rifles harpoons, but for these peoples the best, most honorable occupation remains the hunt. Most of us hunt now to be outdoors and out of ourselves. Hunters of the Arctic don't have to aspire to that condition: The "outside" is where they already are; and the forces that compel them come first from without, from the wild foremost. If you ever want to know what such a hunting life is like, or was like, then what choice is there but to go to where some portion of it is still being lived by the continent's final true hunters— to go there and join in?

> The sun was shining on the sea,
>   Shining with all his might
> He did his very best to make
>   The billows smooth and bright—
> And this was odd, because it was
>   The middle of the night.
>   —*Lewis Carroll,* The Walrus and the Carpenter

In summer up where the Arctic Circle lies well to the south, concealed beneath the bow of the horizon, Carroll's verse is far from nonsense. The simple fact is that the sun *does* shine in the middle of the night, and around the clock. Where it shone when I was there was on the Inuit village of Iglulik on a small barren island under the north end of enormous Baffin Island and off the eastern coastal plain of the Melville

Peninsula (a place so flat that, in the words of a cargo pilot, "when your dog runs away, you can see it for three days"). For more than 4,000 years human beings had lived around Iglulik. Over the level terrain they stacked flat rocks into ubiquitous *inukshuk* ("like a man," with outspread arms), the effigies acting as landmarks or as decoys to funnel the stocky Arctic caribou toward hidden hunters. They lived off those caribou, and seal, whale (both narwhal and bowhead, and sometimes even blue), polar bear, char, waterfowl and seabirds, and not least, *aiviq*, the walrus, which I had come to hunt.

What possessed me to hunt walrus? It certainly wasn't because of any ancient heritage extending back to north country or sea. The first *Qablunaaq* ("big eyebrow"—that is, non-Inuit like me) ships did not anchor off Iglulik until 1822, only to be driven away by a shaman's curse. No more came for almost a century. There was no permanent contact with the outside until the arrival of Christian missionaries in the 1930s. As recently as two generations ago, the Inuit traveled by foot, dog team, or skin boat, dwelling in summer and winter hunting camps and practicing a lifestyle today revered as "traditional"—but which at the time was, to them, nothing out of the ordinary.

In the village where they lived the kids now wore Nike caps and Georgetown sweatshirts and talked in the assumed speech patterns of urban black youth. But on a gravel spit out from the village—three miles by snowmobile across the bay when the ice was solid, but in July a fifteen-mile drive around on a potholed dirt road—stood the white tents of a camp at the edge of the breakup (the edge of the polar icecap itself). There were perhaps two dozen tents—while twenty years before when, as a young Inuit hunter told me, the elders were still listened to, there would have been eighty. Most people now stayed in the village working at "jobs" or, he said, watching television. The hunters in the camp, though, still went out in their open boats whenever the weather was right, to hunt seal and walrus, hunting seal and walrus their millennia-long calling.

Until I went to Iglulik, what I knew about walrus I knew from what I had read. Ancestors of the walrus are found in the fossil record dating back fourteen million years. Since the Inuit first saw the walrus, it has been to them what the buffalo was to the Plains Indians—a source not only of food for both humans and sled dogs but also of an entire array of goods: oil for heat and light; hides (*kauk*) for covering the frames of kayaks; its intestines, according to nineteenth-century naturalist Edward Nelson, for "waterproof clothing, window-covers, and floats"; its bones to become spear points and like products, while the tusks (the *tuugaaq*) were made into lance tips and carved into other tools and into objects of art.

The species name, *Odobenus rosmarus*, derives from the Greek for "toothwalker" and is an acknowledgment of the way in which walrus haul themselves out onto ice floes with their tusks, using them like ivory ice axes. Although it is not unknown for walrus to use those tusks to tear apart seals and even infant whales they have chased down (swimming at up to twenty miles per hour) and caught in their massive front flippers, the tusks serve them primarily as picks for breaking through ice; rakes for clam digging; in dominance displays, in which they lift their heads to show the size of their ivory; in duels with other walrus (which are reported to be brutal[1]); and in defense against polar bear (and sometimes human hunters[2]).

[1] *I have frequently observed them fighting with great ferocity on the ice. They use their tusks against one another very much in the manner that gamecocks use their beaks. From the animal's unwieldy appearance and the position of his tusks, one is apt to fancy that the latter can only be used in a stroke* downward, *but, on the contrary, they can turn their necks with the greatest facility and quickness, and can strike either upward, downward, or sideways, with equal dexterity. I have little doubt but that in the amatory season these conflicts are often fatal.*
—Seasons with the Sea-Horses; or, Sporting in the Northern Seas, James Lamont, Esq., F.G.S., 1861.

[2] *It seemed that the walrus, a huge old bull, charged the boat, and the harpooner as usual received him with his lance full in the chest, but the shaft of the lance broke all to shivers, and the walrus, getting inside of it, threw himself on the gunwale of the boat and overset it in an instant. While the men were floundering in the water amongst their oars and tackle, the infuriated animal rushed in amongst them, and selecting the unlucky harpooner, who, I fancy, had fallen next to him, he tore nearly into two halves with his tusks.*
—Ibid.

AMONG THE WALRUS

Aside from its tusks, there "is one very striking peculiarity connected with the osteological structure of the walrus," wrote the English sportsman James Lamont, Esq., F.G.S., in his 1861 account of hunting off Spitzbergen, *Seasons with the Sea-Horses; or, Sporting Adventures in the Northern Seas*. Mr. Lamont regretted, though, that he "dare not amplify this allusion," his veiled Victorian reference to the walrus's cubit-long baculum, asserted by at least one naturalist to be the largest "in both absolute and relative sizes" of any mammal's.

> O woeful, weeping Walrus, your
>   Tears are all a sham!
> You're greedier for Oysters than
>   Children are for jam.
>   —*Lewis Carroll*, The Walrus and the Carpenter,
>   *verses added by Carroll for an operetta of* Alice

Although they sometimes feed on other sea mammals, walrus are greediest for clams. They can dive to almost four hundred feet, where they root in clam beds with their tusks and bristled muzzles. They pick up the mollusks with their lips, suck in the flesh, and spit out the shells. In a day they can put away as many as five thousand. At day's end, though not daylight's, they inflate large air sacs in their necks that let them sleep upright, their heads bobbing out of the water.

I cannot say why, but something about walrus had always fascinated (or was it haunted?) me. Was it something about their tusks, their size, their unlikeness to almost any other animal, or just all that ice? Reading about them was not going to explain it, though, and only hunting might. So I traveled far north to this place where I could do just that, finally reaching the camp on the spit when it was already past midday—by the clock, anyway. Shooting hours in the High Arctic are not regulated by a timetable listing sunrise and sunset, but by the conditions of weather. When I met my guide—an elder Inuit who spoke, perhaps by preference, little English and who had grown up on tundra and ice and not in the village—he was studying the clouds low on the southern horizon and judging the wind to decide when it would be best to put out after walrus.

Waiting for his decision, I stowed my gear in the plywood hut that would be my accommodations and walked across the gravel to the cook hut where Louise, wife of one of the hunters, ran the kitchen. I drank hot tea and listened to her tell about her job as a primary school teacher in Iglulik. She also told me about her husband, who had taken European hunters after walrus only a week or two before. While they were on the water, adrift, and glassing, a bowhead whale twice the size of the boat spyhopped from the depths. It fixed them with its wary and weary eye, mere yards away, before dropping back into the ocean, its wake tossing the boat like a cork. For several minutes, no one spoke.

Survival suits are mandatory for all hunters, because going into the water without one is fatal, sooner rather than later. If whales didn't turn you over, then there was the chance of a sudden squall. Stepping out onto the rim of an ice floe could mean having it break away under your foot. And the walrus itself was never to be ignored or discounted, even when it appeared to be dead. The truest challenge of hunting walrus was getting to where they could be hunted, and getting back to tell about it. By 4:45 P.M. the elder Inuit had determined from the clouds that it would remain windless, sunny, and chill at least long enough for us to hunt, and he said it was time to go.

> The sea was wet as wet could be,
>   The sands were dry as dry.
> You could not see a cloud, because
>   No cloud was in the sky . . .
>   —*Lewis Carroll,* The Walrus and the Carpenter

I carried my survival suit and my single-shot .450 NE rifle with a 3¼-inch cartridge in its waterproof case to the elder Inuit's boat, tethered to hooks sunk into the ten-foot-high wall of rotting shore ice, and climbed in. A young Inuit was there to assist the elder. After he cast us off we headed the boat southeast, moving slowly over the clear emerald shallows, seeing the rocks on the bottom, eiders in the air, until we reached the deep water in the Foxe Basin below

Fury and Hecla Strait (named for the ships that came in 1822) and got up to speed. A large freighter canoe, manned by two men and a boy in fur-trimmed parkas, waited for us out in the basin, having come from the next village south of Iglulik, and the last for hundreds of miles. With almost fifty miles to travel toward uninhabited Rowley Island to find the walrus, hunters always went with two boats, out of prudence and to share the kill.

In the distance a bowhead breached, spouting steam. Farther off, mirages lifted icebergs into the sky. We passed blocks of wandering, orphaned ice, then slowed to thread our way through narrow leads when the pack closed in. Halfway across we anchored on the edge of a big drift to collect fresh meltwater with which to brew tea on the Coleman stove, Inuit journeys always requiring regular infusions of tea and sugar. Going on, we left the drifting ice and crossed open flat water again until we came to ice blown up against the shore. A mile from the ice the Inuit cut the motors, and we glassed. I saw dark marks on the distant ice.

"Walrus island," the young Inuit said to me, pointing.

> The monsters lay with their heads reclining on one another's backs and sterns, just as I have seen rhinoceroses lying asleep in the African forests.
>
> —*James Lamont, Esq., F.G.S.*

We moved slowly forward until we could see the walrus with the naked eye. The first we got near were cows, to judge by the size of their tusks. Six or eight lolled together on a big floe, flippers up, then rolled to show us the white parallels of their tusks as we approached. When they stood on their flippers to study us more carefully, their hides seemed too big and baggy for their bodies, like that giant suit David Byrne wore in the *Talking Heads* video. Their almost hairless skin was red-pink in the warm sun, from the blood flushed to the surface to help cool them. We spiraled in closer, until they slid off the ice and swam with heads up, keeping their blood-red eyes upon us.

> I noticed one enormous old grey bull, who looked as thick
> as a sugar hogshead, and was by far the largest walrus I had
> yet seen.... [He] carried a very fine and perfect pair of tusks,
> and ... had evidently attained to extreme old age.
> —*James Lamont, Esq., F.G.S.*

More cows were on another, nearby floe, and we circled them as they stared at us. We drew away and glassed more of the ice until we saw three other walrus on a floe. Crossing to them we found three bulls piled on one another, two very large. I looked at the bigger ones in my binocular. One bull had heavy tusks, while the other's were less thick but longer. This second bull was light colored, and like all old bulls its hide was "quite covered with scars and wounds, inflicted ... by the tusks of [other walrus], in fights amongst themselves," in Lamont's words. We came around the floe and cut the engine and drifted in.

The smallest walrus slid into the water and floated beside the floe. The two big bulls stood up on their flippers, looking at us, the lighter-colored old bull lifting its head as high as it could, projecting its tusks straight out. The Inuit nodded now, having decided without a word to me that I should kill the old bull.

> No one who has not tried it will readily believe how
> extremely difficult it is to shoot an old bull-walrus clean dead.
> —*James Lamont, Esq., F.G.S*[3]

[3]*By firing at an old bull directly facing you, it is almost impossible to kill him, but if half-front to you, a shot just above the eye may prove fatal. If sideways, he can only be killed by aiming about six inches behind the eye, and about one-fourth of the apparent depth of his head from the top, but the eye, of course cannot be seen unless the animal is very close to you, and the difficulty is enormously increased by the back of the head being so embedded in fat, as to appear as if it were part of the neck.*

If you hit him much below a certain part of the head, you strike the jaw joint, which is about the strongest part of the whole cranium. A leaden bullet striking there, or on the front of the head, is flattended like a piece of putty, without doing much injury to the walrus, and we sometimes found that even our hardened bullets, propelled by five drachms of powder, were broken into little pieces, aginst the rocky crania of these animals.
—*Ibid.*

I slipped my rifle from its case, turning the scope to 1.75X. Swinging the underlever down, I opened the breech, slid a 500-grain Woodleigh soft into the chamber, closed the action, and set the safety. We drifted closer, the walrus shifting side to side, ready to dive into the sea. I would have to kill the old bull dead on the ice, without its falling or diving into the water, where it would likely sink and be lost. We were within twenty-five yards when the bull with the heavier looking tusks, in front of the old bull, lowered its head and body and turned away, giving me a clear shot at the old bull. Standing in the rocking boat, I put the cross hairs on its head, between the small eye and smaller earhole, and thumbed the safety forward. It was 8:30 on a bright and sunny night.

At the boom of the big rifle the ton-and-a-half walrus crashed onto the ice floe with a shudder. It was moving reflexively, and there was something wrong with its left tusk. Its head jerked and the tusk lifted off the ice, and I could see that it was broken nearly in half. The walrus had snapped it off when it struck the ice, the pieces of ivory lying on the floe. It would never be in a record book after that, which was as it should be. The other bull remained right there, its whiskers bristling, menacing us with its tusks as we landed on the floe, before diving into the water. As we walked up to my walrus, the Inuit made me put an insurance round into its neck.

I knelt then beside what could be, without hyperbole, described as a huge beast, sparse tufts of brown fur over its body, the flippers the size of sofa cushions. On its chest were two sets of parallel raked wounds, signs of its escape from the clutches of a polar bear that had attacked from behind. Was shooting this walrus why I was here?

For more than an hour the four men butchered with a skill that had not yet been lost by watching television. The best meat and blubber would be stuffed into a kauk bag and stitched as tight as a keg-sized sausage. This would be for the prized *igunaq* ("Eskimo ice cream," some called it), the bag buried in the summer in the beach gravel, to be dug up and eaten in January to celebrate the return of the sun. The elder took the task of cutting off the upper jaw, which held the *tuugaaq* (which in this case were *taqijuuk*, "big tusks," even with the broken one) and cleaning the meat from it. Then he removed and fleshed the walrus's peculiar "osteological structure." Two of the others concentrated on quartering and boning the carcass, one of them taking slices of the spinal column to chew on until I asked for a bite—which turned out to be utterly tasteless, even though it was where any potential diseases probably lurked. The fourth drew out onto the ice what looked like a few hundred feet of intestines. Like Lewis and Clark's cook, Charbonneau, he pulled them through his squeezed fist to push out all that was "not good to eat," then neatly braided them into two tight coils, the way walrus hunters, I learned, prepare intestines for transport all around the Arctic.

As the walrus was cut up, a ring seal put its head out of the water—maybe drawn by the scent of blood—and marked the place as somewhere to return to after we were gone. Every few minutes a sound of deep sighing came from out in the floating ice, until a bowhead calf breached some thirty yards from us, swimming past. I looked around for the boy. He had picked up my two long brass cartridge cases and was wearing them like false tusks. He smiled as wide as he could without letting the cases fall out.

That's when I knew why I had come for walrus. Not *to* shoot, but *by* shooting to join with four thousand years of a hunting culture, while it still exists. No more than a dozen Qablunaaq hunters came here each summer to hunt walrus, and to hunt they had to do so as assignees of Inuit hunting rights. That only made sense, because who else but the Inuit had a true right to hunt these strange and wonderful animals?

For a few hours, in a place a long way away, I had been an Inuit by legal instrument, and I hoped by spiritual bond both with them and with the walrus. When we brought all the meat and hide and tusks back to the hunting camp, we found the tide was out when we reached there, just before midnight, so I had to wade in over the flat, cobbled bottom and climb the rotting shore ice. I knew then that my time as an Inuit was done. I looked at the white tents, casting elongated shadows in a sun that could not find a path below the horizon, and hoped that the time of the Inuit hunter was not done. I could hope that the walrus I had killed would, in some way, help those tents be raised next summer. As barren as this land might already seem, fewer hunters' tents in the light of the summer's nights would make it only more so.

APPENDIX

CONTRIBUTORS

With Kansas his birthplace, **Craig Boddington** ("The Best Country") has roamed the world, hunting big game farther and more intensely than any other writer of his generation—and possibly several generations past and to come. Editor of *Petersen's Hunting* magazine from 1983 to 1994, Boddington has written more than 2,500 articles and eighteen books. During a thirty-year career in the U.S. Marine Corps Reserve he earned the rank of colonel in 1996 and was selected for promotion to brigadier general in 2001.

Stephen Bodio ("A Friend of the Devil") is a writer, naturalist, hunter, and traveler. His most recent books are *Eagle Dreams*, about the eagle falconers of Mongolia, and *On the Edge of the Wild*, a collection of essays. He lives with his wife Libby in rural New Mexico, with a pack of sighthounds and several hawks.

Philip Caputo ("The Farthest Away River") was born in Chicago in 1941 and has been hunting and fishing virtually all of his life—he picked up a cane pole at age five and learned to shoot a .22 when he was eleven. After graduating college in 1964, he served in Vietnam with the Marine Corps. Following his discharge, he became a reporter and foreign correspondent for the Chicago *Tribune*, where he shared a 1973 Pulitzer Prize for investigative reporting with three other reporters. In 1977 he quit daily journalism after the publication of his first book, *A Rumor of War*, and has been writing books and magazine articles ever since. His latest novel is *Acts of Faith*.

Susan Ewing's ("Crossing Over") articles, essays, and short stories have appeared in *Sports Afield*, *Gray's Sporting Journal*, *Big Sky Journal*, *Bugle*, and other magazines. Her work has also been anthologized in *Heart Shots*, *A Road of Her Own*, *American Nature Writing*, and other volumes. She is the author of three books of nonfiction and two children's books, *Lucky Hares and Itchy Bears* and *Ten Rowdy Ravens*. Susan lives in Montana.

Sam Fadala ("The Plastic Deer"), born in New York, raised in Arizona, and at home in Wyoming, has in his time been a city fireman and a smoke jumper, a cook and a fence mender, and a college and a high school teacher. Over the last thirty-five years he has written some 4,000 articles on hunting and firearms, especially black powder, for publications from *Sports Afield* to *Field & Stream*, *Outdoor Life*, the *Shooter's Bible*, and scores of others. He is also the author of a novel, *The Last Ride of Shadow Briggs*.

APPENDIX

Humberto Fontova ("The Hellpig Hunt"), born in Havana, Cuba, immigrated to the United States at age seven in October 1961 with his mother, sister, and brother, his political-prisoner father joining the family months later. Married for almost thirty years (to the same woman—Shirley), he has three grown "kids": Monica, Michael, and Robert. He has written for *Sierra, Scuba Diving, Men's Journal, Saltwater Sportsman, Bowhunter, Buckmaster, Boating,* and many other outdoor publications. Currently a columnist for Newsmax.com, specializing in Cuban matters, and for *Louisiana Sportsman,* where his subject is Cajun-Cuban outdoor lunacy, he is the author of the critically acclaimed *The Helldivers' Rodeo* and *The Hellpig Hunt,* from which this story is taken. Humberto lives in New Orleans, despite the loss of his home in Katrina, and continues to indulge his obsession with hunting, fishing, and spearfishing. His latest book is *Exposing the Real Che Guevara and the Useful Idiots Who Idolize Him.*

Robert F. Jones was the author of eight novels, including the cult [*Editor's note: for lack of a finer word*] classic *Blood Sport,* as well as eight works of nonfiction, among them the highly praised *Jake* and *Upland Passage.* His articles and essays appeared in *Sports Afield, Audubon, Time, Life, Sports Illustrated, Harper's, Men's Journal,* and *Shooting Sportsman;* they are included in twenty-five anthologies, among them *Best American Sports Writing, 1995.* He lived in Vermont and died in 2002. His widow, Louise, graciously provided "Brothers of the Wolf" for this anthology.

Ted Kerasote's ("Trophies") essays have appeared in dozens of periodicals, including *Audubon, Field & Stream, Outside, Men's Journal, National Geographic Traveler, Salon.com,* and *Sports Afield.* He is the author of four books. One of those, *Bloodties,* is among the most frequently cited works on the ethics of hunting. His latest book, *Out There: In the Wild in a Wired Age,* won the 2004 National Outdoor Book Award for literature. His newest book is *Merle's Door: Lessons from a Freethinking Dog.* He hunts from his home on the Gros Ventre River in Wyoming.

Chris Madson ("Gorillas") holds a bachelor's degree in biology with a minor in English and an M.S. in wildlife ecology. The Wildlife Society has recognized him as a certified wildlife biologist. He is currently the editor of *Wyoming Wildlife* magazine with the Wyoming Game and Fish Department. During his tenure with the magazine, *Wyoming Wildlife* has won fifty-eight national awards for excellence. He has contributed more than two hundred freelance articles to other publications, including *Audubon, National Wildlife, Outdoor Life, Nature Conservancy Magazine, Ducks Unlimited, Bugle,* and *Pheasants Forever.* He hunts big game, small game, waterfowl, and upland birds.

Playwright **David Mamet**, whose *Glenngarry Glen Ross* won the 1984 Pulitzer Prize, the New York Drama Critics Circle Award, and the 2005 Tony for the best Broadway revival, is the author of the plays *Oleanna, American*

Buffalo, A Life in the Theatre, Speed-the-Plow, Sexual Perversity in Chicago, The Cryptogram (winner of the 1995 Obie Award), and many others. He has translated and adapted the works of Pierre Laville and Anton Chekhov for the stage. For the screen he has written *The Postman Always Rings Twice, The Untouchables,* and *Wag the Dog,* and has been the writer-director of *House of Games, The Spanish Prisoner, Heist,* and *Spartan,* to name a few. He is also the author of children's books, novels, books of poetry, nonfiction works about directing in film and on stage, and collections of essays, including *Make Believe Town,* from which "Deer Hunting" is taken.

For over thirty years articles by **Thomas McIntyre** ("Blind Faith" and "Among the Walrus") have appeared in *Sports Afield, Field & Stream, Outdoor Life, Gray's Sporting Journal, Petersen's Hunting, American Hunter, Sporting Classics, The Hunting Report,* and *The Field* in England, as well as in nearly a score of anthologies. He is the author of the critically acclaimed books *Days Afield, Dreaming the Lion,* and the award-winning *Seasons & Days: A Hunting Life.* He, his wife Elaine, and son Bryan Ruark live in northern Wyoming, where the deer and the antelope still play.

Jameson Parker ("Dining with Bears") received his B.A. from Beloit College in 1971 and spent almost thirty years as a working actor. While he is best known for his starring role as AJ in the long-running hit television series *Simon and Simon,* he has also appeared in numerous plays, television movies, and feature films. Now making his living as a writer, he has written stories and articles for magazines, and has written several outdoor television shows. He has published two books: *An Accidental Cowboy* (Thomas Dunne/St. Martin's Press) as author, and *To Absent Friends* (Willow Creek Press) as editor and contributor. He is married to the singer and actress Darleen Carr.

Aaron Fraser Pass ("Top of the World") has been writing on outdoor topics for more than thirty-five years. Originally employed by the Georgia Department of Natural Resources, he first focused on environmental/conservation issues and general hunting and fishing. Evolving into big-game hunting and technical gunwriting, he has hunted over much of North America and has been published in most major American hunting periodicals. Today, he spends much quality time with setters and double-barreled shotguns, and has given up smoking.

David Petersen lives in a small cabin on a big mountain in Colorado. He is the author or editor of thirteen books about wildlife, wild places, and wild people, including *A Hunter's Heart: Honest Essays on Blood Sport; Heartsblood: Hunting, Spirituality, and Wildness in America;* and most recently, *On the Wild Edge: In Search of a Natural Life.* "The Great Bubba Brotherhood Hunt" appeared originally in *Gray's Sporting Journal.*

David E. Petzal ("Thirty Years with *Cervus Canadensis*") has been with *Field & Stream* magazine in one capacity or another since 1972, which was also the year in which he killed his first elk, a six-pointer, in Montana. Since then he has hunted the awful beasts with varying degrees of success in Colorado, Utah, Wyoming, New Mexico, and Washington. His biggest elk was taken in Utah in 1998, and scored 386 B&C. He regards elk hunting as a character-building experience, much like hitting yourself in the head with a hammer. It's a good way to see just how much punishment you can take.

About himself, **Nick Popovich** says, "At heart, I'm just a kid from a steel-mill town in Pennsylvania. I worked at various construction jobs in various places and am trying to learn how to write and would like to go back to Pennsylvania someday to live again." He says about his writing: "I write about dreams and dreamers and the child inside all people without which child the person is not really alive or capable of being awed." His stories, including "The Rain Crow," have appeared in *Gray's Sporting Journal.*

Ron Spomer ("A Mountain Goat Hunt") has been writing about and photographing wildlife and outdoor adventures since 1975. This has taken him to five continents and several Pacific Islands in search of fur, fish, and game. He has backpacked, kayaked, canoed, boated, floated, and toted guns and cameras over thousands of miles from the high Arctic to the deserts of southern Africa. Spomer's words and pictures have appeared in well over a hundred magazines, as well as brochures, pamphlets, and advertising campaigns, and he is the author of six books on wildlife and hunting. The recipient of numerous writing awards, he lives in Idaho, where the land is more vertical than horizontal.

Mary Zeiss Stange ("The Home Place") is the author of *Woman the Hunter* and coauthor of *Gun Women: Firearms and Feminism in Contemporary America*, as well as being a Montana bison rancher and Skidmore College professor of women's studies. She writes about social and environmental issues for publications ranging from *Montana, The Magazine of Western History* to *USA Today.* She is the editor of *Heart Shots: Women Write about Hunting* and general editor of *Sisters of the Hunt,* the Stackpole Books reprint series of classic women's writing about hunting.

Mark T. Sullivan ("The Biggest Deer in the World") lives with his wife and two sons in southwest Montana. He is the author of six novels, including *The Purification Ceremony,* which *Sports Afield* called the best hunting novel in twenty-five years, several screenplays, a handful of short stories, and numerous magazine articles. He is an avid outdoorsman who lives for adventure, hunting, powder skiing, and August mornings fly fishing the Yellowstone River.

E. Donnall Thomas, Jr. ("Lions in Winter") writes regularly about bowhunting, wingshooting, fly fishing, and wildlife for most major outdoor publications and has authored thirteen books on related subjects. He does all of his big-game hunting with recurves and longbows. He and his wife, Lori, divide their time between homes in central Montana and southeast Alaska. Hounds and Labrador retrievers have largely taken the place of their four grown children.

Samuel Western ("Sheep" and "Foliage and First Blood") has written for *Sports Afield*, the *Wall Street Journal*, *Life*, and *Sports Illustrated*. For twenty years he has written about the Rocky Mountain region for the *Economist* of London. He is the author of the highly regarded 2002 economic history of Wyoming, *Pushed Off the Mountain, Sold Down the River*. In a previous incarnation, he worked in the Swedish merchant marine, as a contract logger in Washington and Oregon, and as a commercial fisherman in Alaska. He's also walked the south flank of Wyoming's Bighorn Mountains for many falls as a professional hunting guide.

Terry Wieland ("Williwaw") is shooting editor of *Gray's Sporting Journal* and author of *The Magic of Big Game*, *Spiral-Horn Dreams*, *A View from a Tall Hill—Robert Ruark in Africa,* and the classic *Spanish Best—The Fine Shotguns of Spain.* In 1999, Wieland was named Leupold Writer of the Year. His latest book is *Dangerous-Game Rifles.*

A Midwesterner by birth, **Bill Wise** ("The Indian Giver") lived east of Chesapeake Bay for fifty-five years. His writing reflects a love of family, friends, and nearby woods and waters. A legendary surfer, Bill was inducted into the East Coast Surfing Hall of Fame. Researching diverse topics such as vintage side-by-side shotguns, ocean waves, and competition pigeon shooting, he was touched daily by new friends and old from around the world through his computer. He continued to hunt whitetails from his wheelchair after his friend's death, the "Indian" of his story. Bill died in 2007.

Jim Zumbo ("Night of the Living Alligators") holds degrees in forestry and wildlife management. He sold his first article to *Outdoor Life* in 1962 and went on its masthead in 1978. He is currently its hunting editor. He has written more than 2,000 published articles and some two dozen books, including *Portraits of Elk Hunting.* Jim has hunted in all fifty states, all but three Canadian provinces, as well as parts of Africa, Europe, and South America. He lectures extensively and hosts his own television show, *Jim Zumbo Outdoors,* on the Outdoor Channel. He and his wife, Madonna, and their two Labradors live in a log home in the mountains between Cody, Wyoming, and Yellowstone National Park.